How I Won The Yellow Jumper

Ned Boulting started his broadcasting career at Sky in 1997, working as a reporter alongside Jeff Stelling on the now legendary show *Soccer Saturday*. In 2006 he was given the Royal Television Society's Sports Reporter of the Year Award. He presents the Tour of Britain for ITV, as well as the inaugural Tour Series, and contributes features and live reports to coverage of the Tour de France.

Also by Ned Boulting

How Cav Won the Green Jersey
On the Road Bike

'Paris, 4 July 2003: My first Tour de France. I had never seen a bike race. I had only vaguely heard of Lance Armstrong. I had no idea what I was doing there. Yet, that day I was broadcasting live on television. I fumbled my way through a few platitudes, before summing up with the words, ". . . Dave Millar just missing out on the Yellow Jumper." Yes, the Yellow Jumper.'

Follow Ned Boulting's (occasionally excruciating) experiences covering the world's most famous cycling race. His story offers an insider's view of what really goes on behind the scenes of the Tour. From up-close-and-personal encounters with Lance Armstrong to bewildered mishaps with the local cuisine, Ned's been there, done that and got the crumpled-looking t-shirt.

Eight Tours on from Ned's humbling debut, he has grown to respect, mock, adore and crave the race in equal measure. What's more, he has even started to understand it.

Includes *How Cav Won the Green Jersey: Short Dispatches from the 2011 Tour de France.*

Ned Boulting

How I Won The Yellow Jumper

DISPATCHES FROM THE TOUR DE FRANCE

YELLOW JERSEY PRESS
LONDON

Published by Yellow Jersey Press 2014

2 4 6 8 10 9 7 5 3 1

First published in Great Britain in 2011 by
Yellow Jersey Press
Random House, 20 Vauxhall Bridge Road,
London SW1V 2SA

www.vintage-books.co.uk

Addresses for companies within The Random House Group Limited
can be found at: www.randomhouse.co.uk/offices.htm

The Random House Group Limited Reg. No. 954009

A CIP catalogue record for this book
is available from the British Library

ISBN 9780224092401

The Random House Group Limited supports the Forest Stewardship
Council® (FSC®), the leading international forest-certification organisation.
Our books carrying the FSC label are printed on FSC®-certified paper.
FSC is the only forest-certification scheme supported by the leading
environmental organisations, including Greenpeace.
Our paper procurement policy can be found at
www.randomhouse.co.uk/environment

Typeset by Palimpsest Book Production Ltd, Falkirk, Stirlingshire

Printed and bound in Great Britain by Clays Ltd, St Ives plc

CYCLING GLOSSARY

Attack

A cyclist making an attempt to break free of the bunch – often for the stage win or to take time out of the leaders, either alone or as part of a small group. Popular places to attack include on climbs or down daring descents.

Autobus

A group of riders, usually on a mountainous stage, banding together to finish the stage within the cut-off time.

Bidon

A cyclist's bottle for liquids, attached to the bike.

Bonk

The much-feared physical condition when a cyclist's body has run out of fuel. Symptoms include light-headedness, hallucinations, fatigue.

Break/breakaway

A group of riders splitting from the main bunch to attack. Will often be chased down by the **peloton**.

Bunch sprint

A chaotic end to a stage where teams engineer their sprinters to the front to contest the stage win. Only certain stages (usually flat ones) will be suitable for a sprint finish.

Cadence

The rate at which a cyclist turns the pedals.

Category one climb

A system of categorising climbs: the lower the number, the steeper the route. **Hors categorie** (literally, without category) is the toughest.

Chamois (chammy) cream

A cream liberally applied to avoid saddle sores.

Classic

A one-day professional bike race in Europe. Many have been running for decades. Famous classics include: Paris-Roubaix, Tour of Flanders, Milan-San Remo.

Cleats

Bits of plastic attached to your shoe that clip on to the bike's pedals. Can refer to the entire shoe.

Cofidis affair

An infamous drug raid in 2004 that was exposed after cyclists' phones were tapped by French police. Multiple riders were arrested and charged with possessing illegal drugs and the scandal rocked professional cycling.

Criterium

A race organised in a city centre that involves multiple laps of a closed-off route. Usually a short race, as opposed to a standard road race.

Directeur sportif

The person in charge of a cycling team, with a similar role to that of a football team's manager.

Domestique

A support rider in a team, whose responsibilities include fetching food and drink from the team car for their leader, pacing the leader up climbs, chasing down breakaway groups.

Echelon

A horizontal formation of riders often deployed in cross-winds. Riders across different teams take it in turns to be in the most exposed position, with other riders being able to shelter and conserve energy.

EPO

A synthetic hormone that allows blood to carry more oxygen around the body and therefore improves performance in endurance sports. Using EPO is a type of blood doping.

Etape

A stage in a multi-day bike race.

Festina affair

A drugs bust in 1998 during the Tour de France where a significant haul of drugs was found in a team car. Nine riders were arrested and many teams were investigated during the race.

Green Jersey

The jersey awarded in the Tour de France to the rider with the most points. Points are awarded to the first riders to reach the end of a stage, or who win an intermediate sprint during a stage.

Gruppetto

The Italian term for the **autobus**.

Lead out

The formation used by a team to get their sprinter to the front before a sprint finish.

Musette
A cyclist's bag of food to be eaten during the race. Often collected by a **domestique** or handed out at a feed station by a **soigneur**.

Peloton
The main group of riders during a bike race, often numbering over 100.

Polka Dot Jersey
Awarded to the 'King of the Mountains' during the Tour de France – the rider who picks up the most points during mountain stages, awarded for arriving first at the peaks.

Rainbow Jersey
Worn by the world champion in their discipline – time trial, team time trial, road race. The jersey is white with a band of five stripes (green, yellow, black, red, blue).

Ramp
The slope where a rider waits immediately before they are cleared to begin their time trial.

Sitting on someone's wheel
The practice of conserving energy by riding just behind another rider in their slipstream, which can reduce effort by roughly 20 per cent.

Skinsuit
The skin-tight outfit riders wear in time trials to be as aerodynamic as possible.

Skis
The special handlebars on a time trial bike which force the rider to adopt an aerodynamic position.

Soigneur
The member of a team's support crew responsible for distributing **musettes, bidons** and administering massages to the riders after a day's racing.

Sportive
A short mass ride open to amateurs, often to raise money for charity.

Sprocket
The toothed wheel that a bike's chain rolls over.

Time trial
A race or stage in a multi-day race where riders compete individually against the clock.

Torque
A measure of power output.

Turbo trainer
A stationary bike used for training or for warming up.

VAM
A measure of elevation gain (usually metres per hour), which is used as an indicator of fitness and speed.

White Jersey
The jersey awarded to the best young rider in the Tour de France.

Yellow Jersey / *Maillot Jaune*
The jersey awarded to the leader of the Tour de France.

To Mum and Dad

CONTENTS

I'd love to say that cycling has always been my passion. It would be advantageous to claim that I had run away from home in the mid-seventies, stowed away on the Zeebrugge ferry, armed with only a Curly Wurly to sustain me and a Kodak Instamatic to record my adventure, in the hope of catching a glimpse of Joop Zoetemelk riding the Flèche Wallonne. But, to my great regret, that would be a lie.

Instead I have had to accrue history, to acquire heritage at double-quick pace.

I was a few days short of my thirty-fourth birthday when I first saw a bike race of any description. It wasn't any old bike race, mind you. It was the Tour de France. And I was there to report on it for television, which meant that I had to at least look and sound like I knew what I was talking about. That confidence trick wasn't always successful.

My first year covering the Tour passed in a haze of angst-ridden confusion and I vowed never to return. Yet, unconsciously, something of the Tour had wormed its way into my DNA. Before I knew what I had done, I agreed to work on the 2004 Tour. Then I ended up covering every Tour between 2005 and 2010, eight Tours in all. I have now spent a total of twenty-four weeks following the peloton round France, gradually growing ever more obsessed with the race.

After the best part of a decade, I might almost claim to understand it, or at least bits of it, from time to time.

I am not the only one to have made this progression. The chapters to come are for anyone who has made a similar journey in following this extraordinary sport. They reflect, to some extent, my transition from novice to devotee, taking in both scepticism and wonder. They also invite a minute inspection of the nooks and crannies of life covering the Tour de France. They tell of champions and car parks, yellow jerseys and filthy socks. They celebrate the race, but they celebrate all the other stuff, too.

That 'stuff' is what makes this a unique event: the millions of fans lining the road, the thousands of Tour vehicles, the villains, the virtuous, the hungry and the hopeless. It's not just about the riders. For the rest of us, it's the mere act of crashing through France, chasing after an event that won't stand still: a series of lurches from incident to accident.

You will notice that, like the Tour itself, this book doesn't follow a straight line. It has a mind of its own, and tends to jump from superstar to supermarket, from the riders to the roadies, from an appraisal of the career of Lance Armstrong to a meditation on the workings of launderettes. My experiences over the eight Tours that make up the substance of this account are necessarily a little disorderly. The random nature of everyday life grinds away at your journalistic endeavour, and leaves it smoking like the red-hot clutch plate of an overheated Renault Espace, immobile and stranded up a mountain. In fact, there's a chapter about just that.

Like those mind-bendingly difficult pixellated designs that were all the rage in the eighties, my hope is that, if you stare at these chapters for long enough, suddenly a fully rounded 3-D picture of the Tour de France will emerge. Fleetingly.

But what of the race itself?

The sport of cycling, not for the first time, faces extreme scrutiny. In fact, it exists in a permanent state of tension. A series of doping scandals involving some of its biggest names has taken cycling's credibility close to the brink. It feels as if the watershed moment, the point of no return, is now both increasingly imminent, and indefinitely delayed.

Ever since I have started to cover cycling, bad news has broken across its bows. But incessant attacks on its integrity, the most damning from within cycling itself, have done little to dull the growing popularity of the sport, particularly in the UK. The unravelling of reputations at the very highest levels has coincided with the emergence of a generation of British cyclists able to compete with the very best in the world and, in the case of Mark Cavendish, thrash them. So even if the Tour has never had it so bad, we, in our British bubble, have never had it so good.

That's not the only ambiguity that has defined my evolving attitudes to covering the race. In fact, there's not much about the Tour that isn't ambiguous. Therein lies the fascination.

A colleague once told me that the only way to follow the Tour is to use the same technique that Inuit people use when faced with the blinding whiteness of the snow. They look at it 'with an off-centre gaze'.

Here are my off-centre thoughts.

Ned Boulting
June 2011

THE CAST

Since the Tour is as complex as a Tolstoy novel, it might help for me to effect a few introductions. Many of the characters in this book are well known. Others, less so. But all are vital to my story.

LANCE ARMSTRONG

Lance – or Larry, as we have dubbed him – is the alpha and omega of the years I have covered on the Tour. Articulate, imperious, stubborn and subtle, he was the reason I became transfixed. Oh, and he won it seven times.

CHRIS BOARDMAN

In his time, Chris Boardman won Olympic medals, yellow jerseys and world records. Track or road, it mattered little. These days he spends his Julys working for ITV. He sweeps up with the same proficiency he used to ride a bike.

MARK CAVENDISH

Cavendish is the rider I have interviewed more than any other. Principally because his fifteen stage wins to date have coincided with my tenure as ITV's Tour de France reporter. For that reason alone, I feel a little possessive towards him. He may not share that feeling.

STEVE DOCHERTY

Steve has produced or directed almost every Tour for British TV coverage since 1903. Here he is, circa 2009, struggling with the concept of a computer. A punctilious man with an understated passion for the sport and an ability to multitask under pressure while wearing perfectly creased shirts.

GARY IMLACH

Gary has covered every Tour de France for the last twenty years. He has presented the ITV coverage since 2002. He is universally accepted as one of sport's most admired and respected broadcasters. He does, however, eat tinned mackerel. And I have to share his lip-microphone sometimes.

PHIL LIGGETT

The Grand Man of the Microphone of the Telly of the Tour. Phil's voice has rung through decades of bike races all over the world, but when July comes, it rings loudest. Silver-haired, silver-tongued, shaven-legged: that's what he is.

LIAM MACLEOD

Liam is a fine cameraman and a splendid fellow. His work has brought to life everything I have done over the last four years of the Tour. An ardent Rangers fan with an Irish-sounding name, his confusion was only increased by his introduction to cycling. Like me, though, he's got the bug.

DAVID MILLAR

David Millar has been my Tour guide. His roller-coaster career has heaped triumph upon failure, rebirth upon disgrace. Lately he has taught me not to believe all that you see. But, equally, that without belief, we might as well all go home.

MATT RENDELL

Matt is one of cycling's great thinkers. Look at him, scratching his chin and musing. Among other books, he has written *The Death of Marco Pantani*, the definitive work on il Pirata's tragic life. On my first Tour, he nursed me through my initiation. Without his knowledge and passion, I would have given up long ago. He is also able to speak almost every language on earth, which in my eyes makes him extremely clever.

PAUL SHERWEN

The other half of the Phil-and-Paul double act. Chipper, chirpy, cheeky and any number of other adjectives beginning with 'ch', Paul's unfailing good humour and faith in cycling makes him a force of nature. As is his ability to talk for hours at a time. Incidentally, he owns a substantial chunk of Africa.

JOHN TINETTI

On my early Tours, I worked with John out on the road. He is a poker-faced, tough Australian, who has surprisingly strong opinions about cycling. He just tends to keep them to himself. He can also run fast. Backwards. With a camera. Filming.

BRADLEY WIGGINS

Wiggins. Long, tall and with an ever-changing barnet. No one expected him to finish fourth in 2009, but he did. In the course of three weeks he made British cycling re-evaluate its ambitions. His achievements have changed the way we think about ourselves as a nation of riders.

BEN WOODGATE (WOODY)

Woody is one of television's top sound recordists. Rich in charm, long on talent and bereft of most forms of seriousness, he strolls through July with a set of headphones clamped to his ears, pretending that he cares about cycling. He drives the car a lot, and secretly quite enjoys it.

LEWISHAM HOSPITAL: PART ONE, AUGUST 2003

'Who won the Tour de France?' This is what they were asking me.

A difficult question: a slippery customer, alive with Gallic guile. It would take some thinking about. But thinking wasn't that easy any more.

I was drawn to the sight of my knees. They, at least, were recognisable. The scars still there from my countless childhood scrapes, but hidden now by straggles of hair. In fact, the whole length of my shins and calves down to my ankles were hairy – something that, while it didn't directly puzzle me, seemed strangely ill-fitted to the moment.

Above the curvature of the kneecap there was a flourish of scarlet, not blood, but something odd and out of place. Elastic. Red elastic, tight too. The red trim of a pair of shorts whose shiny black expanse seemed both utterly alien and entirely familiar.

Cycling shorts. Lycra. Where had they come from? Who had put me in a pair of Lycra shorts?

I jerked my head upright, urgently scouring the antiseptic environment for clues. A tray of metallic bowls. A curtain. Posters of diseased lungs. Nothing informed me. No help at all as my heart and mind raced, chasing after an explanation. Understanding trickled away like sand through my fingers. I returned my gaze to the sight of my shorts, torn slightly on the left thigh. This time I contemplated them with sullen resentment.

I was, I could only conclude, ever so confused.
'Ask him again.'
'Who won the Tour de France?'

A SIMPLE MISTAKE

July 2003. What was I doing in Paris?

I had slept fitfully in the Best Western alongside the old cavalry stables in the Avenue Duquesne. All night long a storm had crashed around, banging the spindly branches of a plane tree against my window. If my sleepless night had been a scene in a film, they would have angled the camera on its side. I would have opened an eye. The clock on the bedside table would slowly have come into focus: 5.40 a.m.

I got up to see if breakfast was being served.

A bitter coffee, a beautiful croissant and several hours later, I sat in the plump comfort of the driver's seat in a brand-new Renault Espace. It was an early summer's day. Paris was enjoying a morning of blazing contrasts. Lumpy clouds rumbled across the city throwing down shafts of deep shade. Otherwise, the sky was painted the brilliant blue of a kid's bedroom. It was two days before the Grand Départ of the Centenary Tour. I was struggling with two new life experiences. The first of these was satellite navigation.

The second was the Tour de France.

A month or so before this moment of solitary fear in a Paris side street, I had been fiddling nervously with a teaspoon in a Soho café, sitting opposite Gary Imlach. He was the seasoned presenter of the Tour de France; I had just been told that ITV would be sending me out to work on it as a reporter. Gary, in between tiny bites of his minimalist Italian biscuit, was doing an extraordinary job of hiding his concern, not to mention alarm, at my lack of preparation. To fill the silence, I opted to speak.

'Lance Armstrong. He's the American cancer bloke, isn't he? Keeps winning it,' I said, feeling that I'd got off to a flyer.

It wasn't long though before I'd exhausted my scant knowledge and was out of my comfort zone. Gary had suddenly started to talk about the team time trial.

'They have teams?' I offered, genuinely surprised. 'I didn't know that.'

Gary mentally dropped his espresso cup. It had been an uncomfortable sort of meeting.

Deciding that the depth of my ignorance wasn't going to subside overnight, I had embarked on a course of doing not a lot. I could have buried myself in research. But I had so much to learn that I decided anything I did this late in the day would have been quixotic, so I learnt nothing. It was a technique that had got me through school and university and I wasn't going to abandon it now.

So I had hastily thrown as much clothing as I could into the biggest suitcase I could find, along with a passport, an iron and some leftover euros I found in a jar in the kitchen. Then I left for France.

Now the day had dawned, I stared slack-jawed through the windscreen as Paris came to life. A street cleaner power-hosed the grime from a petal-shaped grille at the base of a tree. Two American girls deep in gossip waltzed arm in arm. A thin man spat.

I fought through the sat nav menu options and tried in vain to change the language settings from French to English. I felt a sense of rising panic. This was not only my first experience of the Tour, it also would be the first bike race I had ever seen. And only now, with my accreditation swinging from my neck like a noose, did it dawn on me that I might just be the wrong man for the job. I started the engine and drove off, unsure of my destination.

'À *deux cent mètres, au rond-point, tournez à gauche.*'

At least the sense of direction and purpose that navigating Paris gave me papered handily over the cracks of my fear. I had been instructed to head for what is known as the 'Permanence'. An odd name this, since the 'Permanence' is anything but permanent. It is the Tour's headquarters. Logistic and administrative officers, commissaries, media, medical staff, tailors and drivers all need somewhere to work. The Permanence is where this happens, normally situated at imponderable expense in the biggest place they can find. But since the Tour generally moves 200 kilometres every day, the Permanence shape-shifts and re-emerges in another exhibition hall on the outskirts of another town each time. Its permanence is relative.

Parked up and once again outside the comfort of the Espace, I made my way towards the cavernous hall in which I had arranged to meet my colleagues from ITV. Including me, the production team totalled twelve. Most had an average of ten Tours under their belts. Some were closing in on their twentieth.

I entered the brightly lit room, and at a stroke understood that the phoney war was over. Everywhere I could see actual riders with actual bikes spouting actual foreign languages besieged by people who actually knew what they were talking about.

Fighting shy of any encounter that might bring me into close contact with this alien world, I skirted the walls till I found some familiar faces. Gary Imlach was tap-tap-tapping into a Mac, looking useful, absorbed and in command. Sitting opposite him at a desk was my producer, Steve Docherty. He had a long list of stuff he needed to discuss with me. We left Gary to it and went off in search of somewhere quiet.

On the other side of the hall we found a space, which seemed to accommodate a thousand desks. We helped ourselves to a paper cup of nasty Grand'Mère café. It glowered up at me from its awful blackened depths (the Tour eventually inculcates a strong instinct for which freebies to exploit and which to leave, but this was my first Tour, and I had much to learn). Steve sat me down to talk through the first few days of the rest of my life.

Tall, blond and taciturn, Steve had, in one guise or another, produced and directed British TV coverage of the Tour since the mid-eighties. A man from the Borders with a love for Carlisle United, he balanced strongly held beliefs with rare shows of enthusiasm and a deep understanding of cycling. He also came with a reputation for not suffering fools. And here he was, amid the clatter and clutter of the vast French carnival gearing up for action, clutching a Bic rollerball in one hand and a throwaway coffee in the other, facing exactly that: a fool.

He had in front of him a list. His neat handwriting, headlines in CAPS, underlining in red, revealed a portfolio of short reports that I would have forty-eight hours to generate:

NED FEATURES

1) Lance Armstrong: from cancer survivor to champion.
2) The Famous Four: Anquetil, Merckx, Hinault, Indurain. All five-time winners.
3) The Centenary Edition. A Hundred Years of the Tour.
4) The Tour Route, in facts and figures.
5) The Contenders: who can threaten Armstrong?

Steve shot me a glance across the table, which let me know that he didn't expect me to succeed. The glance was superfluous. We both knew that I knew that I would not succeed.

I drew sharply on the Grand'Mère, which by now had grown cold. Instead of swallowing, I swilled it around my mouth, feeling at once how it was staining my teeth black.

The rest of that day passed in a tailspin of activities, none of which were remotely focused or efficient. I scribbled fragments of script on notebooks; I tore them up. I recorded pieces to camera, only to have them scrutinised and rejected. I tried to gear up for what was to come; I failed.

And so it was that the following day, dressed in a poorly ironed shirt, I stood at the start of the Tour de France for the very first time. The streets were lined with people. The 2003 Prologue was about to get under way.

The first thing that I noticed was the noise. The speed came later. It sounded like the drumming of fingers, gaining in urgency. Disc wheels hammering up a cobbled road at forty miles per hour.

First off the starting ramp that day was, I think, some bloke from the Euskadi Euskaltel team (eight years on, and I still struggle to pronounce this team correctly, and normally find a way of avoiding it by referring to them as the 'team from the Basque Country' or some such). He flashed by me, my first glimpse of a racing bicycle. I checked his unofficial time over the 6.5km course displayed on the digital clock over-hanging the finish line. I had no idea what to make of the information. I had no point of reference, it meant nothing to me.

One after one, I watched them finish. It was an odd sight, but exhilarating at the same time. Seen from the front, the rider, clad in his time-trial skinsuit, his back arched and head dipped, flew like a bullet towards me. His energy was pent up behind him in an ordered fuss of legs and lungs serving only to push that millimetre-perfect front wheel over the line. In that instant, an unseen cord unclipped and the cyclist's spine crumpled down. His head snapped upright. His jaw suddenly hung loose to gulp in the restorative air. Each time the cyclist would have a split second of utter peace before the madness of the Tour and of the crowd descended on him.

Overcome by a sudden fit of journalistic diligence, I would occasionally contemplate running after a rider. But when I looked down the length of the road, he would be long gone. Literally, gone.

What an unusual event.

The day wore on. I anticipated the hunched blue of Armstrong flying past. He was the star attraction and would start last of all, with the number 1 on his back, denoting his status as the reigning champion. I wanted to see what all the fuss was about. In the meantime the endless procession of cyclists ground remorselessly on.

I stood alongside the tall, keen figure of Matt Rendell, the writer who has worked for ITV on all the Tours I have covered. The poor fellow had been seconded to guide me through the proceedings. I looked to his every gesture for confirmation that I understood the grammar of the day's events. He had plenty of gestures, including a quite uncontrolled throaty Hispanic holler. Every time a rider he knew personally flew past, he would let rip. I swear that at some point he screamed 'Arriba!' in some bloke's sweaty ear as it fizzed past him.

I marvelled at his enthusiasm. The veins stood out in his neck. Nothing could deflect from his delight as some tiny Colombian climber pedalled over the finish line having posted the ninety-third best time of the afternoon. I could only dream of summoning up such passion.

But frankly, after a couple of hours, my first Tour de France had started to bore me.

Even now, I don't much like time trials. Only occasionally do they throw up much drama but more often than not they just confirm what we have all expected. I sometimes think that they are there solely for the purists, and that I am still too new to the sport to understand the aesthetic. I lose track of the number of times I have been asked to film a guided tour of a time-trial bike. One day I might just blurt out, 'Look, they're very light, and very aerodynamic, all right? That's it. That's all there is.'

The rhythm of that first, long day was suddenly enlivened as we edged towards our 'on-air' time. We would be broadcasting live on ITV1, the big network! From a flat-pack set by the side of the finish line, Gary Imlach would thread together the denouement of the day's events before crossing live to the coverage of the best riders who would all set off in the final hour. Phil Liggett and Paul Sherwen would commentate. In that first year, Stephen Roche, the Irish winner of the Tour in 1987, was our occasional pundit.

My role would be limited to interviewing the winning rider. The hope, and indeed the expectation, was that this might be David Millar, a man I had never heard of and certainly never met. Apparently he was Scottish. Along with Armstrong, so I was told, he was one of the favourites.

I waited, and I watched. My earpiece crackled with Phil's commentary. His was a voice that would provide me with the soundtrack of my summers to come. Yet back then, I barely understood a word.

An Australian called Brad McGee posted the best time. In the all-white skinsuit of Francaise des Jeux, he looked like a kinky time-traveller from a David Bowie movie. He crossed the finish line, and I saw him being marshalled to a holding area behind the podium. There he would have to wait while the final dozen riders threw down their challenges.

Then came a slight raising of the tension. The commentary in my ear spluttered something about Dave Millar starting. In a kind of makeshift tent at the finish line, I glimpsed the TV screen through the hordes of journalists. I saw Millar's long ungainly form bowed to the frame of his time-trial bike, rounding the first corner, the camera mounted on a crane pulling higher and wider as it went with him, until the elegance of the Paris skyline filled the frame.

The split times came through. Millar was in the lead by a fraction of a second. Then, at the second split, the gap had grown. Somehow, viscerally, I knew this was important. He was approaching our finish line hard and closing in on victory and the first yellow jersey of the 2003 Tour de France. I dashed across to the barriers to watch, both delighted and terrified for him.

It was at that moment that my earpiece exploded with noise. Liggett's excitable commentary was drowned out by the off-air expletives of Steve Docherty, Gary Imlach and just about everyone else on the production team.

On the final bend before the home straight, riding over cobbles, Millar's chain bounced off his front ring. In a split second, his challenge was over.

I only found out later, he pulled it back on with his fingers and sprinted hard for the line, but crossed it one-tenth of a second down on McGee.

At that precise moment, every spectator on the route knew more than I did. Everyone on our production team, every viewer at home, was better informed than me. I scampered around, trying to look purposeful by intermittently sticking my finger into my earpiece and frowning. But who was I kidding? Something profoundly unexpected had happened and I had no idea what it was. Yet I was about to be cast in the role of Man-On-The-Spot. I ran back to the side of my cameraman, and stood poised to interview . . . someone. Anyone. About anything. I was ready to impart News, oblivious of the fact that I Had No Idea What To Report. Adrenalin simply plonked me in front of the camera.

Minutes passed. They were filled with tense, incoherent airtime, which Gary Imlach and Stephen Roche on the set had to bridge with talk of Millar's unchaining. There is only so much that can be said about a chain coming off, except for 'the chain clearly came off', and there's a finite number of ways of expressing that, even allowing for Stephen Roche's bizarre Franco-Irish accent.

Millar had long since disappeared. Crossing the line at forty miles an hour, he had carried on at that speed, heading towards the Eiffel Tower where his Cofidis team car was parked up. Matt Rendell, long legs pounding away, had set off after him, shouting into the increasing distance, and with decreasing usefulness, 'Dave!'

My ear crackled again. The voice of our director cut through. 'Have you got anything for us, Ned?'

I didn't know what to say. I think I might have said, 'Yes.' Just to appear useful.

'We're going to come to you in twenty seconds. Stand by. Gary, hand to Ned.'

Then, before I could adjust my collar and compose my thoughts (which pre-supposes that I had any in the first place), Gary Imlach handed over to me 'for the very latest on the David Millar situation'.

The blind eye of the camera fixed me. The red cue light went on.

In the polished glass of the lens a couple of feet in front of me, I caught a glimpse, like the image in the back of a spoon, of ITV's new cycling reporter, silent for a second, and then, in front of the reflected backdrop of ancien régime Paris, starting to talk.

What passed my lips must never be revisited. Some tapes are too painful ever to unearth from the archives. Even if the old adage holds true that one can learn from one's mistakes, there are some mistakes that can break one's confidence beyond repair.

I have been told though, by a friend who was watching in

embarrassed disbelief in a house in Chelmsford, that I uttered words like 'some sort of thing with his bike'. I followed this up, apparently with the killer line, 'kissing goodbye to his chance of winning the yellow jumper'.

Yes, the yellow jumper. That's what I said.

BEING ON AIR

Before sitting down to write this book, I had assumed that my first-ever cycling broadcast had taken place in 2003: that ill-fated live update on David Millar. Now, thanks to my sister Emily, I have found out that I am quite wrong. And, as older sisters tend to be, she is right.

In fact, my cycling pedigree predates that awful moment by some twenty years. In 1984, aged fourteen, I was at home one day in the Easter holidays revising for my exams. This involved a lot of worrying blackheads with tweezers, wobbling backwards on the rear two legs of my chair, rewinding cassettes by spinning a pencil (to save on the Walkman batteries, you understand) and occasionally reaching for a silver spray-can to daub some poetry on my bedroom wall.

Accompanying this teenage idling was the background noise of my late childhood, known as 96.9 Chiltern Radio. It was the sound of Bedford, Dunstable and Luton. On that particular afternoon there was a phone-in: 'The State of Bedford's Roads'. As if local radio in that early afternoon slot wasn't already dreary enough, they had summoned up a debating point with a stultifying lack of potential.

Quite why I decided it was time to phone in, I have no idea. Boredom is the only explanation I can offer. Boredom, with perhaps the added spice of fiddling with my brand-new Marantz stereo cassette-radio player in an attempt to record my broadcast debut. I unpeeled a brand-new TDK C-90 cassette, and slid it into position, then closed the door and pressed the record and pause buttons simultaneously. Now I was ready and I could phone in the station.

To my astonishment, I was put straight through to the studio, where they kept me on hold. Once the production team had established that I was simply a precocious little twerp who meant no harm and was unlikely to swear in the middle of the afternoon to the Chiltern Radio audience, I was told to stand by. I clutched the receiver, sweaty palmed with anticipation (a frailty that still affects my microphone hand).

The music faded down. 'OK, that was Daryl Hall and John Oates,' said the DJ. Probably.

'Now, what about the roads in Bedford?' he went on. 'What about the state they're in? And just what is the council planning on doing about it? That's the topic for the phone-in this afternoon, and we've got a caller on the line. It's Ned, from Bedford. What have you got to say, Ned?'

The roof of my mouth went suddenly very dry. 'Hi,' I struggled to get the word out. A displaced feeling started to overwhelm me, as if I was watching myself from a perch on the ceiling. From this elevated position, I looked down upon myself about to make my first broadcast. This is perhaps the only time that Chiltern Radio has ever been known to replicate the effects of LSD.

'What do you think about it, Ned?'

A fatal, short, and very telling silence. Then I recovered, and began.

As soon as the telephone conversation was at an end, I hung up, and sat cross-legged in my bedroom, my white Solidarnosc T-shirt hanging loosely over a heart still beating hard from the stress of the encounter. After a minute or two, and feeling my pulse return to something approaching normality, I was able to rewind the cassette, and play it back.

It was horrifying. I wince to remember it.

The only other time I can recall a similar feeling was the moment I first discovered the size of my ears. On that occasion, I had been taken for a haircut at the Italian barbers in Foster Hill Road. The comforting hair flaps which, in keeping with the spirit of late seventies boyhood fashion, had kept my ears hidden for a decade were about to be hacked off by an indifferent middle-aged Sardinian barber, wielding a sharp pair of scissors in one hand and a John Player Special in the other. I was struck dumb by the sight of a mildly pornographic calendar and the proximity of a box of condoms. This was a man's world, and I was about to receive a man's cut.

It was only when I got home that I dared to study my reflection in the mirror and analyse fully the extent and significance of this new, extraordinary fact: I had really quite large ears. Things would never be the same again. I could now see me as others saw me.

And so it was when I first heard my voice played back to me. The shock of hearing yourself as others hear you! My voice astonished me; odd, and at the same time intimately familiar. What was indisputable was that I desperately needed my voice to start to break. Dave Taylor's and Jim Briscoe's had gone two years ago, while I still sounded like someone doing an impersonation of my mother. It was humiliating.

I can remember with surprising clarity the gist of the phone call, and there's one phrase in particular, which I can recall verbatim. My sister can too, and she still takes some pleasure in reminding me of it.

'I get around quite a bit . . . by bike.' Like a young Don Johnson from *Miami Vice*. I get around quite a bit. Honestly. In my mind's ear, I can almost hear the DJ quietly restraining his urge to snigger or resign, or both.

'And I was riding along Tavistock Street yesterday, and I hit a pothole, and I nearly fell off.'

'OK, Ned. So you think the state of the roads is terrible, do you?'

'Yes. I do. Really dangerous.'

'Because of the potholes? Are they a real problem for you on your bike?

'Yes. I think something should be done.'

'Right.'

Pause.

'OK, that's Ned from Bedford, who thinks something should be done about the potholes. Next up, it's Supertramp, and "Breakfast in America".'

That episode should have put me off any notion that I

might one day make a living from talking on air about cycling, in any form. But, quite incomprehensibly, here I am, doing just that.

One summer, I think it was in 2004, Kath, my partner, delighted in showing me a TV review in which I was described as the 'Monty Don' of cycling: determined to 'dumb everything down'. This was a bizarre piece of criticism, given that I really don't think I look much like the wizened gardener, and would also consider him to be an expert in his field (literally). But it made her laugh wickedly and with just a hint of scorn, which you wouldn't normally expect from a supportive family member.

Prior to this engagement, I had worked almost exclusively on football programmes, with a brief foray into the extraordinarily forgettable world of women's golf. (Not forgettable, I hasten to add, because it's played by women, but because it's golf. The 2002 Oslo Open is a week that will endure in almost no one's memory.)

Football, though, was a game I had learnt how to read and write. Phrases such as 'overlapping wing-backs' and 'playing off the shoulder of the last defender' formed part of a language I could not only understand, but also express with cliché-strewn abandon. I could talk a passable football, even if I still couldn't play it.

But initially in this shrill, garish, bullet of a race, I couldn't move without a grammar book, a primer, a dictionary and a babelfish stuck in each ear. For a long time the language of cycling remained stubbornly foreign to me.

As the dust settled on my first Tour, I had vowed never to return to cover the race. I reflected in a lengthy debrief with our producers that the work I had produced over the month of July 2003 had been the worst of my career. I would still stand by that assertion. What made that admission still worse was that they agreed.

By the end of the first week, when the Tour had delivered us up to the very top of the Alps, I was sick of the sound of my voice. The problem was a collapse in my self-belief, the illusory arm bands that keep the TV reporter afloat. Quite when, or how, I started to learn to swim, I am still not sure. And even after eight years, I have the odd moment where the old sinking feeling returns.

Talking to the camera is a strange business. What you see on the screen only tangentially relates to reality. Even though it may be our words and our mouths that articulate them, at the same time there is a confidence trick being played by presenters. It may be our faces that we stick in front of the lens, but we are just pretending to be us. It's like being a ventriloquist's dummy who looks strikingly like the ventriloquist; a clone almost, manipulated by the original from which it was cloned. Less Rod Hull and Emu. More Rod Hull and Rod Hill. All presenters have to create a fictional persona, which is close enough to the truth for them to feel comfortable, and yet different enough for them to be able to carry out the functions required of them without being shambolic. The end product that pops up on the telly is a fairly true-to-life version of the person whose name appears in the caption below.

A 'real' report, from a 'real' me, would be peppered with unacceptable amounts of fumbling around and lapses into linguistic disarray. These are the bits that, generally speaking, have to go when you're a TV presenter, even though they are often the bits that make you most human. Over the years I have tried to allow these back into my delivery, like letting weeds take seed in lawn to lend it a more natural look. But you don't want to overdo it.

Likewise, the 'real' Gary Imlach might be tempted to close the show by simply, bluntly speaking his mind, rather than using the wonderfully spiked baroque constructions that are his trademark.

There's a subtle difference. This is Gary Imlach being 'Gary Imlach'. And frankly, no one will ever do it better: eloquence, precision and, most importantly, humour. As Gary grips the microphone, he does so with the archetypal iron fist in a velvet glove.

When I was preparing for my second Tour, I spent two days locked in a little broom cupboard just off Piccadilly Circus, surrounded by boxes of tapes from twenty years of Tour de France coverage. Most of them stretched back to the years when it was Channel 4 who broadcast the highlights show. In those days, Gary did my job, with Phil Liggett fronting up the coverage.

It was an education watching Gary's contributions. Two features stick in my memory. In one he was riding a bamboo bike around some Dutch town. The act itself broke a long-standing personal vow never to allow himself to be filmed on a bike. It was delivered in Gary's inimitable dry deadpan, and it dripped with irony.

In another little film, he had stopped at some remote rural location, which was on the route of the Tour the next day. There, by whatever means, he found himself steering a pedalo out into the middle of the lake to help the mayor of a virtually non-existent hamlet attach a huge floating sign depicting the name of the village to a mooring. The sight of Gary sitting in a white plastic boat pedalling out into a murky lake set a benchmark for strangeness to which I still aspire.

On the 2010 Tour, Gary was presented with a trophy from the Tour for twenty years' service. Christian Prudhomme, the Tour director, appeared to have no idea who Gary was, since he's not a very visible presence outside the confines of our truck. But it was a fine moment, rendered all the more amusing by witnessing Gary's almost total discomfort with the proceedings.

Gary eshews cliché. He has a style that is all his own. He stands wilfully apart. But the Tour provides a big enough canvas for his highly individual space to exist and still leave some blank room for others. With time, I realised that it was possible for Gary's fine brushstrokes to sit alongside my Jackson Pollocks and have understood that our contrasting approaches may have nudged the entirety of the production in a new direction.

You might argue that on my first few Tours I was trying

too hard. What now seems self-explanatory to me, at first seemed deeply mysterious. My efforts often fell short of clarity. I shudder to recall some of them.

My quest for ground-breaking TV once had me sitting outside a café somewhere in one of those hard-to-define areas in France's vast interior, lining up nine sugar cubes into a paceline, and rotating them across the table so that each cube took its fair pull at the front. I was bringing the team time trial to sugary life. My enthusiasm for metaphor didn't stop there. I had them in an echelon, too. Diagonally stretching out across the tablecloth, from saucer to ashtray, sheltering the other cubes from a notional sidewind.

Stretching the conceit to a point way beyond the viewer's patience, I discarded cubes one by one, as they were 'dropped' by their sugary teammates, succumbed to punctures or snapped forks. Then, with a brilliant flourish, I rounded off the epic by deliberately tipping the contents of my coffee cup over them all, soaking the white tablecloth on which they were arranged.

This was high-pressure television, since for obvious enough reasons there could be just one take. Not only that, but once the grand crème was dripping from the margins of the table and we were hurriedly dismantling the camera equipment, we had to fend off a tirade of perfectly justified abuse from an understandably terse waiter. His moustache flickered disdain. I suspect the five-euro tip we left for him was taken out the back and shot. I didn't dare ask him for a receipt so I could claim back the cost of the coffee.

As I said, it was early days.

At about the same time that I started to become a regular contributor, Chris Boardman also started presenting for ITV. Even if his world records, world championships, yellow jerseys and Tour de France stage wins meant that he was marginally better placed to talk about cycling than I was, he still had to learn about telly. He too has had to follow an arc of learning, especially in the uniquely cobbled-together world of ITV's broadcast operation.

Here's a revealing picture for you. When Michael Owen was still playing for Real Madrid a few years ago, he was flown by private jet from Madrid to Liverpool and back again to sit in the football studio for a couple of hours as pundit on a Champions League match. By contrast, last summer on the Tourmalet, the former Olympic gold medallist Chris Boardman stood around for a couple of hours ankle deep in mud and wearing a bin bag to keep out the rain so that we could all help load up the truck at the end of the day. Like your dad packing the family car before a holiday, I suspect he even enjoyed it.

Watching him go about his day, you can see why he achieved everything he did. Chris has a habit of applying an aggregation of marginal gains to almost everything he turns his hand to: writing scripts, taking photos, running a multimillion-pound bike business or eating lunch (all of which he is prodigiously good at).

He's part of the team, although on the other hand, he obviously isn't part of the team, since he's actually done the stuff that the rest of us just talk about. He will only discuss his own career when asked and even then reluctantly. But despite this, he is still capable of the odd bold claim to his own prowess.

'How many kids have you got, Chris?'

'Six.' A deadpan face looked up at me from behind his Sony Vaio laptop. 'I've only had sex six times as well. I'm just extremely efficient.'

It took me a while to be able to read his dry sense of humour. It might take my parents even longer. On my birthday in 2005, the ITV team were all enjoying a sun-drenched rest day lunch together in Courchevel. I was moaning about the fact that no one from home had contacted me to wish me happy birthday. Chris put down his beer, grabbed my phone, scrolled through my contacts list to one labelled Mum and Dad, and dialled their number.

'Mr Boulting. Hello, it's Olympic Gold Medallist Chris Boardman here. Just ringing to remind you that it's your son's birthday.' I imagined my dad standing in his kitchen a thousand miles away, frowning at the receiver in puzzlement, before hanging up.

Nothing fazes Chris. He exudes the kind of absolute certainty that surely only comes with having been the best in the world. He generates a kind of density of purpose in his dealings with you, which is matched only by the density of his actual body. Although he is no longer at his racing weight, Chris has by no means gone to seed, and in fact he's in very good shape. He stands perhaps an inch shorter than me. One day on a ritual run, I asked him how much he weighed, guessing it was a little less than my weight.

'Eighty kilos.' I was amazed. It was eight kilos more than me. I looked at him disbelievingly. 'I'm just very dense,' he explained. He opened up a little sprint, and left me for dead as we turned for home. The man has lungs like wheelie bins.

Certain things are immutable though. Phil Liggett is one such thing. A silver-haired, silver-tongued supremo in shorts. It has taken me many years to grow used to the sight of a man of some considerable years who routinely shaves his legs.

Frankly, on that first Tour, I was still at the stage where the shaved-leg thing was making me writhe with mirth and misunderstanding. I would chuckle at all those smooth-skinned men in shorts all over the place, and I was troubled by visions of them all in their bathtubs, wreathed in bubbles in the style of a Camay soap advertisement, stretching their legs skywards as they glided their razors down their shinbones. I was reminded of a passage in Matt Seaton's excellent book *The Escape Artist*, in which he ponders the practicalities of leg-shaving. The question for Seaton was not so much why as where to stop. How high should the shaved area extend? Should it stop as soon as is necessary, at the line of the shorts, creating a hairy-trunks effect? Or should it perhaps extend much higher, possibly even incorporating, well, everything?

As is clear, I was still scarcely able to conduct a conversation with a hairless-legged man in shorts without inadvertently glancing at them. I'm over that now, except when I am talking to George Hincapie, whose varicose veins at the end of a day in the saddle look as if a family of vipers has crawled under his skin and begun to feed on his calf muscles. They are among the Tour's greatest sights and, like the twenty-one switchbacks of Alpe d'Huez, will one day be numbered for posterity and given plaques bearing the names of famous domestiques who never wore the yellow jersey.

But Phil with hairy legs is unimaginable. He paces around the race with a huge, bouncing gait, easily straddling five feet with each stride. He is known by all, and spends his days flitting from truck to truck, servicing the English-speaking world with its cycling commentary requirements. From Perth to Pennsylvania, Cape Town to Carlisle, the Tour de France sounds like Phil Liggett. With his partner Paul Sherwen they have a cult following in the USA, the size of which would make Marilyn Manson proud.

It took years for Phil to remember my name. Years. I was first introduced to him back at the Permanence in Paris in 2003. I have to confess that his name meant nothing to me, just as mine meant nothing to him. He was a ball of

enthusiastic energy. Snapping up my accreditation he studied
it closely and, seeing to his satisfaction that it had the requisite
number of stars and special stamps, his first words to me
were, 'Have you got yours yet?'

I had no idea what he meant. He took me, almost literally
by the hand, to the other side of the vast hangar where the
Tour's administration had set up shop, and, pushing through
a phalanx of oddly dressed Belgian journalists, led me to the
front of a queue, where a nice lady gave me a plastic bag
emblazoned with the Crédit Lyonnais logo. Phil patted me
on the back and smiled. 'There you go, Ben.'

And with that he vanished, lost in a sea of cycling corres-
pondents. It would be days before our paths crossed again. I
looked in the bag. It contained a limited-edition wristwatch
commemorating the centenary edition of the Tour. I still have
it, unopened, in mint condition. My youngest daughter was
born that year and I have it in mind to pass it on to her, so
that she can put in on eBay when she's a student. She might
get enough for a few pints and a curry.

I suspect Phil must have boxes in the attic full of such tat.
I wonder if he ever takes it all out and gazes at it with nostalgia
and pride. I doubt it.

The most striking thing about Phil though, and this is what marks him out as uniquely adapted to the role of cycling commentator, is the way his brain works. Freudian psychology hypothesises the existence of the Über-Ich, the super-ego, which acts as an inhibitor to the expression of our id, our most primal instinctive drives. Without this facility, we would be wildly prone to acts of self-expression, which would mean that life would be unlivable. We would give vent to every passing impulse, no matter how much we would be better served by keeping our thoughts to ourselves.

It's safe to say that Phil's Über-Ich is not very high func-tioning. At best, its batteries need changing. At worst, I think the whole thing needs ripping out and replacing. He operates seemingly without any interface between what is thought and what is expressed. In most of us, this would be catastrophic. But Phil is a benign man, and the worst that his unconscious can throw at us is a mild expression of concern that the weather might be about to turn a little cooler than he had anticipated.

The great benefit to him of this slight malfunction is that he can talk. In the beginning was the Word, but before that there was Phil.

You'll see him at breakfast commentating his way through his choices at the buffet table.

'Marmalade perhaps today or some honey maybe no had that yesterday it'll be the jam today and maybe a croissant but not a chocolate one had too many of them for tea and besides need to watch the old waistline ah hello Ned how you doing son Ullrich for today I reckon pass us the butter . . .'

Sometimes you're not sure whether he's talking to you, talking on the phone, thinking out loud or actually commen-tating. You have to study closely the nuances to determine whether these are musings or actual communication.

'Going to be hot today yup for sure Armstrong to make his move bloody iron couldn't get the damn thing working and the sat nav packed up last night reckon that final climb'll splinter them today had too much cheese last night woke up bloody thirsty in the night too think Hushovd'll edge it today don't you Nick, er Ned. Ben. Morning all.'

Morning, Phil.

Yet, even on those early Tours, his voice was bedding itself into my unconscious. Accompanied by Paul Sherwen, the pair of them go through the gears as the stage reaches its end. As the bunch chases the break, the algebra narrowing, the equation of the inevitable catch holding steady, it's Phil's voice that will rise to prominence, and which signifies, more than any other sound, July and the Tour de France.

There's a section of the show in which Phil and Paul answer viewers' emails. The office in London filters the best ones, and faxes (yes, faxes!) them through to our truck parked in a field somewhere in France. (If they could find a way of installing a telex machine in the truck, we'd be using that instead of laptops.) The two commentators, sitting side by side in a ridiculously cramped studio, gaze up at the camera, read out the questions and answer them. In doing that, one of them has to pull off one of television's trickiest feats: the art of looking pleasantly interested in what the other person is saying while not actually looking at them.

Occasionally these sections will be illustrated with some expert opinion. Men like Rolf Aldag, Graham Jones or Laurent Fignon, while he was still alive and working for French TV, will be consulted. Sections of their interviews will then be dropped into the coverage in answer to a particular enquiry. There came a time on the 2009 Tour when a viewer asked for my opinion.

I had written in a column for the ITV website at the beginning of the Tour that Lance Armstrong had no chance of winning it. But after a week's racing and a succession of things going his way, that prediction looked far less secure. I was being asked if I still stood by my statement.

Phil read out the email, and threw it over to me, posing the question like this. 'Well, let's find out the answer. Ned, what do you think? Can Lance Armstrong still win the Tour?' I had recorded an answer in which I concluded that, no, he couldn't, and wouldn't win it. Then, in the final edit the answer was grafted on to Phil's question, and the show then went on its course.

It was an important moment for me though. My opinion had been sought and had been deemed worthy of voicing. And what's more, I was right. Armstrong couldn't win the Tour that year, and he didn't. It wasn't perhaps the hardest call to make in the history of sporting predictions, but it was a start. It had taken me the best part of a decade to muster the self-confidence to make a major judgement I could justify.

Phil had even got my name right. Someone must have written it down for him in his notes.

These are the voices and the faces of July then. In the company of Gary, Phil, Paul and Chris, I have become absorbed with the sport, and will gladly corner anyone at any party anywhere in the world and talk endlessly about the Tour, whether I have been invited to or not. A bore has been spawned.

But still, even now, when I am about to see the little red cue light at the front of the camera flick on, I feel much like that fourteen-year-old boy, sitting on the carpet in the middle of his bedroom, clutching the phone and holding his breath.

THE YELLOW BOOK

At Arsenal Football Club's shiny north London home, the Emirates Stadium, there is an area between the two dressing rooms and the tunnel. It is an empty space, really, white-washed and unremarkable. But here's the interesting part: this nondescript architectural afterthought is known as the 'Sterile Zone'. I should explain. There is no actual need to scrub up with disinfectant, or pull on McDonald's worker-style hairnets before entering. It simply means that there is a particular type of person who may not enter: the journalist. If I weren't so care-worn and gnarled, I'd be faintly offended.

At the end of a match, we wait outside the Sterile Zone with our noses pressed to the glass of a fire-door, watching the players trudge off the pitch, and then re-emerge from the changing room a little later, washed, dressed and pomaded. Then, generally speaking, they disappear without talking to us. Arsenal, by the way, are one of the more obliging football clubs, but our contact with the players is every bit as regulated as the word 'sterile' suggests.

Recently, I have been forced to conclude that football players don't actually exist. At least not in the way that you and I would define existence. You need a strong grasp of quantum theory to understand the ephemeral nature of their being. After they plug in their iPods and board the coach, they reappear almost instantly in a hotel so exclusive it can only be glimpsed for nano-seconds by scientists working in the CERN large hadron collider. Or they disappear from view via a wormhole located at some regional airport normally reserved for the military. Either way, they just vanish.

But cyclists are real people. And they sleep in real hotel rooms. The proof for this can be found in *The Yellow Book*.

Handed out free of charge to all accredited personnel on the Tour, this indispensable volume contains all the vital practical information that is needed to navigate the route in a car, trying to keep pace with the peloton. Written in hilariously bad English there is a token amount of historical guff and the potted histories of start towns. But, critically, it also lists the hotels in which the teams are staying every night. With addresses and telephone numbers.

An open invitation to stalk them!

The first time I was handed a *Yellow Book*, I was astonished. Even at night and over his breakfast the next morning, the likes of Lance Armstrong would be afforded no peace by the Tour. It's a wonder they didn't cut 5,000 copies of his room key and hand them out with every book.

The helpfulness doesn't stop there. Most teams will pin a photocopied list of names and room numbers to the wall of the entrance lobby. This speeds up the check-in procedure as the riders get back from the race. But it has the, perhaps, unwitting side-effect of enabling journalists to doorstep them as they nip from room to room.

In fact, it was in just such a circumstance that I once spent an awkward minute or two in the company of Eddy Merckx. I'd actually been looking for his son, Axel. I'd found out his hotel room number, and was just approaching the door when his dad appeared, leaving the room. He nodded curtly at me. I was suddenly overcome with embarrassment. The last thing I wanted to do was give the five-time Tour de France winner the impression that I was stalking his son. So I walked on, thinking I could duck round the corner and head back once the coast was clear. The only problem was that Eddy turned and walked in the same direction as me, at the same time and at roughly the same pace.

Eventually we arrived at the lift. To complete the charade I felt I ought to get in. Eddy joined me and together we stood in silence. I thought of a dozen things to ask him. I didn't ask any of them. Then we got out of the lift together and crossed the foyer together. He then left the hotel.

I sat down, and tried to figure out how long I should leave it before I went back up to Axel Merckx's room and tried again.

The Tour de France inhabits a kind of 'infected zone', a space without coherent jurisdiction. The laws that govern journalistic etiquette are often vague. Sometimes they are non-existent. That's not to say that they don't apply. It's just that no one is quite sure how they might apply, because no one knows what they are.

It is in and around hotels where the public and the private lives of the Tour de France mix. Here is the uncomfortable middle ground, where athletes pad in their sponsored leisurewear across the shining floor tiles of hotel lobbies, greeting family members who have flown in for a visit, mingling with riders from opposing teams, ordering caffè lattes, and battling with wi-fi access codes. Along the endlessly repeating corridors above, behind closed doors, there are other riders, dressing wounds and grimacing through their massages.

This is where, in theory at least, the din of the race withdraws, and the riders are granted a little sanctity. But not much of it. Show me the hotel foyer, and I'll show you the journalist, waiting in ambush.

The first time I ever had cause to strap a pot plant to my head and apply foyer-coloured camouflage paint to my face was after that momentous cock-up on the streets of Paris back in 2003. To compound my agony at having downgraded the *maillot jaune* to a mundane item of knitwear, I had now been sent off on a mission to winkle David Millar out of the security of his hotel room, just so he could relive the moment all over again for the benefit of our viewers.

I had discovered, by consulting *The Yellow Book*, that Millar's Cofidis team were to be housed twenty kilometres south-east of Paris in a 4-star auberge. We had set off through the thinning Paris traffic, while Matt phoned as many of his contacts as he could, including Millar himself, whose mobile remained resolutely switched off. When we'd finally reached the place, there was no sign of him. The receptionists gazed upon us with deep suspicion as we skulked around outside the lobby with a clatter of equipment, all wearing the same pitifully needy expression. It was already late and we were hungry. Lean, wild dogs at the door.

While I gazed impotently around the place looking for salvation to jump out from behind the concierge's polished desk, Matt had been busying himself outside the hotel. He'd interviewed French mechanics as they hosed down the time-trial bikes in the drying sun.

Dinner time came and went, without so much as an amuse-bouche to share between us. Gloom settled in. We stopped talking to one another completely. Matt's phone remained mute. The expressions on the faces of the hotel staff shifted imperceptibly towards a position of sympathy.

This was my first experience of an evening shift on the Tour: staking out some poor sod in a hotel whose only wish is that you would give up and leave him alone to his massage and his evening meal. And all the while you too are thinking that all you really want is to give up and leave him alone to his massage and his evening meal. Yet your duty is to wait and observe, through half-shut doors giving a glimpse into restaurant rooms, how everyone else in the world is rounding off their day with conviviality and claret.

Cofidis riders had been observed meandering to and from the dinner table. But not Millar. At some point Matt stepped up his assault on the Scotsman's privacy by obtaining his room number and ringing his bedroom phone. Once again I was staggered to see how easy this was.

Suddenly, at about 9.30 that night, Matt's rabbit-and-hat trick worked. We spotted the tall, awkward figure of Dave Millar loping slowly towards us across an interior courtyard in a baggy Cofidis tracksuit. Grim-faced, he shook our hands, and then talked at some length about his disappointment.

It was all down to Matt, of course. Watching his tireless efforts in the lobbies of hotels has taught me a great deal about persistence.

If the meerkat is at home in the desert, then Matt lives for the hotel foyer. I have spent countless hours in his company on evening duty, making nuisances of ourselves under the tut-tutting gaze of the receptionists. But while I have felt irritated, bored and discomforted by the experience, I strongly suspect Matt has enjoyed every second. When all trace of adrenalin has been and gone, and all conversation dried up to irritable grunting, Matt Rendell is the only member of our quartet who can still retain his focus, eyes on stalks and head flicking from side to side as he nervously tracks the comings and goings in the foyer.

On another occasion, we were trying to get an interview with Millar's former directeur sportif Francis van Londersele.

We had been hanging around in his hotel for what felt like hours, mainly because it had been. We had doorstepped riders having massages, we had knocked on the doors of empty hotel rooms, checked the gym, the pool and all the rest of it. We kept returning to the foyer, where Matt would take up his favoured position. It was an area of carpeted flooring slightly to the left of reception which afforded a view simultaneously of the front door, the restaurant, the bar, the stairwell, and with a half-step forward and a crane of the neck, the entrance to the toilets.

Nothing escaped his notice. No rider could slouch by with his hands in his pockets and his gaze directed to the floor without Matt clocking his presence, instantly calculating his usefulness to the cause and accosting him with a beaming smile and outstretched hand. Fearless, he is. And he has been known on more than one occasion heartily to greet absolutely the wrong rider with entirely the wrong name.

'Federico!'

'No.'

'Manuel?' He gets it right eventually.

For the umpteenth time, he dialled van Londersele's number and this time it cut through. *Francis? Allo. C'est Matt . . . Matt du Foyer.*

Matt du Foyer! The aristocrat of the media stakeout, a titled hack. Brilliant. Just thinking about it still brings me out in a smile.

There were still other occasions when I suspect I owe His Foyerness my broadcasting life. Late one evening, well after the highlights show had been put together and sent back to London for broadcast, Matt and I were called into the truck by Steve Docherty. We shot a glance at each other. This is almost always ominous, doubly so, when everyone else in the truck is told to get out, so that there can be no witnesses. We feared the worst.

Inside the dark of the truck, Steve looked up at us. 'What stories have you got for me for tomorrow?'

Matt cleared his throat.

Rashly, I spoke up. 'Well . . .' but then I realised instantly that I had nothing to say.

I tried to buy time within the sentence itself, which rarely works. '. . . I was thinking that there might be some value in doing a piece which in some way reflects what people are saying about . . .'

Matt backed me up. 'Yup. That.' He nodded his agreement. Steve looked back down at his running order for the next day, which featured a blank item where ours should be.

'Get to a hotel. Get me some Aussies. I want Aussie riders. In a hotel. I want banter.'

We were stranded at the top of a mountain. It was already quite late. We were miles from any hotel with Aussies in it. This sounded as close to impossible as any task I had been set on the Tour.

'OK, Steve, no problem.' We left.

As we sat in traffic inching down the mountain, Matt phoned as many people as he knew in World Cycling, who even had a tangential connection with anyone or anything Australian. We didn't reach the hotel of the Française des Jeux team much before 9.30 at night.

To my amazement, though, once again Matt had done his thing. He led the way, as behind him we clattered into the hotel foyer, trailing wires and dropping batteries as we went. Breathlessly, we arrived at the designated hotel room, aware that riders and team staff were beginning to turn in for the night and that our appearance stretched their definition of open access way beyond what might be considered reasonable. Nervous of what reception awaited us, we knocked on the door.

We needn't have worried. Within minutes, Woody was pinning a microphone on Baden Cooke, and his roommate Brad McGee. These weren't just any old riders. Cooke showed me his collection of green and white jerseys, all packed away in his suitcase. McGee trumped that by laying out a clutch of yellows on his bed. And being Aussies, once they saw the red light for 'record' blinking on the front of the camera, they couldn't resist a bit of showing off. So we even got our banter. TV requires banter, you see. It's a necessity.

This strange encounter had all taken place in a tiny, hot room. The two riders shared this limited space in an airless hotel in the foothills of the Pyrenees, and they had sacrificed what little privacy they might have enjoyed to oblige a British TV crew. By the time we left them it was nearly eleven and they had to try and prepare for the next day's stage. We took our shoes off, and padded down the corridor.

So it is that, half-guest, half-pest, we go about our half-welcomed, half-intrusive business, unsure of where we stand or how far we can push our luck. The Tour de France has a knack of keeping you in a state of perpetual uncertainty.

But at least it isn't sterile.

INTRODUCING ARMSTRONG

'Lance. If I bet a hundred dollars that you would one day be President of the USA, would I be wasting my money?' I posed the question on the eve of the 2005 Tour. I wasn't being sycophantic; I was just curious.

His answer was archetypal Armstrong. He picked me out from a very big crowd of journalists in a hall, paused for a moment, and then spoke slowly.

'I have no plans to move into those circles.' He paused. Everyone at the press conference thought he was finished. 'But if the bet wins, do I get my cut?'

I've kept that tape, just in case.

I first glimpsed Lance Armstrong in 2003 at the centre of a scrum of camera crews, snappers and reporters that had formed around him in the blink of an eye. The whole ridiculous fleshy circle was drifting across the open expanse of an empty exhibition hall in Paris like a cyclone inching its way over the Atlantic. At the eye of the storm was Armstrong, small but in very clear command, despite the chaos raging around him.

I was astonished by the scale of the interest in him. I had only marginally heard of this man just a few weeks prior to arriving on my first Tour. Now I had come face to face with the insatiability of the media's appetite for Armstrong, and I couldn't believe it. I had been given my instructions to get some shots of his arrival at the hall in Paris where the Tour had set up shop two days before the start of the race. I had naively imagined being able to sit him down, one-on-one for a few minutes, to introduce myself formally and to start to build some sort of working relationship with the man whose endeavours were about to shape the pattern of my first three weeks on the Tour.

What I hadn't envisaged was getting a thick ear from a Flemish photographer and my toes stamped by an Italian radio presenter.

Armstrong, in 2003. Madness in a moment.

The man himself looked almost a little amused by the insanity enveloping him. Down the years I have often felt this. That he has been quietly delighted by the absurdity of the scenes that unfold before him day after day on the Tour. Television crews will stop at nothing to be the first ones to thrust a microphone under his nose. Radio's no different. Everyone wants a bit of him and, this being the Tour, you can get close enough to take a bit, too. Yet, to me, he remains uncompromised, aloof. Not haughty, just amused.

On the 2009 Tour, the first year of Armstrong's much-hyped

comeback, Matt Rendell found himself in pole position in the most almighty bundle that formed within seconds of the American's Astana team completing the team time trial. This time, rather than the conventional scrum, Armstrong had disappeared into the heart of a moving mass of bodies. The whole seething entity was proceeding at jogging pace. Armstrong, in the middle, was flanked by a dozen CRS French riot police, who were in turn encased, like the core of a Scotch egg, by an outer layer of reporters and cameramen. At the front of this absurd sight, Matt's cameraman John was running backwards, filming, while Matt, attached to him by a microphone, was being lifted off his feet by the ever-tightening circle of bodies. At the point at which he lost all contact with the ground and was literally being carried aloft, he caught Armstrong's attention. Instead of framing an insightful enquiry about the General Classification, he beamed broadly and launched into the best question ever asked of Lance Armstrong: 'Lance, doesn't this ever strike you as completely ridiculous?'

Armstrong, caked in the drying sweat from a roasting Montpellier sun, smiled the briefest of smiles. 'Yeah, well. It does make me miss lying on the beach with a beer.'

Indeed.

In 2004, for some odd reason, we started calling him Larry. Not that he was ever aware that he had acquired a new nickname. We certainly never said it to his face. No, we were far more subtle than that. We said it behind his back.

It's hard to remember just how the name Larry stuck. Certainly there was an element of debunking about it. Lance sounds epic; Larry just sounds suburban. But actually, it had more to do with his relationship with the singer Sheryl Crow. After his marriage to Kristin, his first wife, fell apart, he hooked up with Sheryl. I understood that she was famous on a global scale, and had been responsible for the 'sun coming up on the Santa Monica Boulevard' but we all kept forgetting her name. I was convinced she was called Shirley. I still think she should be. And Larry would be just right for Shirley.

As luck would have it, we were allocated the Novotel on the outskirts of Liège as our hotel for the two days prior to the start of the 2004 Tour. Sheryl Crow, Lance Armstrong and the rest of the US Postal Team were staying in the same hotel. It was the first and only time we were ever billeted in the same place. It worked out pretty well, at least for us.

After twenty-four hours, and largely due to Matt Rendell's blossoming relationship with Armstrong, we had secured an exclusive sit-down interview with Crow, or Sheryl, as I kept intoning to myself to stave off the awful, but very real danger of slipping up and calling her Shirley.

When the hour came, we set up the camera in the appointed room and waited for the lady to arrive. Which she did, right on time. There was little that I remember from that interview save for one quote.

'I think it's incredible, just getting out and meeting people, particularly in France, how much love there is for Lance Armstrong. How they just totally love the man.'

I felt a judder from behind me, as John, who was shooting the interview tried to control a fit of cynicism.

After the interview, Woody posed for a photo with Crow, presumably because he didn't often get the opportunity to be seen next to people shorter than him, and we all said thanks and went our separate ways.

Later that evening, we were all caught in the lift together: Matt, John, Woody, Larry, Shirley and I. Armstrong said something nice about Matt's latest book to Sheryl. Then the banter subsided, and we all started not concentrating on what her name wasn't. It was a long twenty seconds.

There is an aura that surrounds Armstrong. I have known three men in my life who have possessed it in equal measure. Sir Alex Ferguson, Lance and the headmaster of my secondary school, C.I.M. Jones (I never knew what the C stood for, let alone the I and the M). When Larry left the Tour for the first time in 2005, he took some of the race with him, and diminished its standing by his absence.

In 2007, when we reached Paris for the final stage, there were rumours spreading like wildfire that Lance was in town, ending a two-year absence from the Tour. The retired champion had, seemingly, arranged with the US TV Network OLN to take a ten-minute turn in the commentary box alongside their regular team.

Now this was remarkable news. ASO (the Tour organisers) and Armstrong were like a newly divorced couple, enjoying the freedom after their years of mutual dependence. An uneasy cohabitation during his racing years: France never really took to the American, and the feeling was often mutual. Suffice to say, when Armstrong decided to drop in on the Champs-Elysées, as far as the Tour was concerned, he wasn't welcome.

To this day, we don't know how he did it, but there was talk that he'd smuggled himself onto the race in the back of a Discovery Channel team car. I wouldn't rule it out either. Like José Mourinho who, it was claimed, jumped into a laundry bin, threw towels over himself and was wheeled into the Chelsea dressing room to circumvent a UEFA ban, Armstrong has always had a showman's ego.

So, there I was on the Champs-Elysées, tipped off about Armstrong's imminent arrival, waiting for at least an hour at the back of the commentary truck with a cameraman. Facing the wrong way. Inevitably.

By the time I'd noticed him, he'd stolen a march on both of us and we were charging to get past him so that I could fire in a question. John and I were now running backwards, fast. After a two-year abstinence from chasing the Armstrong sound bite, I was suddenly back in business.

'Welcome back to France, Lance. Have you missed it?' I thrust the mic in his direction, still trotting backwards.

I never heard his answer, because suddenly I was lying flat out among the TV cables and the dog shit, having tripped on the root of a tree.

I did, however, see him stepping politely over me, offering an apologetic smile, edged with a veneer of amusement.

Later that day, just as Armstrong was completing his stint for OLN, there was a sudden loss of power to their commentary box. All their communications went down. To this day, no one has been able to explain why it only affected the Americans, but needless to say, the conspiracy theories have been entertaining.

I have other memories of Armstrong, which are more dignified than falling over in front of him. At home above my desk,
I have framed the front page of *L'Equipe* from 12 July 2003.
The headline reads 'Armstrong, oui mais'. The picture beneath
shows Armstrong in yellow for the first time that Tour,
answering questions in front of a forest of microphones at the
summit of Alpe d'Huez. He looks, if not jubilant, then care-
worn. I am in the picture too, straining forward to catch his
eye and get my questions heard. Behind us, the unnatural
blue of the Alpine summer sky lights the scene with infrared
intensity.

Armstrong, oui mais

Même si le Texan a parfaitement contrôlé les débats, il n'a pas été souverain.

This is how I often remember Armstrong. It was my first
Tour, and my first exposure to his nature. The climb that day
had been won by Iban Mayo, who had attacked and ridden
away from the bunch. Further down the switchbacks of the
famous mountain, Armstrong had been furiously repelling
attack after attack from riders like Tyler Hamilton and Joseba
Beloki. He neutralised them all. After the podium protocol,
he stood in front of us, empty with the effort, his eyes almost

betraying tiredness, as he questioned his rivals, 'Are they racing the Tour?' he wondered. 'Or are they racing me?'

The grip he held them in. By the end of his reign, during the fag end of the drab 2004 and 2005 Tours, his power in the peloton was unquestionable. No stage was gifted, no breakaway allowed, no lesser rider accorded his hour on the stage without the volition or at least tacit permission of the champion.

Since the races themselves were among the dullest Tours, we spent much of the time on the sniff for something else to talk about other than the castration of the opposition: a fading Jan Ullrich, about to be discredited; Ivan Basso, a good friend of Armstrong and too close to him for anything other than what looked like a rather neutered challenge; Tyler Hamilton and Floyd Landis, former teammates who were ekeing out the embarrassing final chapters of their careers.

And so it was that we leapt on a little scandal which played itself out over the closing days of the 2004 Tour, a race that was decided even before Jean-Marie Leblanc had penned the word 'Paris' on the route map. It was revealing, in that it threw Armstrong's true nature into sharp relief.

Filippo Simeoni was a rider with a problem. A tall, awkward, emotional man with a decent, albeit doping-tainted, career both behind and before him. He was riding out the end of an anonymous Tour in the garish colours of the completely underwhelming Domina Vacanze team. On Stage 18, he fancied a bit of the action.

Simeoni had previous form. After admitting to doping offences a couple of years prior to that, he had testified in an Italian court that Dr Michele Ferrari had, on a number of occasions, prescribed him EPO. Ferrari had worked closely with Lance Armstrong. This testimony naturally enough reflected badly on the Texan, who reportedly denounced Filippo as a liar. Simeoni promptly started proceedings against him for defamation. Brave, especially when you have to spend three weeks alongside the man, riding to the edge of collapse, up and down mountains in the searing summer sun. Armstrong counter-sued but in the end both men withdrew their cases.

That day six riders broke away, not one a threat to Armstrong's lead. Nor was Simeoni when he attacked and rode across to the break. But the yellow jersey was enraged. He tore off the front of the bunch, hammered across to the breakaway, and informed them that he would stay there for as long as Simeoni was part of their number. Behind them on the road, T-Mobile, the team of Jan Ullrich, had to react and, unsure of how this might play out, they hit the front and started to bring the race back together again.

The original six pleaded with Simeoni to relent. Eventually, wordlessly, the Italian sat up, and dropped away, Armstrong alongside him. T-Mobile called the chase off, and as the bunch swallowed up the two riders, Simeoni fell back through the peloton and, it is said, was spat at repeatedly.

Nothing and no one moved in those years without Armstrong's say-so.

At the finish line, the story of what had happened was tearing through the media village. We were trying to get our accounts straight, each of us running through the dense under-growth of high voltage cables coiled around the hundreds of broadcast vehicles, snatching a rumour from the Dutch, a fact from the Danes and a tip-off from the Italians. The chatter had thrown up a story, which, if confirmed, would give some more substance to the Simeoni feud.

Back in April of that year, it was rumoured, during the Tour of Georgia, Lance Armstrong's people had contacted Mario Cipollini, the pantomime-camp king, flamboyant sprinter and leader of the Domina Vacanze team, and asked him in no uncertain terms to make sure that Simeoni was not part of the Tour roster. This would have been a preposterous intervention. A grudge is one thing, but this would have taken it into very uncomfortable territory.

The reason that we, in the media, were drawn to this story was simple enough. There was in those years an unspoken sense that we were all subject to the Armstrong Orthodoxy. He was big news. And as a result of his endeavours year on year, the Tour grew bigger. The bigger the Tour, the better our job prospects, our security. Why rock the boat?

This issue, though, enabled us to touch on controversy; to hint at a different way of reporting on Armstrong. We had bitten our lips, buried our more cynical instincts, but this suggestion of bully-boy tactics on the part of Armstrong worked as a pressure valve. We were letting out a little air, without running the risk of a full-blown puncture.

By now the breakaway had been whittled down to three riders who were passing under the flamme rouge, which signifies that a kilometre is left to go. They were sweeping towards the finish line near the Place de la Liberte in Lons-le-Saunier. A twenty-six-year-old Spanish domestique named Juan Miguel Mercado outmanoeuvred his nearest rivals to win the stage. To this day, that is the greatest result of his racing career. He sailed across the finish line, arms aloft, pursued by a camera team from RTB Belgian TV, but obdurately ignored by the rest of us who smiled apologetically at him before returning our attentions to the sinuous run-in, in the hope of snatching Armstrong the moment he arrived.

We waited for eleven minutes and twenty-nine seconds, the history books tell me, before Thor Hushovd announced the arrival of the main bunch by winning the sprint. Behind him, and flanked as ever by his guardsmen Hincapie and Beltran, came Armstrong, left leg extended on the pedals as he drifted in.

The scrum ensued. An undignified tangle of cables and lenses. Armstrong looked grim, as he studiously ignored us all, which wasn't hard since no one was actually addressing a question at him. Yes, microphones and cameras were thrust in his face as he jostled his way through us to the podium area, but not a single question came his way. Instead, we fought among ourselves. I trod on the ankle of a French radio reporter; German TV tried to wheel the shopping trolley that houses the generator for their wireless TV signal through the pack of sweating and stressed journalists; Norwegian writers went elbow to elbow with a Basque snapper. It was laughable. Only the main man wasn't laughing.

He disappeared through a gap which appeared miraculously in the barriers, sending the whole ghastly entourage sprinting 150 metres round the outside of the compound to the official media area. All this was played out to the sarcastic applause of the watching public, whose scorn I understood. I would have laughed too. At the mixed zone we waited for his officially sanctioned appearance. This was in no doubt. The wearer of the yellow jersey, along with that day's stage winner and all the other jersey holders, are obliged by the Tour organisers to make themselves available for interview. Even Armstrong.

Most days he obliged us, and would only shirk his responsibilities when there really was nothing to say. This was his fourth day in yellow, having memorably loaned it out to Thomas Voeckler for ten days in the middle of the Tour. This close to the end of the Tour, and after relatively few days as wearer, the sense of routine had not yet settled in, and there was still much to talk about. Not least, of course, his extraordinary spat with Simeoni. Armstrong's not a shirker, we thought to ourselves. He would come.

He didn't. We waited till the protocol was done with. However, as the uninspiring strains of the Tour's ponderous anthem cranked up for the final time over the PA system to close out the ceremonials, we caught sight of the leader of the Tour de France hopping on his Trek bike and making for the exit to the compound. Like a plague of accredited locusts, we took flight and ran after him.

Yet Armstrong vanished. He was gone. We'd looked everywhere for his team car. We'd considered all the avenues he could have turned into. We'd asked the right people and kept our eyes open, but we had drawn a blank.

Just as we turned and filed back towards the TV truck. Just as we were hatching a version of events that might explain, or even justify, the fact that the 'Finish Line Crew' was returning to base without the big interview of the day, we ran into him.

He was at the centre of a small knot of cycling journalists. The guys from the press had trapped and encircled him with their Dictaphones. We joined the circle, our microphone suddenly swelling the numbers. I held back with the questions to gauge the tenor of the conversation.

There was a difficult balance to be struck. Lance had clearly been spotted and persuaded to talk by a pack of writers. I had to respect that fact. Understandably, perhaps, the written press have a high regard for what they do and a fairly obdurate disregard for the work of TV and radio. They resent our privileges. They resent our facile lines of questioning. They resent our demands for space (have you seen how big our cameras are?) and, frankly, they sometimes just resent us. Now they had cornered the main man on their own, it was made clear to me, from the scowls of disapproval, that he was theirs, and theirs alone.

I listened.

'Lance, another day in yellow. How does it feel?'

'Lance, talk us through the closing stages.'

Where was the question? Had I missed it? I could tell from the knitted brows of the writers that all the while they were holding their recorders close to Armstrong's lips, they weren't listening to a thing. They were formulating a plan of attack. They were scheming, manoeuvring the conversation to a point from which they could launch their attack and fire in the silver-bullet Simeoni question. Armstrong looked to me as if he was fully aware of what was going on, too. The unasked question was the elephant in the huddle.

This was a rough-and-ready encounter, which was taking place in a public place on neutral ground. There were no chaperones or media officers. He was alone and so were we. There was no barrier to keep us apart. We were face to face and inches apart. This type of confrontation, when it comes to it, is not without its tensions. The Simeoni question would stir things up for Armstrong. It would invoke the spectre of his association with the wrong people.

'What went on between you and Simeoni, today?' I could wait no longer. And in an instant, I knew for certain that no one had asked him that question yet. Their microphones all inched forward a notch. We were bunched together so tightly now, that we might have been rehearsing a world record attempt to see how many people you could fit in a telephone box, only without the telephone box.

He looked right at me. Very close. 'I just follow on the wheels.'

And with that, he broke into the broadest of smiles. He seemed pleased with the joke, and enjoyed a little ripple of sympathetic laughter from some of the onlookers. Then he turned half away from me, a dismissive gesture designed to close the chapter. His smile appealed to the other guys to chip in with a different line of enquiry. I knew he didn't want to hear my voice again, but that if I hesitated for a fraction, he would take that as a sign of weakness and ride off.

'There is a rumour that you asked Mario Cipollini that he shouldn't be selected . . .'

He'd turned back to me now, and he didn't wait for me to finish my question. 'That's absolutely not true.'

'Not true?'

Filming to my left, I found out when I reviewed the footage later, John had started a slow zoom, ever tightening into Armstrong's taut features. 'One hundred per cent not true. Absolutely not true. How can I ask a team who to take? I can barely control that on my own team.'

Our encounter was finished. For once, I felt, it had been a score draw. In his long and winning Tour career, Armstrong had enjoyed many great days. This wasn't one of them. I rushed back to the truck, with the tape. My throat was dry.

Elsewhere, amidst the debris of the splintered peloton, Matt had cornered Simeoni.

'Yes, it's true. Cipollini did everything to keep me out of the Tour team.' He looked bruised, but coherent. 'Armstrong showed what sort of person he is today.'

We ran both interviews in full. Gary Imlach's carefully chosen words that closed the programme that night were among the best I have ever heard in a sports programme. He touched on Armstrong's greatness before going on to say, 'Armstrong needs grudges the way that the *Flying Scotsman* needs a steady supply of coal.' He continued, 'What we saw on the road today was the most powerful cyclist in the world using his status to take revenge on a man who won't make in his career what Lance is going to make this month.'

It was the tail end of only my second Tour, and I was now recognisable to Armstrong. Up to this point, I had really only had cause to celebrate the man. Now I had been brought face to face, literally, with something different: Armstrong continuing his battles off the bike. From that moment on it's possible that he became more aware of me in the press pack. I certainly felt that the ground had shifted a little, and that our subsequent encounters were defined by the lines we had drawn that day. As a journalist, the taped encounter left me a little exhilarated, but, in equal measure, uncertain.

EN ROUTE

There is a misconception among my friends and family back at home that I spend every July stopping off to sketch a Roman viaduct, or perhaps to take in an open-air opera in some town square. Pure fallacy. There is nothing very charming about following the Tour de France. For the most part, getting around the route of the Tour de France involves sitting wordlessly in a hired car that belches diesel fumes into the atmosphere, while wondering which type of sandwich you might choose from the service station, if the traffic ever starts moving again.

At the beginning of each Tour the three of us, sometimes four, when Matt is in our car, have to confront the reality of thousands of miles in front of us. There are routines to observe, conversations to beget and forget, old jokes to be revisited, new ones to develop (although this is becoming a rarer occurrence).

July is made up of moments like this.

Matt is at the wheel, accelerating hard and missing gears with insouciant abandon. I am in the passenger seat beside him. A heap of photocopied A4 sheets detailing our itinerary spills uselessly across my knees. A week ago, they were all bound in a sensible folder, but chaos has consumed them. Woody is fully engaged in our hunt to find a bed for the night. He leans forward from the back seats, trying to help us navigate. Liam, iPod in ears, slumped against the door, eyes half closed, is praying to the French god of food, Michelin. He won't say much until we've arrived.

But, even though we've only just started, it's worth stopping here. A freeze-frame of our grey Renault Espace trundling up a charmless provincial industrial estate in search of human comfort. Following the Tour.

Let me begin with luggage.

Suitcases are such hateful things. They represent misery in bulging plastic form. Heaved with loathing from pillar to post, and left in the back of the car to melt in unreasonable temperatures, their glowering presence makes manifest your distance from home. The long expanse of their zips reminds you of the distance to be traversed before home is reached again.

Experienced Tourists can probably date suitcases to the exact stage. Like trees add a ring for each year, so our cases accrue the scurf of daily decay. One year, the strap on my big blue one finally broke. I laughed at it. I literally stood there on the damp pavement outside the gloomy Hotel de la Croix Blanche in Tarbes, laughing scornfully at a bag.

They are dictators: they impose their will; they determine your happiness.

Like a stiffening bovine corpse left out in the summer's heat and allowed to rot, a suitcase will start to swell. By about day five, this becomes a problem. Inside it there is a burgeoning pressure, a building up of noxious gases: by-products of a rot that has infected clothes left for dead. Generally speaking, it starts with the socks.

At first, it's manageable. Prologue socks can be easily contained. But a day of pounding up and down the streets of some prestigious regional capital in pursuit of riders on carbon-fibre bikes will grind a pair of Gap ankle socks into a state of compacted and frayed filth. Some simple rules should be observed that will help contain the carnage if diligently followed. A little suitcase husbandry is critical.

So, listen up. Should you be lucky enough to sit down for dinner in the comforting surroundings of a brasserie, your socks will need changing before you head for the bar. Do this as soon as you get to the hotel room. Pair them up in their saline filth, roll them together and slip them inside the compli-mentary plastic sack that is meant for your laundry order. This can be found by sliding back the door to the left of the desk with the leatherette wallet containing information on how to dial internationally using the phone on your bedside table.

Should you find yourself in a hotel too modest for a laundry service, don't despair. Underneath the desk with the telephone on it, or just to the right of the door, you will find the waste bin. Take out the small white bin liner. This will do for a few days but won't last longer than that, as it will tear. Or simply melt away.

Then unzip the inner lining at the top of the suitcase and slide the bagged-up socks in there. If the Tour starts in the temperate gloom of Belgium or Brittany or, indeed, Britain, you might get a few days' grace before the plastic starts to degrade, allowing them to infect the healthier tissue in the main body of the case, spreading their malignancy. But be warned: by week two, there will be nothing left that doesn't look, and smell, like it's been stuffed down the back of a couch.

It is a kind of slow misery, watching the disorder begin, gain a foothold and then ride roughshod over all the best intentions.

Back at home there is a rhythm and a structure to the process of packing. Over the years, it has become a source of some pride to me. Packing has become a work of great finesse, very different from the wild overcomplication of my first year on the Tour. Shorts are in their rightful place. Shirts, too. Pants, adapters, and chargers; the multiplying mutant strands of twenty-first-century life. Everything neatly displayed and in pristine order.

Then there are the nonsense items; all the other nuts and bolts. They are signifiers of a perplexing naivety taken on the trip in a spirit of wild optimism, and then neglected the whole way round. This can be a sketchbook or a pair of swimming trunks, but most years it takes the form of a thick and impenetrable novel. Two years ago, it was *Crime and Punishment*. I read as far as the crime, but by the time we'd reached Limoges, I'd given up on the punishment.

It is a trip of three and a half weeks, if you include the days spent filming before the start of the race. It can feel like months. A rider once told me that he too sits in his hotel room of an evening after yet another gruelling stage, opens the route book at the relevant page, and measures with the pad of his thumb the thickness of pages passed, against that of those remaining. Reaching the halfway mark is like the first glimmer of dawn after a long and sleepless night. You suddenly become aware that it is possible that this whole thing might, at some distant point in the future, end. You know, actually end.

There are daily irritants. For me, the most challenging of these is the need to appear passably turned out in front of the camera. Some people are born presentable, others have presentability thrust upon them. That's me. The effort to appear even remotely tidy – smooth of chin, slick of hair and sporting a pressed shirt – leaves me weak. And, routinely, I fail.

Let's leave aside the problem area of my face for a moment, which tends to sport an angrily burnt nose, and eyes that permanently bear the wrinkles of another dreadful night's sleep. No, the thing I struggle most of all with is my inability to iron.

The battle starts even before I leave for France. I stalk the big clothes shops of Oxford Street, picking up polo shirts and wrinkling them to see how quickly and smoothly they unfurl. I know what I am looking for, even as the security guard eyes me with suspicion. Never mind the cut and the colour, are they easy-iron? But I've never cracked it. I might buy half a dozen new shirts each summer, only to find that at least four of them won't be fit for purpose and will end up at home, adding another layer to my polo-shirt mountain.

I crave polyester. My dreams are woven in simple nylon.

How I envy Gary Imlach. He has amassed, during his twenty-odd years of Tour experience, a collection of shirts that are as unchanging and timelessly uncrumpled as Phil Liggett's smiling face. The trick he has refined is to wear his 'non-broadcast' shirt in the air-conditioned gloom of the TV truck while he is scripting, thinking and generally preparing. His 'broadcast-quality' shirt, that is to say the favoured shirt singled out for the purposes of the day in question, hangs patiently on a hook behind him. Late on in the day comes the moment when the scripts are printing off and he's ready to leave the truck, find a scenic backdrop and record the closing to the show. Then, and only then, does he slip on the unwrinkled shirt, and stroll out into the sun. Perfect.

The only time this really couldn't work was on the Tourmalet in 2010, when a deluge meant that the only sensible clothing was a bin bag. Still, he'd managed to iron his hair.

I quizzed him about his regime once. He told me that his first decade covering the Tour had been spent in much the same despair as mine with regard to ironing. Until that is, he discovered 'steaming'. It seems he used to hang the shirt on the shower rail in his hotel room, carefully adjust the angle of the head and the trajectory of the hot water stream, and then, after setting it to 'Unbelievably Hot', allow it to run until his accommodation resembled an Istanbul hammam. Seemingly unconcerned by the 92 per cent humidity that built up in his bedroom, Gary was able to leave for work in the morning buoyed by the knowledge that he would not be plagued by crumpledness, confident that his journalistic acumen would not be undermined by a crap collar. These days, he's refined this down to one of those portable hand-held steamers, which he wields with extraordinary dexterity.

I, on the other hand, iron. I iron on desks, bedside tables, sink tops, chairs. Sometimes I iron on ironing boards, although these occasions are rare. Any half-decent forensic scientist could track my progress round France by recording the distinctive scorch marks left by my travel iron on the work surfaces of cheap hotels. They are cloven hoof marks of a ruminant hack.

Ironing involves forward planning. However late I might finally get to bed, the need arises to think about tomorrow's shirt. It must be ironed right there and then. It cannot wait till the morning. The reason for this is simple enough: the iron travels with us. There is no time in the morning to allow it to cool down naturally. A hot iron, even if wrapped in a stolen hotel towel, should never be placed in your luggage alongside a nougat-related confectionery gift supplied to you by the Office of Tourism of Montelimar. Really, never.

I would like to say that I have become adept at this down the years, but it would not be true. Any casual observer of our Tour coverage will recognise the wilting collars and ragged seams that characterise my sub-standard attempts at grooming. But assuming that I have managed to get down to the breakfast room wearing a shirt that doesn't draw open ridicule or even hostility from my colleagues, the next hurdle I have to overcome is the ritual of the morning bad moods.

Over an endlessly repeating cycle of croissants and stubby baguette ends garnished with pats of butter unfolded from foil wrappings and miniature pots of *confiture de fraises*, I have to confront the daily disparate psychopathologies of the crew with whom I share my professional life.

If Matt is with us, then he has normally jumped the starting gun by a good hour, found a local newsagent, and committed to memory every word of at least three newspapers in three different languages. His mind is fizzing with cycling minutiae, as he juggles breakfast and deep thought. He pushes his laptop's luck by sloshing coffee and orange juice around the table. He has cycling on his mind, and cannot conceive of a world not similarly obsessed. At this hour, he struggles to find like-minded conversation partners.

'You know what?' No one answers. 'The thing about Juan Antonio Flecha is this . . .'

'Not listening, Matt.'

A moment later, he understands his error of judgement. 'Yeah. Suppose so. Yup.'

Liam is always last down. Breakfast for him is the slow unfurling of a frown. It is his chance to emit silence.

Generally speaking, at the agreed hour of our departure, negotiated at midnight the night before in the lobby of the hotel, Liam will be loading up salami and soft cheese onto another baguette. As he heads for the car, he is still sloshing a steaming cup of black stuff and mumbling profanities about the quality of the coffee in French hotels.

Woody, having drained the orange juice dispenser dry, will have passed through almost unnoticed, save for a sneezing fit. He has a habit of sneezing three times, one after the other, and turning each individual sneeze into a foul-mouthed (nosed?) profanity. Atch-anker! Atch-ollocks! Atch-osspot! Just the three, and then he'll let it rest, before silently mixing a pot of honey into a plain yoghurt.

Still, he has his uses. He's the one who remembers to bring the squeezable Marmite with him from home.

On certain rare occasions, my colleagues might actually ask what we're doing that morning, who we would be chasing. They might feign interest. But if I start to explain the nuances

of the cycling story with too much journalistic enthusiasm, I will be met with the 'Partridge-shrug'. This takes its name from Alan Partridge's famous restaurant scene and is a gesture of such complete indifference that it withers the soul and diminishes both the shrugger and the shruggee. And so it is, lost in our private little worlds, that we load into our vehicles the stuff which we had unloaded only hours before.

And on we go.

We learnt long ago to switch off the voice on the sat nav. Our own monotonous blather is bad enough. There's no need to add another voice to the drone, especially if it belongs to someone who doesn't actually exist and can't chip in to buy the coffees. The downside is that we often sail blissfully past our motorway exit, adding an instant 30km to our journey. But it's our choice, and frankly we're too proud to accept the error of our ways. Besides, the car is our home for a month, and we have become unusually protective of its individuality.

The ITV crews travel round in three identical Renault Espaces. I say identical, although it hasn't escaped my notice that some are more identical than others. It appears that the car designated to convey Gary Imlach and Chris Boardman around France has tended, over recent years, to boast leather upholstery, whereas the others don't. It's not a complaint, just an observation.

These cars take such a hammering on an annual basis, it's a wonder anyone will let us rent them at all. In fact, it appears there is only one rental garage in the whole of France that is prepared to entertain such a patently loss-making undertaking.

Every year, the production team has a struggle on their hands with the particular branch of Renault Location who insist that they no longer want our business. Every year, though, some sort of deal is struck. The usual clincher is the publicity card.

ITV producers: 'But, you must understand. These cars will be driven by ITV's team of high-profile presenters covering the Tour de France. Money cannot buy such exposure. The marketing impact back in the UK for Renault should not be underestimated. It must run into many, many pounds.'

Renault: 'Ah, well, of course that changes everything. Please feel free to abuse our brand-new vehicles as much as you wish, and return them in an almost unusable and pretty much unsellable state. Also, don't worry about the flood of traffic offences that will reach us by post long after you've fled back to London with your tails between your legs. It would be our pleasure to settle all your debts with Police Nationale.'

I'm pretty sure that's how the conversation must run. Only in French obviously.

The worst job on the whole of the Tour, which I have managed to swerve so far, happens on the Monday morning after the final stage in Paris. Someone, normally Matt since no one else volunteers, has to return the car to Renault at their hard-to-find depot somewhere behind the Gare du Nord. This much he has learnt: don't wait for them to ask questions. Drop off the keys and run.

One time, when reversing the car out of the subterranean car park underneath the Place de la Concorde for its final journey home, Matt got too close to a concrete pillar and completely destroyed the entire left side of the car. It had made it all the way around France with no visible damage, until the very last movement when Matt delivered the *coup de grâce*.

By some extraordinary coincidence, Mike, our engineer, managed to do the same thing to another car in exactly the same place four years later, only without the same impressive degree of violence. He posed for a picture. For insurance purposes, of course.

On my first Tour Woody tried to back into a frankly non-existent parking space on the top of Alpe d'Huez, and in doing so, tore a ridge four-foot long down the length of the passenger side of the vehicle, ripping off the wing mirror. A couple of days later, Matt drove the same car firmly into the back of a family saloon in the foothills of the Alps. Undeterred by his own obvious guilt, he leapt out of the car, arms flailing wildly and levelled furious accusations at the driver in front, neatly raising the temperature of the encounter to boiling point. Apart from internal bruising and mild concussion to its head gasket the Espace made it back to Paris in one piece. However, I suspect the young family who we shunted into disrepair may still be stuck on the hillside waiting for assistance. If they are reading this: sorry.

On another occasion, we let Liam drive. Years would pass before we ever let him try again. It was his first experience of getting up a mountain on race day, something that takes a lot of practice. On the morning of a big stage with a summit finish the road crawls with cyclists trying to ride the climb for themselves. There is no way of knowing how many there are on any given day. But it is many, many thousands.

They are, it goes without saying, insane. On any other day of the year (provided the mountain hasn't closed for the winter) they could tackle the ride in relative peace, passed only by the occasional chalet maid in a Renault Clio. They could freely enjoy the uncluttered sights and smells of the mountainside. But on race day, they form part of a vast crowd of cyclists veering all over the road, terrorised in turn by the ghastly clamour of a thousand accredited Tour vehicles. All manner of cars, vans and trucks, steered by drivers on the verge of exhaustion, gasp for air up the mountain as they nose through the crowds, edging people either into sheer rock faces or as close to the abyss as they can go. Into this craziness, and on his first Tour, we pitched Liam.

Now, I am no mechanic, but the Renault Espace has a shocking clutch. After no more than ten minutes of inching up an incline in first gear, you start to notice the smell. The trick is to stay in gear as long as you can, and if you have to stop (which is pretty much always), nip it quickly into neutral and pull on the handbrake. Just never, ever, sit on the clutch.

Unfortunately, Liam hadn't got the hang of this. Despite our increasingly emphatic advice, he persisted with his clutch foot flat to the floor. The more we implored him to lift it, the less he seemed to listen. No more than a quarter of the way up, he was muttering to himself like a battle-shocked Vietnam veteran drinking alone in a Milwaukee strip joint. He stared fixedly ahead, sweat running in rivulets down his temples, as the car filled with the distinctive acrid smell of smoking clutch plate.

Suddenly, as we rounded a tight, steep corner, from somewhere underneath the bonnet a volcanic cloud of white smoke billowed, large enough to ground temporarily all flights in and out of France. We came to a halt.

Liam remained sitting, a gentle rocking motion had set in, and the shadow of a disturbing smile played across his lips. We had stopped mid-switchback and now sat blocking half the road, as exhausted riders, firing volleys of abuse in our direction, streamed past us. Instantly a bottleneck of Tour traffic started to form behind us.

To the spectators at the side of the road, we became a source of delighted amusement, a useful boredom reliever. Our smoking engine continued to betray our incompetence. A Dutch TV crew, in a non-smoking car, managed to nudge past us, stopping briefly to tell us that the clutch plate was by now probably white-hot, and that if we attempted to move, it would shatter like a plate of glass. Their best advice was to 'get the lid open and maybe piss on it a bit'. We smiled our thanks, wound up our windows, and sat tight. A little island of Britishness marooned in a crap French car.

Descending is another thing altogether. Queues fifteen miles long routinely form on mountainsides, consisting of a dangerous mix of accredited and non-accredited vehicles. With the right-hand lane chock full of stationary traffic, and the left lane empty of vehicles coming back up the mountain, sooner or later one of the Tour vehicles (usually a champagne-coloured Citroën belonging to France Télévisions) will pull out of the queue and start to hurtle down the wrong side of the road at breakneck speed. Instantly, it will be joined by a dozen others. The trick is not to be the first car in the illegal convoy speeding down the wrong side of the road. It's best to be in second place. That way, they, not you, take the impact of any head-on collision.

This terrifying practice has been severely curbed over recent years by the police, which is not altogether unreasonable. But some of the irresponsible thrill of touring has gone with it.

If Woody drives most of the time, I tend to sit in the front passenger seat. I normally have a little left-over scripting and thinking to do as we race towards the finish line. With my laptop perched on my knees, I fight a growing urge to vomit. As soon as I have finished whatever it is I have to type, a Pavlovian response to French motorways kicks in, and within seconds I am asleep, dribbling gently down my collar.

This is when someone, usually Liam, will lean over with their camera phone and film me snoring as my head bobs up and down. I have almost a dozen clips of me on various motorways in France sleeping in this manner, down the years. They document a soft decline into narcoleptic middle age.

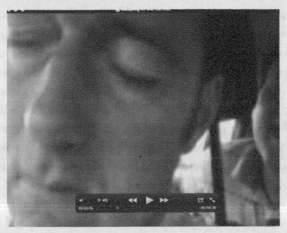

When he's not filming me, Liam is either ranting about the
uselessness of Glasgow Rangers' latest signing, sleeping or
tuning his ukelele. If he is feeling chipper enough, we will
then be treated to a burst of inappropriate music in the style
of George Formby. 'Total Eclipse of the Heart' by Bonnie Tyler,
for example. It works well sung at high speed in a cod-Wigan
accent.

Each stop off for refuelling can be a source of tensions as
we mimic the dysfunctional emotional dynamics of a family
on holiday with their teenage kids. We take turns to play the
Sulking Teen, although I normally favour the part of Strict
Dad.

I have a mania for efficiency in these stops, resenting
each and every second spent in the queues and aisles of a
French motorway service station. So it is that I have taken
recently to manning the petrol pump, while Woody, who
keeps the float, goes in to pay. In this way, I get to send the
other two ahead to sort out/acquire/indulge themselves in
whatever way they feel is appropriate. Then, when I have
cascaded sixty-odd litres of stinking diesel into the bottomless well of the Renault Espace, I can join them in the shop,
safe in the knowledge that they have already had time to

peruse the shelves and make up their minds about what it is that they crave.

Woody normally panics. Sensitive to my impatient streak, he has already queued to pay for the fuel, trousered the receipt, and loaded himself up with comfort food. And that's when the panic sets in. He will always come back with at least one item that betrays a rush of blood at the till. This may take the form of an awful yoghurt-based French drink. Strawberry Yop is often the weakness of choice, or a random confectionery with a vaguely insulting name, like Pimp. Or Plop.

The two of us will be back in the car then, and ready to go, before Liam has come back. Occasionally we will catch a glimpse of him moving from aisle to aisle behind the glass of the shopfront, shimmying between rows of querulous school kids. We know perfectly well that he is looking for coffee. We know, also, since nothing much surprises us any more about each other, that he will return eventually with a brew that in no way matches his exacting standards.

And so, in the end, he will reappear cradling a small plastic cup full of something dark and forbidding, which matches his scowl. That face he pulls, with its distinctive jutting out of the lower lip and sinking of the angle of the head to sixty-five degrees is known as *'faire la tête'*. It takes its name from a chef in a restaurant in a village in the Pyrenees who didn't want us to sit down for dinner because it was nine o'clock already and he couldn't be arsed. The waiter implored us to be quick in choosing our meals, because, he said with a flick of his head in the direction of the kitchen, the chef *'dans la cuisine, il fait la tête.'*

It is in this manner that we progress around France, with ninety euros in the glove compartment nestling next to our passports, for presenting to the gendarmes when they inevitably pull us over for something or other. We keep the correct money for the fine so as to save time. It works well.

The motorbike cops in their bright blue and slightly camp jeggings appreciate how quick we are on the draw. Money. Passports. Licence. Sign here. Apologies. *Au revoir. Et bon Tour!*

Time must be saved at both ends of the day. It slips through your fingers.

It sounds simple enough, but it's not always that easy beating the race from the *Départ* to the *Arrivée*. If we have been filming at the start village, we have to get going five minutes before the race leaves or risk getting stuck behind it. The Tour puts up signs that point to the preferred off-race route. We hunt for these amidst a forest of brightly coloured and often contradictory signs pointing to various car parks, for the teams, for the caravan, for the race officials. The 'Hors Course' signs aren't easy to find in a strange town, which has been almost entirely shut down for the day and features random roadblocks around every corner.

Add to that the well-intentioned ignorance of local volunteers stationed at each roadblock, and it makes for a frazzled exit. They are often as unfamiliar with the layout of the town as we are.

'Excusez-nous, madame. On cherche l'itinéraire hors cours.'

'C'est pas par ici. Alors . . . je sais pas.'

'Brilliant. Thanks.'

Suddenly we'll spot the correct sign to 'Hors Course'. It's generally met with an excited whoop of 'Whores Cors!', using the same highly amusing pronunciation that means Bagnères-de-Bigorre is rightfully known in our car as Bangers-de-Big Ears. And Pamiers is Pam Ayres. Obviously.

On arrival at the finish line, there's a similar problem, in reverse. In an unfamiliar town, getting as close as you can to the TV compound to cut down on the distance you have to lug the camera equipment requires skill, persistence, instinct and brinkmanship. Things can get fractious. I will be desperate to get parked up and get going, since normally I have to feed a story back to London immediately on my arrival at the TV truck. Liam, however, conscious of the fact that his is all the heavy gear, will look for the closest possible parking space.

Eventually, inevitably, we lose our bottle, dump the car and run. Usually we leave it parked slightly diagonally, half up on a pavement, with one wheel hanging off the kerb outside a fire station or a hospital or some building of minor importance. But in provincial France, Tour accreditation is like having diplomatic immunity. Only once have I ever received a ticket on a bike race in an accredited vehicle. And that was on the 2010 Tour of Britain, in King's Lynn.

And after the day's work, the pressure continues. Released from duty, we throw our kit back in the car and fire up the sat nav. This moment is key. The details of that night's accommodation are entered. We hold our breath as the route is calculated. It could be anything from twenty kilometres to a hundred.

It might take ten minutes or two hours. It might mean dinner and wine and chat. Or it might mean a sandwich from a petrol station before unloading all our equipment from the car in the dead of night.

Either way, Unloading Must Happen. Buried back in the mists of time, some equipment had been stolen from one of the Channel 4 crew cars parked up overnight, and ever since then, perhaps understandably, the edict has been handed down that the vehicles will be emptied of their contents, which, to be fair to the production company, would probably cost close to £50,000 to replace.

Because of the zero-tolerance policy on left luggage, the only thing to be nicked in my time on the Tour, from the back of an otherwise empty car, has been a crate of tinned mackerel and several bags of raisins belonging to Gary Imlach. For Gary, this spelt dietary disaster, and reserve supplies had to be freighted out from London.

But banging huge, heavy flightcases up narrow, uneven staircases at ten o'clock at night while tired and hungry is not very much fun.

On reaching a hotel, one of our number has to assume the role of designated spokesman, and ask the bewildered receptionist the same hideously repetitive question in babyish French every single night. Is there a chance, the merest of slim hopes, that there might just possibly be a secure ground-floor storeroom, where we can stow the gear without the need for lugging it all up to the fourth floor? No? I thought not.

Every year before the Tour departs, I make a mental note to look up the word 'storeroom' before leaving for France. Every year I forget, and, therefore, every year we are reduced to making do with the less-than-adequate *petite chambre*.

It's always funniest, though, when it's Woody who takes on the asking. Quite unabashed, and a little impatient, he throws in a loose smattering of English words to pad out the bald spots in his sentences, and to give the listener the impression of casual fluency without actually being either casual or fluent.

'Err. So. Yeah. *Bonsoir. Une* question. Um, just wondering *avez vous une* . . . (wait for it, here it comes) . . . *petite chambre pour* you know, um, all that stuff really. *La*.' He would point at one of us grunting past him carrying a tripod, smirking a little.

'*Non. Désolé.*'

'OK. *Merci.*' He'll flash a tiny exasperated continental-style smile. 'Bugger.'

Cultural immersion, Tour style.

And once the gear is stowed away, once the curtains are drawn, and the day is done, it's time to find a flat surface to do some ironing.

FRANCE. AND THE FRENCH

Faced with a sunset in Provence, perched on the warm stone of a ruined fort in a rare moment of calm, as the race swooped through the flatlands that divide the two great mountain ranges, a thought articulated itself: this really is quite a lot better than Bedford, isn't it?

I am not claiming that my Francophilia is even remotely exotic. It simply means that I conform to a determinedly middle-class stereotype. You just need to observe the long lanes of traffic queuing on any given day of the week to get on the ferries at Dover. There you will find the busy-looking couples of middle England, fretting in and around their Volvo. He is trying to affix the GB sticker without creating any air bubbles, she is organising the passports and reservations into a sensible folder. There are the mildly bored kids in their early teens gazing through the rear-seat windows into the quayside drizzle. France is the impassioned, year-on-year, genetically self-fulfilling love affair of the English middle classes. It's in the script.

'Have you got the traveller's cheques?'

'They're in the glove compartment.'

'We should aim to get to a bank before eleven. You never know when, or how long, they'll close for lunch. Where are the passports?'

'In the glove compartment.'

'Good. Excellent. All set then. There'll be a *péage* coming up soon. Have we got some euros?'

And so on. Beam deflectors, Michelen guides, nougat. The cricket on the World Service, crackling into oblivion as the Parisian Périphérique draws near.

Back in the early eighties I had been just such a child, on just such a journey. The first trip abroad I ever made was through Calais, and down through France. I was astounded, the first time we stopped for a toilet break, to be introduced to 'pétards', or 'little farts', literally translated.

They are, for those who don't know, miniature sticks of dynamite bundled together in bright red little packs of ten or twenty, which you could buy at tabacs. I swiftly discovered that four of them, stuffed in the passenger-door ashtray of a Datsun and ignited, would blow the door clean off its hinges, and cause apoplexy in the middle-aged parent attempting to steer his right-hand drive car down the wrong side of the road. On that same trip, too, I was introduced to the bidet, and even established what they were used for. Not before I had established beyond any doubt what they weren't used for, I have to confess.

But it was the sight of kids only a couple of years older than me riding motorbikes without helmets, playing pinball with such precision and flair that they could even lift the table three inches in the air and drop it down again without activating the tilt mechanism, and speaking actual French that impressed me most. This was a grown-up country, with real genuine cool. Authentic, original cool. I was from Bedford, had two spots on my chin, and wore a pacamac. I yearned to be French, with all that might bring with it.

'Lucky bastards.'

'Who?'

'The French. Lucky bastards.'

Someone always says it. It's a recurring mantra, a leitmotif of my working life on the Tour de France. It's the signature catchphrase. Somewhere just south of Lyon it will get aired in the airless car for the first time, and from that day on, it is a thought that is verbally expressed daily, sometimes even hourly.

The Hexagon, as cycling's sentimentalists delight in calling it, has it all. From the green lush north, to the pines and sand of the west, with two vast mountain ranges and the French Rivieira thrown in for good measure. And even if the French have got questionable taste in leisurewear, they've got the Tour de France by way of compensation. Even those French people, who don't care about cycling, still care enough to know that it's on. And who might win it. They have to. It's in the small print of their contract, part of their duties as citizens of the republic. Like passing the time of day with neighbours in boulangeries.

One day we were in a pretty town called Saint-Fargeau. It was a typically beguiling little place, complete with a trickling stream, an oversize château, a chocolatier, and an esoteric museum (in this case, for some inexplicable reason, it housed France's foremost collection of early gramophones). We were filming a day ahead of the Tour's arrival. At about four o'clock, we headed to a bar to watch the closing kilometres of that day's action. The next day, the circus would descend, and Mark Cavendish would claim yet another stage win.

The TV was on. In the far corner of the bar, a Canadian family perched around a Formica table heavy with Coca-Colas. They were chatting a little too animatedly about their plans to visit the Museum of the Gramophone. Aside from them, the bar was not exactly buzzing. There was a barmaid polishing glasses in the manner of an extra from 'Allo 'Allo. But she wasn't the only cliché in the room.

There was the most perfect example of an Old-Boy-At-The-Bar. I sat next to him. He actually wore a beret and a red neckerchief. I was delighted. We both stared at the screen. A hundred kilometres to the west, a helicopter was pulling back to reveal a long peloton, stretched out at the front end into single file. HTC-Columbia was beginning to get the chase organised. My friend was watching, absent-mindedly chewing his lunch. By way of conversation, I asked him if he was enjoying his salami sandwich.

'C'est bon, votre pain?' I enquired smilingly.

There was a pause of quite extraordinary length during which he chewed and gave the impression of utter indifference to my question. I held my smile. It began to hurt.

'Non,' came the surprisingly honest reply. 'Trop sec. Il manque du beurre.'

He glanced a little savagely at the barmaid, who shrugged her indifference back at him. He looked profoundly irritated. After all, there's nothing like a dry, unbuttered salami baguette to take the edge off your enjoyment of the Tour.

Undaunted by his overt unwillingness to engage in light-hearted bar-banter with the sunburnt English fool sitting beside him at the bar, I ploughed on.

'Vous aimez regarder le Tour?' I offered, throwing a sideways nod in the direction of the TV screen to eliminate any room for misunderstanding. There was another, even longer pause. I became unsettled. Was this a deliberate snub? Had he failed to understand my French? It turned out that he was formulating his reply. When it came it was succinct and left little margin for ambiguity.

'Non.'

Munch, munch. Dry crumbs tumbled from his lower lip onto the counter below. It made me thirsty just to watch him.

I allowed what I considered to be a dignified length of time to elapse before I threw in the towel and left some money on the bar for my coffee. At the door, just before I stepped outside into the glaring sun, I glanced back at the hunched shoulders and silhouetted shape of the beret that belonged to my taciturn friend at the bar.

Then the perversity struck me. Despite his protestations on both counts, there he was. Eating his dry sandwich. Watching the Tour. As if he had no choice.

In the end, that's the point I suppose. There's no getting away from a race which prides itself on getting round all parts of the country as often as it can. It is, after all, the Tour de France. Not the Tour de Anywhere Else. (Although there is a curiously irritating habit for minor races in far-flung non-francophone countries to name their races using the French conjunctive 'de'. The now defunct Tour de Georgia is the worst offender. A fine race, I have no doubt, but an ill-judged name.)

So, to be fair to the French, they did the 'de' bit a long time before anyone else had even grappled with the concept. And they still lead the way. Strange though this may sound, it sometimes slips your mind when you're on the race that you're in France, such is the international bubble that you inhabit. It's only when you chance to look in detail at the faces in the crowd that you remember what this event means to the host nation. The hours spent waiting at the roadside, enduring baking sun or torrential rain, putting up with the unbearable clamour of the tannoys and the frenetic hell of the Caravane Publicitaire. Grandads, old dears, families with youngsters decked out in as many free sponsored hats as they can get their heads in; some of the lengths gone to just to catch a glimpse of a mediocre French cyclist coasting by at 30mph.

The closest equivalent to this kind of patient enthusiasm for a sport in which the home nation so massively under-achieves is the British Wimbledon obsession. There is a common currency in the Henmanite campers outside SW18, and the dedicated Tour fan who will travel hideously over-crowded roads just to get a glimpse of Laurent Brochard. Except that, where the queues outside the All England Lawn Tennis Club might be a mile long, on the Tour de France they stretch over hundreds of miles.

And yet, one of the curiosities I have become familiar with over the years has been this: there appear to be two parallel Tours.

One is the global game, the Armstrong-driven explosion of blue-chip sponsored, mega-corporate transatlantic teams with a diversity of nationalities among the nine men on the team and their followers, as well as the hundreds of millions of fans worldwide. The other Tour is French. Decidedly, reso-lutely, determinedly French.

It comes down to national pride, I guess.

On the morning of 6 July 2005, everyone in the media village was glued to TV monitors, tuned to their respective national broadcasters. It was an important day, one that had been widely talked about, particularly in the French press. That day, every major station in Europe would be carrying live pictures from Singapore where the result of the bidding process for the 2012 Olympics was about to be announced.

Certain that London was the outsider, and a little indif-ferent to it all anyway, I was scooting around the place mopping up little errands here and there, trying to stave off a late-morning hunger. The race was still hours from the finish line. As the announcement drew close, however, curiosity got the better of me. I stopped by a makeshift studio, which had been erected by RTBF, the Belgian TV station. I stood under an awning as a drizzle was beginning to fall, fingering a small Paris 2012 souvenir badge, which I had been handed and had placed in my pocket as a keepsake.

'The International Olympic Committee . . .' Pause. 'Has the honour of announcing . . .' Longer pause. Across the tented village of the media compound, I could hear the simultaneous translations into Spanish, Italian and German. 'That the games of the thirtieth Olympiad in 2012. Are awarded . . .' final pause. '. . . to the city of London!'

Londra!

The camera cut to a side shot of the hall, with the most undignified jumping-up-and-down going on from the British delegation. Where I was standing too, there was an audible reaction, reaching us from further afield.

London!

A large crowd had gathered along the finishing straight, even though there would be a long wait before the race was due to finish. They had made their way there hoping to watch the announcement on the big screen, and then share in the inevitable party, which would follow Paris's triumph.

Londres!

Now their day was ruined. There were wolf-whistles and some shouting.

I lingered a little in front of the Belgian monitors, watching a bizarre three-way hug featuring David Beckham, Seb Coe and Ken Livingstone, each of them wearing the kind of beige suit normally only ever seen for sale on the market down the Walworth Road.

Unexpectedly, I felt a little reflected glory. The Belgian crew started drifting back to work, patting their congratulations on my back as they passed. My inflated sense of self-importance grew a little more. I guess they weren't really crediting me with making the key late-night interventions that had swung the whole thing London's way. They were Belgians after all, so I think they were probably just very pleased to see Paris missing out.

I gathered up John and Woody and we spent the next hour or so putting together a short package of vox pops to reflect the reaction among the locals to London's success. I don't know what I was expecting really. We were in a town called Montargis, a little to the south of Paris. During the Hundred Years War the Earl of Warwick laid siege to the town for months, until the residents got their act together and sabotaged the dykes and reservoirs in the local area, flooding the enemy lines and killing hundreds of Englishmen. Had the bloodlust been dispelled over the following 500 years? Or would their descendants still be hell-bent on exacting retribution for English perfidy?

I strolled up and down the finish line, microphone in hand, stopping every now and again to offer in broken French, 'Vous souhaitez sans doute feliciter Londres!' I wasn't totally sure that they would wish to congratulate London, but I felt they should be offered the opportunity.

It seemed, though, that they didn't feel the same way. Reactions varied from grudging acknowledgement that London might be a reasonable venue, to frank and forthright allegations of deceit and vote-rigging. One man looked directly at the camera, and drew his finger across his neck as if to cut the viewer's throat. I stopped and spoke to one of the Tour's legendary figures: the Cochonou salami-man. Small, permanently irate, and moustachioed, this terrifying elderly man spends every July pedalling a tricycle up and down the final kilometre of each stage handing out flimsy chequered sun-hats and miniature sample-sized cellophane-wrapped salamis to the waiting throngs. I have on a number of occasions tried to steal salamis from his basket only to get caught in flagrante and chased off in the style of a sped-up Benny Hill sketch. So I should have known he wouldn't react with any great friendliness to my approach.

'*Je m'en fous d'Angleterre! Je m'en fous de Londres!*' His words were garnished with fragments of Cochonou salami as they flew in my direction. Garlic, salt, fat and hurt pride.

'*Je m'en fous de Blair!*' he added. And then he spat on the ground, in the manner of a man pretending to be a small, angry Frenchman, made all the more compelling since he actually was one.

There's a bit of me that understands his anger. His nation invents a great race and wins it a lot. Then they invite the rest of the world to come and join in and they stop winning it altogether. And now he is faced with this idiot from English TV trying to wind him up about the Olympics. As if he wasn't irate enough already. And would everyone please stop trying to nick his salamis.

But away from the vitriol, there is a touching faith about French support for their cyclists. The fact that they still care about an event their riders seem genetically incapable of even threatening to win does the nation great credit. In the years that I have covered the Tour, French success has been limited to bit parts. Their participants tend to be attendant lords, that will do to swell a progress, start a scene or two. Like going for a gold medal in curling at the Winter Olympics, the French seem to have been busying themselves with competing for the lesser prizes, in the sober knowledge that the big one will elude them for years to come.

Not that that doesn't have considerable appeal. Recent Tours have featured heartening, brave rides from Sylvain Chavanel, Brice Feillu and Geoffroy Lequatre to name a few. But they have also been characterised by the slow, saddening decline of Christophe Moreau. Moreau is a national treasure, we are led to believe, although I am not so sure. By and large, the French cycling public, despite their yearning for a hero to emerge, aren't daft, and I can scarcely accept that they have genuinely warm feelings towards 'the greatest French rider of his generation'. A man who has five top twelve finishes on the tour to his name, Moreau has been masquerading as a contender. Since returning from a suspension for doping he has been holding his own only up to a point with the main men in the mountains. That point invariably would be the first major acceleration. With battle raging up front between the likes of Evans, Sastre and Schleck, French TV would treat the viewer to long, loving, lingering close-ups of Moreau falling off the back and riding all on his own in a world of pain. 'There's Christophe Moreau again, struggling already to hold the wheel.' Every year. Even the French must have become sick of it.

But while Moreau confessed in 1998, his Festina teammate Richard Virenque, stretching credulity among swathes of the media, maintained his innocence. Not everyone believes him. For me, Virenque was another symbol of the impotence of French cycling. Year after year his targeted assault on the polka-dot jersey given to the 'King of the Mountains' was as predictable as it was repetitive. But the stick-insect son of Morocco carved out an extraordinary niche for himself. Seemingly ignored by the main riders, by dint of being half an hour adrift in the General Classification, he swept up intermediate climbing points on middling climbs, possibly because no one else could be bothered. 'Oh go on, then,' I imagine them thinking to themselves, 'give it to Virenque.'

He scooped up seven polka-dot jerseys in an era where not many other French riders were showing themselves. He won stages. He should have cemented his place in French hearts.

And, perhaps he did. For a portion of French cycling fans it never mattered that Virenque was morally compromised goods. I would often spot the Virenque fans on the Tour and was fascinated by what could possibly draw them to support him. Amidst the sea of painted names on the tarmac, the LANCE LANCE LANCE and the BASSOs and ULLRICHs, there would always be a fair smattering of ALLEZ RICHARD, often with a surprisingly neat tricolour painted alongside.

These would have been the proud handiwork of the die-hard caravanners, those French families from Rennes or Le Mans, who would have driven to their allotted switchback days before the arrival of the race, braced the vehicle with stones against gravity and then begun stolidly eating their way through a mountain of merguez, scowling at the new arrivals. Each day would bring more and more caravans from Holland and Germany, cluttering up their view, and bit by bit ALLEZ RICHARD would be swamped on all sides by an invasion of foreign-sounding names. It was a metaphor for the race itself, and it would have been enough to make them retreat ever more deeply into their morning's edition of L'Equipe, shaking their heads in despair. These were the people who represented Virenque's natural constituency.

Virenque can be astonishingly forthright. He once recorded

a chat show on French TV where he gave quite possibly the most honest answer any sportsman has ever given, an answer that recently has been echoed by Floyd Landis. This was the exchange between Virenque and the presenter Thierry Ardisson:

Q: If you were sure of winning the Tour by being doped, but knew you wouldn't get caught, would you do it?
A: (without blinking) Win the Tour doped, but without getting caught? Yes.

It's a wonder that corporate France still holds enough faith in the man to crave association with him. These days he has contracts with a sticky glucose drink (fair enough) and with a pharmacy (yup, I can see that, too). But there's one French business that will be forever Virenque. The years of his triumphs were the heady days when the polka-dot jersey was sponsored by the supermarket chain Champion.

Since Virenque seemed to own exclusive rights to their prize, and even appeared outside of the Tour in their TV commercials, they were intimately associated with the man, and were clearly pleased with the return on their investment. Their sponsorship of the event seemed to grow with each passing year. Each intermediate King of the Mountains point would be festooned ever more garishly with Champion's logos, and kilometre after kilometre of barricades leading up to each line would all bear the same supermarket's name. We fondly imagined that Virenque was by now so indebted to the sponsor that he had to spend every hour God sent working for them. We speculated endlessly about how every morning Virenque would put out hundreds of Champion barricades, before he was allowed back to his hotel for breakfast. 'Virenque was up early again,' one of us would

invariably comment driving towards a finish line past acres
of Champion signage.

Since his racing career ended, he has been working for
Eurosport, where, for me, he invites unflattering comparison
with the late, great Laurent Fignon and the idolised Laurent
Jalabert, the pundit on France Televisions, whose urbane
charm has won him universal admiration. But at least he
doesn't have to put out all those barriers every morning.

Which brings us to Thomas Voeckler: the anti-Virenque.

Few riders inspire as much affection and genuine respect
as Thomas, the man with the widest beaming smile in world
cycling. He has a naturally engaging temperament and an
inclination to good manners, which puts us all to shame.
There have been times when I have wanted to jump over the
barricades and give the man a hug. The most recent of these
came on the 2009 Tour when he held off Cavendish and the
marauding HTC-Columbia train to ride out a solo win into
Perpignan. It was a stage that the Manxman would have
underlined three times over in red ink as a banker win. It
would have been the last thing Voeckler would have wanted,
naturally, an unrestrained hug from an English journalist. But

that's the kind of reaction he provokes in people, not least the French. This is a man who they properly worship. He's also the only rider I've ever asked to sign anything. I have a poster at home advertising the Grand Départ of the 2005 Tour in Voeckler's home department of the Vendée. He's been Photoshopped onto it so that it looks like he's riding over water. How fitting.

It's hard not to talk of this guy in the diminutive. Pick your patronising cliché; it probably applies. But as Matt has often turned to me and angrily pointed out, the man deserves and demands our respect.

His coming of age was in 2004. His was the kind of gutsy almost-achievement that you would more readily associate with English cricket teams. It bears comparison with Mike Atherton's mind-bending powers of concentration as he ground away at the crease over the best part of two days to save a Test match against South Africa in 1995. To cricket purists, that was deemed to be one of the greatest innings of all time. This is what Atherton wrote about his career-defining moment: 'I was in an almost trance-like state. It was a state of both inertia and intense concentration and I knew that I was in total control.'

Never mind Voeckler, the whole of France, through his 2004 endeavours, entered an 'almost trance-like state'.

Voeckler claimed the yellow jersey on Stage 5. He didn't win the stage, Stuart O'Grady did that, but he was part of a breakaway group in which he was the best-placed rider in the General Classification. Armstrong, containing the pace of the peloton and mindful that greater challenges lay ahead (he was always the master of targeted effort), had let the break get twelve and a half minutes up the road, allowing Voeckler to coast home in fourth place on the stage but straight into the yellow jersey.

Sitting wrapped up in a kagool to stave off the chilly

Normandy winds, I pondered this scenario as I frowned at the TV monitor showing Voeckler, the 'virtual yellow jersey'. Just one year into my life as a cycling correspondent, my internal mental slide-rule was still too undeveloped to cope. I found it hard to calculate how the race could now be led by a man who had so far finished no better than fourth on any stage. I failed to understand the strange honour that was about to be bestowed on the short, awkward-looking rider from a team sponsored by a brioche bakery.

Don't these temporary wearers of the yellow jersey feel a little sheepish? Aren't they just a little embarrassed that their achievement has only come about because they've been deemed to be too irrelevant to anyone in the race who really mattered? Glancing across at Chris Boardman, who had been the temporary custodian of the *maillot jaune* on three occasions in the past, I felt like asking him what on earth all the fuss was about. Of course, Chris had actually won his stages to win yellow, so the comparison might have seemed disrespectful. And anyway, he was dozing off.

France, unlike Chris, seemed to be beside itself with excitement. The Voeckler story was only just beginning. It reinvigorated the home nation's love for the Tour, and taught me much about the nuance of the race; the pack of cards, which gets a daily shuffling.

Voeckler was about to become a great star, a national icon, by the time the Pyrenees reared up in front of the race. On Stage 13, to La Mongie, half his advantage was wiped out. But the next day, up to Plateau de Beille, Armstrong threw down the gauntlet and said, 'Go.' His regiment of blue-clad US Postal riders forced a brutal pace, their leader majestically sitting in behind them in shades. Voeckler, number 129, slipped off the pace immediately, rocking from side to side in an awful ungainly effort, up and out of the saddle before collapsing back down again. His yellow top was completely unzipped and flapped at his sides. He licked his lips, and sometimes looked as if the pain was forcing his eyes closed. He knew he had a certain amount of time he could afford to cede to Lance Armstrong if he wanted to remain in yellow, but, with each passing minute, he was shedding it.

In the final eleven kilometres he knew he could lose five minutes, but no more. Far ahead of him on the road now, Armstrong and the Italian climber Ivan Basso were alone. The mountainside was encrusted with campervans disgorging hundreds of thousands of spectators, many wearing the orange of the Basque country, all of them straining to get a view of Voeckler as news of his determined rearguard action swept through the race. In our truck too, watching at the finish line, our team had only one eye on Armstrong, the story was now all about Voeckler's suffering and his spirit. We were all transfixed.

Still the road bore upwards, and the heat baked down. With five kilometres to go, Voeckler found a slight kick. He stood up again in his pedals and powered past a backmarker who couldn't hold the pace. A great cheer went up. Lance Armstrong won the stage, comfortably riding past Basso in the final 100 metres. He looked barely out of breath. Now Voeckler knew what he had to do. Armstrong had set him his target. He could lose no more than five minutes, four seconds. A team car drew up alongside him and shouted encouragement. As he entered the last 500 metres it was still in the balance. He lowered his frame onto the drops and tried to time-trial home. That burst of pace was enough. As he rounded the final bend, he knew he was safe. Weakly he punched out his triumph, clawing at thin air. His expression was caught halfway between delight and despair. A twin-faced gargoyle.

In that instant, France fell in love with Thomas Voeckler.

I fell in love with the way France had fallen in love with Thomas Voeckler, and came within a whisker of falling in love with Thomas Voeckler myself.

I don't care how dry a salami sandwich might be. Try watching that without caring.

THE GO-TO MEN

My childhood was not so very unusual. I watched a lot of television, which wasn't as easy as it sounds, since there wasn't very much television to watch. BBC1 only came on during the hours its director-general deemed appropriate for people to be watching telly. ITV was considered too risqué, and we could only get BBC2 if my dad stood right in front of the fire holding the aerial fully extended above his head. He could only ever manage a few minutes of that at a time.

Some of what I remember best, though, is watching sport. And, just as smells can trigger the strongest memories, so too can the voices of commentators. I can reflect on seminal experiences set against drama unfolding in the voice of David Coleman. Of course, there was also Bill McLaren, who sounded like toast and Marmite and drizzle tapping on the windows. There was Murray Walker, three words from whom would leave me arranging the cushions on the couch for a Sunday afternoon doze. And Brian Moore, whose tones always call to mind crackling hopelessness on a distant football pitch, as England tossed it away again.

But for some reason it is Coleman and the athletes of the early eighties who hold sway in my imagination. Coe. Ovett. Cram. Daley Thompson. And Shirley Strong.

Shirley Strong. The plucky hurdler who used to sneak off after her races and smoke fags in the stands with her fans. I can even recall to memory the kind of chuckling 'good-old-Shirley' indulgence with which Coleman would embellish live pictures of her chuffing away on an Embassy No. 6 in between heats at the Gateshead athletics stadium.

'There she is, Shirley. Relaxing as only Shirley can.'

It's because we believed we knew them as people that we cared. Whether or not we actually did know them is barely relevant.

'Ho, ho. Typical Shirley.'

We differentiated in our hearts and minds between the super-smooth, urbane Sebastian Coe and the edgy rough diamond Steve Ovett. Television threw into sharp relief their differences as men, their characteristic weaknesses and strengths as athletes. Coe's considered eloquence in front of the camera mirrored his friction-free movement as he accelerated off the final bend. Ovett's pointed, tense shoulders when he ran spoke of frailty but also of unreadable brilliance. He never looked fast, he just was. He spoke little, and with barely concealed reluctance. But I will never forget the moment he turned to the trackside camera after winning through to the 800m final and etched out the letters I L Y to his girlfriend Rachel into the dark air. It was, to my young eyes, shockingly intimate and weirdly compelling.

We really start to care when we glimpse the human story. These tokens of self, these quirks and tricks and foibles are vital to our appreciation. Television knows this. This is why we go on the hunt for personality.

On the Tour, this often means we go after David Millar and Robbie McEwen. These two careers have wound and slowly unwound during my spell on the race. To my impatient desire to understand the sport, they brought the words. Over the years they are the men who have dropped into my microphone the verbs, nouns and adjectives that lend cycling its meaning. They are my go-to men.

Something of Robbie McEwen's personality is left behind each time he stands before a camera. Close your eyes after he has just delivered a withering evaluation of a rival or a damning appraisal of an underperforming teammate, and you will still see the after-image of his face burnt into your vision. You will see his high cheekbones, his thin lips toying with the notion of a smile, and his bright little brown eyes fixing the interviewer. Rat-a-tat-tat.

I have great admiration for McEwen. And that's why on the 2010 Tour, my only encounter with him left me feeling irritated with myself. I was busy trying to grab a cross-section of opinion from as many riders as I could the morning after 'Chaingate', Alberto Contador's somewhat Machiavellian attack on his closest competitor, Andy Schleck. The Luxembourg rider had lost his chain just as he was turning the heat on his rival. Contador took advantage of Schleck's misfortune to ride past him and into the lead of the Tour de France. It was, some said, ethically questionable. Some riders, admittedly not many, saw it as a breach of etiquette.

I saw Robbie by his team bus, and came bowling over to him. Even though he expressly told me he was on his way to sign in for the day and couldn't stop, I went ahead with my interview.

'Should Contador have waited, Robbie?' I asked. I thrust the microphone at him. He paused a second.

'I don't know about that, mate. I didn't see what happened. I'm too concerned about my own race to have an opinion about that,' he told me, as he rode slowly enough for us to walk alongside him.

Before I knew what I was about to say, I replied, 'That's unlike you, Robbie.'

I just blurted it out. I didn't mean it to sound sarcastic. But that's how he took it, understandably. He looked scornfully at me, shook his head and peddled off. I hope he's forgotten about that the next time our paths cross.

He has made a few enemies in the peloton, I am told. And I have to confess that it's sometimes not hard to see why. He must be a nightmare out on the road – verbal, feral, wildly unpredictable, risk-ready Robbie. My early years on the Tour saw McEwen dominate proceedings. In the lull between Erik Zabel and Cavendish, McEwen was the man, hitting the front of the sprints at the very last second, timing his efforts to perfection.

What I loved most about his style was the way in which he fed off the efforts of other teams. His Silence Lotto sprint train, such as it was, was a fractured affair, which seemed either never to form at all or to dissolve in the face of greater organisation from other teams. So, more often than not, Robbie would jump on the wheels of opponents' lead-out men or appear from nowhere through a knotted mass of riders already at maximum effort in the closing fifty metres. He was the street urchin of the sprint.

But in the media melee, he is a gentleman. More times than I care to mention, McEwen has saved me from drawing a complete blank. You get days when the only notable faces to be presented to the media after a stage are difficult-to-interview Spanish riders, or worse: Vladimir Karpets. Then Robbie will appear, heroically, from behind the podium clutching a bouquet and an ugly glass statue from the sponsors. He'll make his way languidly towards you, look you full in the eye, crack open a Nestlé Ice Tea, and wait. He is like my guardian angel . . . a fact that I recognised early on in the first week of my first Tour, in another moment of broadcasting confusion pertaining to jerseys.

In 2003, from Stage 1 onwards, McEwen wore the green jersey for five days, before eventually relinquishing it to his fellow Australian, Baden Cooke. Early on during that sequence I went face to face with the bristling sprinter for the very first time. Nothing more substantial than a microphone separated us.

I was aware, because it had entered into Tour mythology, that he had delivered a wry one-liner to my predecessor. She had asked him during a live interview after McEwen had won a stage: 'Robbie, where did you get your energy from for that final sprint?'

To which he had replied, without blinking, 'Breakfast.' And with that he'd walked away. The reporter, for various unrelated reasons, never returned to cover the Tour.

I went one better. I promoted him. 'Robbie,' I opened, brilliantly. 'What plans do you have now you're wearing the yellow jersey?' This last bit was decidedly less brilliant given that he wasn't actually wearing the yellow jersey. Colour-blind I may have been, but at least I hadn't put him in a jumper.

Unaware that I had made the slip at all, I listened with

foolish nodding intensity, while McEwen reeled off a complex, fluent, analytical answer. It was all about maximising wattage when required, minimising wasted effort, seeing opportunities, being aware of dangers, feeling his way around the race and, for want of a better cliché, taking each stage as it came.

Happy that I had got the required answer to my question, I thanked him, and headed away, only to be called back.

'You might wanna do that again, mate.'

I spun around. McEwen wore the same poker face. Only the merest flicker of amusement in his eyes betrayed what he really thought of my daft question. 'Yellow jersey?' he said, in that signature Australian way of turning a statement into a question. For emphasis, he glanced down at his bright green PMU jersey, and then surreptitiously from side to side, as if to check we were alone.

'Oh. Yes. Right.' He took another long draw on his Nestlé Ice Tea. 'Thanks, Robbie.' This time it was my turn to check left and right to see if I was being laughed at.

We rerecorded the interview, inserting the correct colour. I thanked him again, and entered a position of negative equity with respect to Robbie McEwen. I am still not sure I have broken even.

The following year McEwen allowed the cameras to film him having his wounds dressed. He'd fallen a few days prior to that, and had huge areas of skin missing from his thigh, hip and buttocks. It made for extraordinary, excruciating viewing, which we actually had to debate whether or not to screen; in particular the moment he stepped under the shower, and screamed, yes, screamed, as the water spilled across his open wounds. A showman, perhaps a show-off. But all the better for it.

He was also capable of moments of Napoleonic anger. I recall a deluge in Arras. It was 2004, Stage 4. This time, McEwen was indeed wearing yellow. Or as far as I could tell, for it was the kind of rain that not only blurs the image for the TV cameras, it soaks your eyesight too, water bouncing off your head, and streaming down your nose. The team time trial that day was won with a sapping degree of inevitability by US Postal. In effect, it killed the race as a spectacle. The following morning *L'Equipe* ran a cartoon that featured two French cycling fans under dripping umbrellas watching Armstrong's blue train whizz past them. One is turning to the other, and asking, rather demoralised, 'Yes, but do you think he'll win in 2005?'

McEwen's Lotto team had ridden a stinker. They crossed the line in disarray. With sodden, miserable expressions, they rode on into a congested run-out area. The barriers ended fairly soon after the finishing line, and the riders were almost immediately confronted with the prospect of teetering on their precious bikes through throngs of underwhelmed and very wet locals, with thighs and lungs scorched raw from the exertion. I was positioned at the sweet spot, that area defined after much deliberation, but by common consensus among my small crew, to be the most propitious place for eliciting sound bites from riders too weary to care or too naïve to get away. The run-out area is cycling's equivalent of no-man's land, neither totally public, nor restricted to the accredited members of the Tour. It's like the lanes of traffic in and around multi-storey car parks where no one is quite sure who has priority or right of way, and, if push comes to shunt, who has jurisdiction.

Sure enough, McEwen appeared in the middle distance, free-wheeling at jogging pace through a parting sea of kagools and umbrellas, with his helmet dangling loosely from his left hand. As he skimmed past me, I thrust an ITV microphone his way and muttered something approaching a formal declaration of surrender. I knew as well as he did that there was no point in talking to the proud sprinter who hated time-trialling's rigours with a passion and who had just seen his anaemic team give up without so much as a whimper. I pointed my microphone in his direction with as much conviction as a Quaker would point a machine gun.

A thick, rain-heavy thunder cloud rumbled overhead as the miserable man slid past me with a face that reflected its greyness. I noticed a teenager in a huge yellow rain-poncho lurch forward and try to swipe his water bottle. He failed, and McEwen barely noticed. The kid wasn't alone. A couple of yards to his right, as McEwen sped past, an accomplice in a brightly decorated blue poncho also tried his luck. He was more precise and his grip on the precious plastic flask was more robust. McEwen felt the tug on his frame. Stopping abruptly, he leant over the frame of his bike and lurched towards the offender, snatching the bottle back from the Artful Dodger, who looked suitably humbled. McEwen rounded on him, castigating him in fluent French, before remounting, and, after a couple of pedal turns, noticing that his bottle cage was bent, dismounting again, and unleashing a tirade of Flemish, uncertain clearly as to the provenance of his assailant, before finally settling on the discourse-ending 'Fucking idiot!'

I applauded him inwardly, from the comfort of my raincoat, which had been so rained on that the following morning I threw it in a bin outside the Gothic wonder of Amiens cathedral.

David Millar doesn't tend to throw things. But he does allow words to tumble out. Mercifully, now that he's reached his mid-thirties, he's started to grow out of the post-teenage phase he indulged in, in which every post-ride analysis was peppered with US-based teenisms. 'Awesome ride, but I'm thinking, like, dude – you're well maxed out here. Freaky.' That was pretty standard fare in 2003.

So too was a bronchitic cough that used to preface each

and every interview with him by the side of the road after a stage. Collapsed in the footwell of his team bus, or bent double by the barriers just past the finish line, he would gesture to us on our arrival that he needed a second or two to compose himself, before rattling out the most terrifyingly varied sequence of rasping coughs, spitting two or three times, fake vomiting, retching and then turning towards us with eyes on stalks in anticipation of the question to come. We renamed his team 'Coughidis'. We were funny like that.

Spluttering or not spluttering, Millar was in constant demand in those days. Young, gifted and articulate, he was sought after not just by us, who claimed him as the only Brit on the race back then, but by the Americans, too, as well as a host of other nations queuing up for a word. He was often a highly prized guest on the 'Velo Club', a live post-race show on France Télévisions, broadcast in front of an enthusiastic audience from a huge collapsible studio erected near the finish line each day. His opinion, even then, was worth hearing.

These days, for right or wrong, David Millar is the philosopher king of the peloton. The bitter experiences behind him have left their mark, no doubt about it. But they have also knocked the petulance out of him, and made him into a thoughtful, patient correspondent. Few riders during the Tour de France will sit with me and discuss exact types of EPO, its availability, detectibility and effectiveness. Millar will.

I think back to the moment in 2004 when he took the first tentative steps towards rehabilitation. He had been summoned by magisterial order to the court rooms in Nanterre, in the west of Paris, where an investigation into his case had begun. It was two days before the start of the Tour. Millar would be playing no part. He had confessed to taking EPO and was about to begin a two-year suspension.

We had set our alarm clocks early and driven down from Liège to be there. Arriving just after the session had begun, we set up shop outside the main entrance to the courtroom, and waited. Five hours later, we were still waiting for Millar to emerge. I decided to take matters into my own hands and went inside the building. Quickly enough I established the exact location of the room in which his hearing was taking place. It was all happening behind an anonymous door leading onto a wide, empty corridor on the fourth floor of a tall building. Every now and again, smartly dressed state functionaries would come and go from room to room. But otherwise I had the corridor to myself. There was a wooden bench outside the magistrate's office. I sat down, and within minutes I was asleep.

Some time later, I awoke. The door had opened, Millar and his lawyer were already halfway to the lift. In the seconds before I understood where I was and what was happening, I caught sight of Millar, unfamiliar and curiously young-looking in a suit, glancing back at me, white-faced. I caught him up as he was getting in the lift to go down. His lawyer held the doors open for me. We travelled down the four floors together in silence. Then, as the doors opened, Millar turned smartly on his heels and exited through a pre-arranged back door. His lawyer went outside to hold an impromptu press briefing, sparking panic in Woody, who was still a hundred metres away, on his way back from buying some sandwiches for lunch.

Millar's two years in the wilderness cost him his best years. They almost undid him. Yet his honesty has dragged him through to the other side much the better for it. He's become the archetype of what TV types cynically call 'good value'. Millar 'on doping'. Millar 'on Armstrong'. Millar 'on time-trialling'. Millar 'on cheese/Pink Floyd/haemorrhoids'.

The last time I talked to him at any length, he was hobbling across the restaurant terrace of a Novotel somewhere near the Alps. Mechanical problems early on that day had meant he'd been dropped by the race, and had ridden solo for 160 kilometres just to avoid elimination. He had finished stone last.

France Télévisions had a new trick up their sleeves. Every evening, back at the riders' hotel, they would conduct a long interview with the 'lanterne rouge' of the day, before bestowing upon the unfortunate rider a red jersey to symbolise his last place in the race. The riders were expected to find it all riotously funny.

We too were waiting for Millar that evening. From the far side of the terrace we watched on as the preening French reporter conducted his surely-far-too-long interview. He then rounded things off by commandeering two of the Novotel's receptionists to march out in front of the camera to present Millar with his new red jersey before forcing him to pose podium-style with a girl on either cheek. It was excruciating.

Yet by the time Millar hobbled over to where we had set up, he had not only shifted gear but language too, ditching his fluent French for his languid English. We sat down for ten minutes with him, with the camera rolling, during which time he gave us as memorable an account of the suffering of a Tour rider as I have ever heard.

Millar's travails bookended my first Tour. From his near miss in the Paris Prologue, to a filthy wet time-trial victory in Nantes, his failure and success framed the scales of emotion that the race could elicit. I was impressed. So much greater, then, was my disappointment when I learnt of his doping. It abruptly called into question the veracity of all that I had witnessed. For some time I was left uncertain of what my attitude should be towards David Millar. Instinctively I liked him, yet there was that absolutist voice in my head, which always nagged, 'Doper!' But Millar himself has offered up over recent years such a convincing, clean version of himself that it is hard, even for his most obdurate critics, not to feel a

little warmth towards his gung-ho approach, and self-aware-
ness. Judgements harden eventually. His solo attack on Stage
1 of the 2007 Tour from London to Canterbury when he
stayed away through colossal crowds in Kent was typical of
the instinctive, passionate rider he was becoming. 'Spine
tingling', was how he described that particular suicidal
breakaway. It was.

But it wasn't until Stage 6 of the 2009 Tour into Barcelona
that I realised fully what cycling now meant for him. Part of
a breakaway, which seemed doomed to be caught, Millar had
decided to attack with twenty-eight kilometres remaining.
With ten kilometres to race, it looked fleetingly like he might
have cracked them. In fact, he held the race at bay right up
until the flamme rouge, and only then was he engulfed.
Afterwards I was delighted to hear him tell of his pride and
pleasure in the ride, rather than his disappointment.

'Riding into Barcelona, with a million people on the streets.
Wow. It was special.'

Experts at the game, then, Millar and McEwen. They are
both men with sufficient savvy to remain in firm control of
their media images. But they are also men with enough character to warm to the task, and to bring the bike race into
people's front rooms, for which I am forever grateful to both
of them. It makes my job a hell of a lot more enjoyable.

And perhaps, thirty years from now, someone will think
back to childhood summer evenings, and Phil Liggett calling
home Millar and McEwen.

GLENN

I was standing by the side of the pitch in Lyon. The Stade Gerland, the strangely moulded concrete and white-rendered home of Olympique Lyonnais, was slowly filling with fans. The evening had just started to turn chilly after a day spent in spring sunshine checking out Lyon. We'd had lunch in the Brasserie Georges, the converted railway station, which is now a noisy restaurant. A few hours before kick-off, I'd had a perfect coffee outside, in the company of Peter Drury. We'd watched on as songbirds, heading north again from Africa, stopped off to try and snatch biscuits from sports reporters' tables. It had been a fine day, in a fine city. I was warmly anticipating watching two good football teams tear into each other. It was the quarter-final of the Champions League. It was also 14 April 2005.

I became aware that my phone was buzzing. I looked down and saw that I'd missed a call. It was from Steve Docherty.

His flashing name on the screen puzzled me. I couldn't imagine what could possibly prompt him to call me at such a time. I normally wouldn't hear from him until much closer to the Tour. So I rang him straight back.

He picked up after one ring. 'I've got some very bad news. Glenn Wilkinson is dead.'

I didn't know what to say. Steve elaborated.

'He died at home. His funeral is next week. Just to let you know.'

I stared across the pitch. PSV Eindhoven players were warming up close to me. Guus Hiddink was standing sentinel, watching his charges snapping the ball around in tight groups. Dew was settling on the grass, picked out by the xenon-white wash of the floodlights. The evening was gearing up for its drama.

Glenn was a cameraman who had worked on my first two Tours, and many, many more before that. He had been a big presence on the production team. And he had just died.

There is no appropriate place to hear such things. News like this forces itself on you, cramming a certain time and place with meaning it cannot hold.

The Tour had taken me here before. Two summers previously, I had visited the Stade Gerland. It had been on my birthday, 11 July 2003. Alessandro Petacchi had stormed to his fourth stage win of the centenary Tour on a long, wide avenue right outside the stadium. After the podium ceremonials, Glenn and I made our way to the interview zone. Slightly dreading another meeting with the big Italian and his tendency to deadpan his way in flat-noted Italian through interviews, and tiring of his workmanlike success, we cursed him under our breath. Besides, the Tour was a week old and we were getting irritable. We waited in the heat for our allotted thirty seconds with the big man, me with the microphone poised, Glenn with his camera slung over his back like a rocket launcher in a Rambo film.

That was the day I discovered that getting bored with Glenn Wilkinson was much better than getting bored without Glenn Wilkinson.

He was a restless presence with an eye for mischief. For no good reason he started experimenting with pronouncing names of Spanish and Italian riders in a thick and implausible Geordie accent. Marry-Owe Chippowe Lee-Nee. Jo-Sabre Bell-Ockie. Alice-Androwe Pertackie. It became a feature of the rest of that Tour, and the next one. Indefensibly childish, wickedly funny, and typical of Glenn. The joke has stuck, and has broadened out these days to include Wan Antowniowe Fletcher.

On my second Tour, Glenn had invested in a set of comedy teeth. Not in itself a comic triumph. But the thing is, they were seriously convincing teeth, crooked, yellowed and gnarled. He always kept them stuffed in his pocket for easy access. He'd pop them in at a second's notice. Instantly, he'd assume the vacant posh smile of Harry Enfield's 'Tim-Nice-but-Dim' character. In this guise, he would introduce himself to complete strangers on the Tour who were never able to work out if the guy was for real or not. German colleagues were most impressed, his mannerisms conformed neatly to their notions of how the inbred British aristocracy should behave.

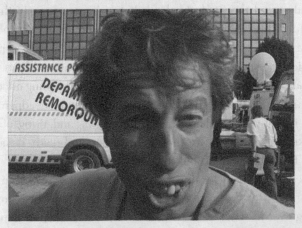

A week or so after his funeral I had to get a new photo taken to supply to the Tour for my press accreditation. By way of paying tribute, I too bought some comedy gnashers. Then, feeling a little self-conscious, I sat behind the pull-across blue curtain in a booth in an unloved corner of Boots, staring at my toothy reflection in the glass, trying to recapture the Wilkinson aura. The joke fell flat, really, but for the next three years my ID carried a picture of me sporting a fantastic set of front teeth.

At the end of a long day, if we made it to a hotel in time for a drink and an evening meal, there would be a great sense of urgency. We would dump our bags, and reconvene seconds later at the bar. All of us, that is except for Glenn. It would take thirty, maybe forty-five minutes before he appeared, a freshly laundered Gap short-sleeved shirt turned up at the collar, his luxuriant wavy hair bouffed up in a style, which would in itself have earned him the guillotine during the French Revolution, and enough aftershave to kill a horse. He'd clap his hands together in elegant delight, and then, mincingly, order a strange aperitif in a too-high voice. We would smile at him. All was well in the world: Glenn was down for dinner.

To have been there in Lyon with him would have been fine. Instead I was thinking about his death. The football came and went. I went about my work a little unsure of myself, a little off-balance. When the last interview of the night had been concluded, I struck off on foot, opting to walk the half-hour back to our hotel on a ring road outside Lyon centre. I left that stadium behind me.

Later that summer, Gary Imlach wrote some simple words about him when he put together a short piece reflecting his contribution. The obituary ran during our coverage of the next Tour. Gary said something along the lines of: 'If you've been watching the Tour over the last twenty years, you'll not know this, but actually you've been watching Glenn.' Those words led into a montage of some of his finest shots and dramatic scenes which he and his camera had captured down the years. It was a rich mix: LeMond, Fignon, Hinault, Roche, Boardman, Indurain, Armstrong. Fields of sunflowers.

Glenn had been involved as far back as the Channel 4 days. This was clearly a halcyon era, of which I am constantly being reminded. From time to time the rest of the crew break into a nostalgic riff about the old theme tunes and generally the way things were. To this day, I meet people who will wax lyrical. 'The Tour de France? ITV, you say? I remember when it was on Channel 4. That was a wonderful show.' We get regular viewers who actually think they're still watching it on Channel 4. They've got every reason to feel tricked though. This is mainly because exactly the same people are still making the show. From the executive producers, Brian Venner and latterly Carolyn Viccari, to the commentators, Phil and Paul, to Gary Imlach. And the cameramen: John must be close to getting a medal for his twenty. Glenn had been approaching that too. His most memorable years were the late eighties and early nineties. British TV, for whatever reason, enjoyed a certain amount of preferential status.

One of the ways in which this manifested itself was that Channel 4 was given a place for a motorbike on the race. It fell to Glenn and his admirable pilot Patrice Diallo to fill the spot.

Riding a TV bike in the middle of a race of the size and scale of the Tour de France peloton is a hellishly complex, as well as a dangerous, proposition, requiring a deep understanding for the fluid dynamics of the sport, as well as Kevlar-coated courage.

There is no equivalent in other sports. Aerodynamics dictate that as soon as you put a motorbike in a race, it will have an effect that can influence the outcome of the event itself. Draughting on the back wheel of a *moto* is a not uncommon phenomenon, and can lead to anger and accusations of cheating among the peloton. For this reason the motorbikes are watched with exaggerated attention by the commissaires.

But daring is the thing and Glenn had it in abundance. Standing up on the back of a motorbike, facing backwards with a lump on your shoulder that weighs as much as a sack of spuds, while travelling down a rain-soaked alpine pass at seventy or eighty miles an hour takes some doing. On a big descent, the motorbikes have to crown the summit some way ahead of the race, for the simple reason that they cannot go as fast as the men on roadbikes. That's why you'll rarely see the close-up head-on shot which Moto 1 would normally offer up with the peloton in full flight down a mountain. Yet just getting ahead of the race takes great skill and courage.

An understanding had built up between Glenn and Patrice. They trusted each other implicitly. A light tap on Pat's shoulder from Glenn was all that was needed for complex messages to be passed from one man to the other. It might mean to pull alongside a particular rider struggling up a climb. It might signal that Glenn wanted to pass by the whole peloton to shoot along the line, or pull ahead at speed, gain a couple of kilometres on the race, and jump off to frame up a static shot and allow the Tour de France to rattle across the frame. All this was well understood between the two men, treading always an intuitive line, which meant that they were valued and respected practitioners, liked and trusted by both the race organisers and the riders.

Patrice is a big long-haired French rider from Orange, with dark skin, deep brown eyes and uniquely convoluted ethnicity, who gets through his day by chuckling and singing to himself good-naturedly. He has little English. Glenn had a similarly sparing lack of French. Despite nearly two decades following the great race through France, Glenn's French was still infantile. As if stuck on an unending school exchange trip that had started in 1982, he still had the language skills of an O level schoolboy on the lookout for cigarettes and flick-knives to smuggle back on the ferry.

I last saw Patrice on Mont Ventoux in 2009, four years after Glenn's death. He had grown a wonderful beard which, he said, was 'off-centre, due to the crosswind'.

A curious pair they made, then. Pat, always in ancient leathers, no matter how hot the weather, and Glenn, with his Home Counties looks and an accent to match, a twitching ball of energy, full of mannerisms and tics and quirks.

'Bonshore, mon ammeee.' He would announce with a flash of his naturally substantial white teeth. 'Je swee avec le meediar.' This was his favourite gag of all. Announcing to anyone who would listen and plenty who wouldn't, in the loudest, most braying British accent he could muster, that he was 'Avec le meediaar.' He was brazen, and unencumbered by embarrassment. I have no idea what Patrice made of it. But I suspect the big man was always inwardly amused by his preposterous teammate. He would smile indulgently.

Glenn had stopped filming out on the race a couple of years before I joined the team, partly because I suspect the privileged place which he'd enjoyed for years was withdrawn. British riders were achieving next to nothing in the early years of the twenty-first century, and therefore British TV had no right to expect a motorbike place. They'd rather give it to the Germans. These days, in fact, only the French and the Americans get to place a motorbike on the race.

But equally, I suspect that Glenn had had enough of the danger. He had two young boys at home, and perhaps he just didn't need it any longer. Instead he opted for the less adrenalin-filled, but equally highly pressured, world of framing Gary Imlach against an alpine backdrop or a Norman church.

He died very suddenly one afternoon from heart failure. He was aged forty-four. At his funeral, his two boys sat in their collars and ties in the front row, their hair neatly parted, their shoes polished. They stared into the middle distance, inscrutable. The church was full to bursting. Somewhere, at the back of the congregation, was Patrice. Ridiculously, Patrice was wearing a tie with his leathers, hastily put on in the car park after he had ridden overnight from Provence to Surrey.

In 2003, the day before the Tour, I sat in a vast press conference listening to Lance Armstrong hold court in measured, serious tones. He was speaking of the race he was about to win for the fifth time, and he was paying it respect. 'The Tour has been everything to me. I've seen it all. Courage. Fear. Love. Even Death.' He was referring back to an event in 1995. Descending the Col de Portet d'Aspet, Armstrong's teammate Fabio Casartelli had lost control and fallen at great speed headlong into a sharp-edged concrete pillar marking the edge of the road. He hadn't been wearing a helmet, and that killed him.

It is a stark image; a watershed moment in the modern-era Tour de France. Casartelli's folded body lies at an oblique angle across the tarmac. He appears to be holding the backs of his knees, drawing them in. There is too much blood on the road.

I remember asking Glenn about it once. There weren't many times in Glenn's helter-skelter life when you could goad him into seriousness. But, on that occasion, I was struck by the sudden shift in him. Stuff goes on out there on the road. And to most of us, most if it will remain hidden most of the time.

He knew and understood a great deal more than he ever acknowledged. I spent only two Julys with him. I wish there had been more.

THE LINGO

He looked my way. He stepped my way. He spoke no English. I had no other option but to address him in his native tongue.

'Alessandro,' I repeated needlessly, playing for time. '*Una bella vittoria!?*' Half question, half statement. It would have to do.

I beamed at him and thrust my microphone in the direction of Alessandro Petacchi, the winner of Stage 3 of the 2003 Tour de France. He started to speak.

'*Si . . .*' But, I confess, the rest was lost on me. I nodded along as if I understood, bravely facing down the salvos of quick-fire Italian being sprayed in my direction. I felt not the slightest discomfort. On the contrary, I was beginning to see that stuff like this happens on the Tour, the natural habitat of us charlatans and linguistic chancers.

The Tour de France is a cacophony of polyglot noise. For obvious enough reasons, the mother tongue of the race used to be French, but that's not quite as true now as it once was. Although continental pro-riders have always been enviably multilingual, there was once an understanding that French was their common currency. Now that doesn't necessarily stand up to scrutiny. The race doesn't really know what language it should speak. Norwegian? German? Spanish? Italian? Russian?

There used to be a distinctive feature of our production, which, sadly is no more. Some viewers remember it fondly and call for its reinstatement. But, for others, its disappearance has been a cause for celebration.

We used to film almost every rider staring directly, if sheepishly, into the camera and delivering the killer line: 'Hello, I'm (insert rider's name here). You're watching the Tour de France on ITV.' These little introductions would play before and after every commercial break. Since English was seldom their mother tongue, the variety of ways riders would find to mangle this simple message was a source of constant wonder.

'You see Tour de France in TVI. Thank you.'

'Hello. This is the Tour de France. I am watching TV.'

'This is ITV's Tour de France on the BBC. Hello.'

I am deeply respectful of each and every rider who ever obliged us in this way. I admire their courage, mostly because I share their shortcomings.

These days everyone just has to muddle through, and muddling through is especially invigorating when you neither speak nor understand the language in question.

Nowhere is this muddling through more widespread than in the interview pen. This is essentially an area about the size of two table tennis tables, demarcated by the same kind of agricultural fencing that usually encloses sheep before they're dipped. That sometimes seems to be a fair reflection of our status in the eyes of the men in charge. Recent Tours have featured the French team Agritubel. This fencing is precisely

team Agritubel. This fencing is precisely the sort of product Agritubel they manufacture. I often wonder whether the Tour cuts a deal with them to provide free housing for the ladies and gentlemen of the media in return for a place in their race.

On arrival in this undignified cage every day, there are handshakes and nods of acknowledgement. There are brief exchanges of gossip and little flurries of laughter between fellow journalists sharing a joke. It is a cocktail-party atmosphere, with a nervous edge. Over many years, I have become familiar with this international melting pot. I have started putting names to their faces.

Frankie Andreu, the perfectly groomed, white-toothed, deeply tanned American reporter. He was a teammate of Lance Armstrong in his pre-cancer Motorola team, and he would be thrust into the spotlight when the testimony given by Frankie and his wife Betsy threatened to implicate Armstrong in a doping scandal. Armstrong was later cleared, but how Andreu maintained a functioning relationship with the Texan with all that flying around I will never know. But he enters the pen, and, in the nicest possible way, always takes up the prime spot, at the corner nearest the area behind the podium from which the riders will eventually emerge. No one challenges his pre-eminence. He is clearly the alpha male.

Then there is Mike Tomalaris, Tommo. He is the lanky legend of SBS and hosts the coverage in Australia; a man with a broadcaster's haircut and a perpetual air of confused amusement playing over his lips. He is a kind, funny man. There were times, even through my first Tour, when he would bow to my superior knowledge. I sometimes bumped into Tommo half an hour after the end of a stage when he would give the impression of being only dimly aware who had won. Time pressure never weighed too heavily on his shoulders.

There's Dag Otto, from Norwegian TV, who drives a car with his own face all over it. We teased him once on the way to the car park: 'Which one's yours, Dag Otto?'

'That one over there.'

'Really?'

Then there's Jorgen Leth, the famous Danish film director who now slums it as a cycling reporter and who'd rather have been directing Brecht at the Copenhagen National Theatre than bumping shoulders with me. There's Bernd, the twitchy German, and his perspiring ineffectual colleague Thomas. And Alessandra De Stefano, the first lady of Italian cycling. A cosmopolitan flock standing about in their pen, ready for dipping.

I have become fascinated by the nuances of living in a kind of fully functioning scale model of Europe. I pride myself on separating from some distance the Austrians from the Swiss, simply by their footwear (Austrians practical, Swiss needlessly flamboyant). I understand instinctively that you can approach the Danes at any time, but the Italians can be tetchy, and the Norwegians often like to have a snooze in the afternoon, so it is best to leave them alone.

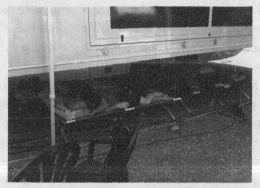

It is a daily delight to be surrounded by a dozen different languages competing for pre-eminence. I have became sharp at realising that the Dutch can speak all of them, but while the Swedes can converse in very passable French, only Germans from southern states like Swabia, Bavaria or Hessen will trust themselves at all to speak the local tongue.

The Americans would if they could. But they can't, so they don't. The French grudgingly break out in a little English if they ABSOLUTELY HAVE TO. The Italians are the same, although they understand more English than they let on, which I find a bit sly. The Belgians watch Formula One on their tellies and don't mix much.

The Brits, well we're up for anything really, even if it stretches way beyond our capacity. Not much of a stretch, come to think of it.

One of the biggest linguistic challenges I had was to interview Jean-Marie Leblanc, the former General Director of the Tour de France. A blustering, bald, portly, trad-jazz clarinet-playing former Tour rider who ruled the roost for years, it was an honour to have made his slightly overbearing acquaintance. He was a towering figure really, who presided over the Indurain and the Armstrong years, over drugs busts and riders' strikes, demonstrations and machinations.

But his lasting legacy as far as many of us were concerned in the media, was the introduction of the 'detachable lanyard'. The word lanyard may conjure up images of ship's chandlers and nautical knots, but in the narrow little world of sports events it means one thing only. It is the brightly coloured, often sponsored necklace of polyester from which your laminated accreditation is hung by means of a clip. A sub-standard lanyard can spell all sorts of bother, for if the accreditation drops off and gets lost without the wearer noticing its departure, days of bureaucracy can ensue before a replacement can be issued. Thus, the lanyard is, for the month of July, your professional life. I have been known to shower still wearing it.

The relief when you can take it off and pack it away for good in Paris is the same feeling you get when someone turns off a poorly tuned radio: until it's gone you'd never realised how irritating it had become. After a decade in this line of work, I have a collection of these things from all sorts of events, which, up until the time I wrote this, I have never admitted to. I suspect all my colleagues are the same, and that somewhere back at home, perhaps in the attic, they have a dedicated Lanyard Wall, and dream of walking their grandchildren up and down it, regaling them with tales of sports journalistic heroism.

Jean-Marie Leblanc's contribution to the development of accreditation accessories was to design a lanyard with a cunningly designed clip which would detach if tugged hard enough. The official line was that this was a safety measure designed to prevent hapless journalists from getting snared up in a rider's handlebars and dragged down the tarmac by the neck. But we didn't believe that for a second. We suspected the Machiavellian Leblanc had designed it in order to remove his enemies, and to rule by fear.

He had been seen on a number of occasions, it was darkly rumoured, to instantaneously remove someone's accreditation at the flick of his meaty wrist. One deft movement, and the offending journo's summer was over, quite possibly losing him his job. The stakes were high: you didn't mess with Him.

Mentally, I tried hard to prepare intensely for those rare occasions when the multilingual Matt Rendell was not around and I would have to interview Leblanc. As a rule, we only ever bothered seeking out his opinion if there was a matter of some controversy to discuss. I was conscious of being in the presence of a man who had complete control over his thoughts and their expression. He joined them up. He was a joined-up man.

His answers soared, exquisitely constructed and spoken with a precision and clarity of accent that left you in no doubt of his absolute Frenchness. He was elegant and exact, but just below the silky surface of his speech, you would occasionally become aware that his words carried the furious threat of a butcher with a meat cleaver in his hand. Talking to him was like going back to school.

In conversation with Leblanc, I would occasionally attempt to rise to the occasion, daring to use words that I was only half-sure of, like '*néanmoins*', or '*d'ailleurs*'. I would try to get as close as I possibly could to the distinctive aspirated whistling noise that real French people so effortlessly tack onto commonplace words like '*perdu*' and '*tendu*'. I might even, on a good day, have contemplated letting fly a casual subjunctive.

With other resolutely French French-speakers on the scene, I am more typically inhibited.

At the start of the 2008 Tour I tracked down Bernard Hinault, who, in 1985, was the last Frenchman to win the Tour de France. He was known as The Badger, a nickname that implied feral aggression. I wondered if he'd taken the same approach into his post-racing career.

A busy man at the best of times, Hinault is in constant demand on the Tour de France, where he has a contractual arrangement with the organisers to turn up and be Bernard Hinault. Really, he is the only man for the job, and the French public can't get enough of him. I was aware of a queue of journalists, well-wishers, sponsors and other accredited Tour types building up behind me.

That year the Tour started in Brest, at the most westerly extremity of the country. This was Brittany, Hinault's country. I wanted to talk to him about the characteristics of cycling in that part of the world, which is battered by Atlantic winds most of the year. I wondered whether the rigours of the landscape had forged a distinctive type of man: no nonsense, bluff and a little gruff.

No sooner had I embarked on the interview than my French just fell apart, and was left in a heap of broken little words on the floor in front of him. What did for me was the whole Brittany thing. I struggled with the pronunciation of 'Bretagne'. I forgot that the adjective was 'Breton', and not 'Brittanique', an error that became all too apparent when I ended up asking him if all Breton riders consider themselves to be fundamentally British.

The Badger looked at me with thinly disguised pity.

And in 2010 I came face to face with Laurent Fignon for the final time. A few years previously I had conducted a similarly shambolic interview in French with him at his hotel complex in the Pyrenees. He'd been a gentleman, and had refrained from showing open scorn. Perhaps because he knew that I was basically plugging his business. But also, I imagine, because he was curious to see how much longer I could continue groping around in the linguistic darkness before I finally broke down in front of him. I wondered during our last interview if he remembered our ridiculous encounter.

He seemed to be well enough in the summer of 2010. But he wasn't. A month or two later, cancer claimed his life. With him went a large portion of France's cycling heritage.

But where Fignon's memory is revered, others are less

fondly remembered. Take, for example, Jan Ullrich: the earring-wearing, freckled, seemingly humourless German whose repeated capitulations in the face of Armstrong's dominance in the mountains characterised my early Tours.

Ullrich showed a disinclination to speak any English, which led me, not unreasonably, to believe that he couldn't. Why should he after all? He'd grown up in East Berlin in the eighties, where learning English was an act of relative decadence. He'd spent most of his racing years in German-centric teams built in his image, and lived and trained in the mountains of southern Germany. The man was as retro-Deutsch as a faded denim jacket.

This shouldn't have mattered. After all, I had a good knowledge of German, having spent a few formative years in the early nineties in Hamburg, gazing into the dregs of Bier glasses wondering what to do with my life. So, I felt a little drawn to Ullrich, my ersatz-countryman. I claimed him, in fact.

There was much I liked about him. I liked the way he flattered to deceive. I found him to be frail, human, charmingly charmless. In some ways, he was the anti-Armstrong, prone to fits of pique, breathtaking weight gains over winter, and with a propensity for slapstick: most memorably flying through the rear window of his team's support vehicle when out for a training ride two days before the start of the Tour.

And yet, he and I never hit it off. In three years of covering those Tours that Jan Ullrich contested, I didn't actually interview him once. Not once. That's a pretty remarkable record really, given the fact that he finished second, fourth and third in consecutive races before disappearing feet first into a quagmire of doping scandals from which he never emerged.

I don't know what it was, but he always managed to swerve me. In big media bundles, I would hold my microphone into the middle of a clump of others, and would fail to get a

question in. He would never look my way. Then, at the very
last second, I would throw in my effort, just at the moment
where he would be turning on his Adidas heels and getting
back on the bus. I was always too late.

There were two occasions when he did speak to ITV but
I was there at neither of them. The first of these came when
quite unexpectedly, a day before the start of the 2005 Tour,
Jan Ullrich sat down in front of Matt to do an interview. To
this day, no one knows why.

With the realisation of his mistake beginning to dawn, Jan
stared at Matt. And Matt stared back, both men trying to
establish who was the more surprised to find themselves in
that position. Not one to shirk a linguistic challenge, Matt
embarked on an interview in German, one of the few languages
he hasn't mastered. He emitted a few words, judiciously
sprinkled with occasional coherent meaning.

'Jan. Wie ist das Problem mit Ihrem Knie?' [How is the
problem with your knee?] This was a perfectly reasonable
start. Except that Matt faited to pronounce the hard K at the
beginning of 'Knie', coming out instead with the English
sounding 'Nee'. A minor mistake, but one that rendered his
accent ridiculous, just as it would be if a German asked in
English, 'How iz ze problem viz your K-Nee?'

To give him his due, Ullrich did well not to laugh.

On another occasion, on a finish line of a transitional stage
in the 2005 Tour, Matt grasped the nettle and, with the camera
rolling, posed the almost-intelligible question, 'Jan. Was ist
gepassiert?' Which would have sounded like this to Ullrich:
'Jan. What gehappened?'

Don't geknow. Now gebugger off.

But what of Alessandro Petacchi? Well, to my great disappointment, he has learnt how to speak a little English. In
2010, when he had a month-long flirtation with the green
jersey, eventually winning it, we came face to face often

enough. Although some of the mystery had gone, both from his answers, as well as from my questions.

'Alessandro. Congratulations. Are. You. Confident. That. You. Can. Win. The. Green. Jersey?'

'I don't know. It will be very difficult, I think. Cavendish is very strong. So is Hushovd. But I try. It's normal, no?'

It may be normal. But it's not half as fun.

FLOYD LANDIS

The winner of the 2006 Tour de France was Oscar Pereiro*.

He will, sadly for him, always be known as Oscar Pereiro-Asterisk. The other man in the race that year, the man who crossed the finish line in Paris quicker than anyone else, was Floyd Landis.

Do you remember Scooby Doo? There's a visual headstart. The wildly twitchy eyes, the peculiar little smile, and the crazed attempts at facial hair and the screechy voice. Norville 'Shaggy' Rogers clearly shares some genetic material with Floyd Landis.

I often think about him, now he's made it his fate-bound mission to bring Lance Armstrong to his knees. I recall the day of his downfall. My memories are sharp, high-definition pictures. They are worth revisiting.

It was Thursday 20 July 2006. I ambushed him in the

morning outside a modest chalet in Saint-Jean-de-Maurienne. We hadn't actively chosen the ambush mission, you understand. There was no great sea of hands volunteering to doorstep the man who had tossed away the Tour de France when he had cracked and haemorrhaged time the previous day. In fact, it was only a sense of duty, an obligation to the narrative of the race, that led me there. There was that and the fact that Steve Docherty had told me to go and do it.

No, this was going to be hard. I had to interview an unhappy millionaire cyclist dressed in a tight-fitting nylon leotard emblazoned with the name of a Swiss hearing-aid manufacturer. That much I knew. But what I didn't know was that he was about to rip the race apart, and then himself.

The crazy thing that morning, as we pulled our dusty, battered Espace into the gravelled car park, was that the Caisse D'Epargne team was billeted in the same hotel. In other words, Oscar Pereiro, the heir apparent to the 2006 Tour de France, was sleeping no more than few yards away from the man who had gifted it to him. Who knows, they might have passed each other the previous evening, in the carpeted corridors en route to the dining room, massaged and tired and wearing flip-flops. Would they have exchanged a glance? Would they have said hello?

There was a larger-than-average media throng present, as well as a good smattering of interested members of the public. They had made their way there to anoint Pereiro. Pereiro's movie-star good looks, rich, dark eyes and admirably chiselled sideburns were just the tonic for a Tour that was adjusting to the vacuum of life after Armstrong. Here was a rider who had some talent, but also immense good fortune on his side. His lead had been granted to him when the peloton failed to take him seriously enough to warrant chasing down. He held on for two days, before ceding the lead to Floyd Landis. But that wasn't the end of it. On Stage 16 to La Toussuire, Landis cracked spectacularly under the strain of defending his yellow jersey. He lost eight minutes as Pereiro held firm and reclaimed the race lead. It was a thrillingly unexpected turn. Here we had a story to tell that was forged from fallibility – the polar opposite to the calculated successes of Armstrong's domination.

It was one of those mornings when we timed our arrival to perfection. In other words, we were very nearly too late. Just as Woody and John were plugging in and fumbling around with their kit in the back of the car, Pereiro emerged from an inauspicious side door, to whoops, cheers and whistles from the largely French crowd. He looked cool. He looked measured. He looked every inch a man in command.

We stopped him in his tracks as he tried to board his team's black bus. He had one foot on, and one foot off the steps. I can't remember much of what he said to us, because, to be absolutely honest, I wasn't remotely interested. I was practising the time-honoured journalistic technique of only pretending to listen, while all the time my senses were sharpened for the arrival of Landis. I was aware that at any second he would appear. Icarus on a bike.

Success is so much less attractive as a story than failure, especially when the failure had been so emphatic, the humiliation so public. What had taken place the previous day had been a very complete form of dethroning. Yellow jerseys are seen as an invitation to attack, but the wearer normally has it in him to respond. Prior to Landis's collapse, I had only ever seen riders hurl themselves at the edifice of Armstrong's unbreakable will, and achieve nothing. Moths to a flame. So, at least for me, this was new.

After such a loss, in what frame of mind could Landis possibly be?

A flash of Team Phonak green. Unnoticed by almost

everyone, Landis had emerged blinking into the bright alpine sunshine, and was already hobbling his way towards the privacy of the team bus. I thanked Pereiro for his time, politely cutting short one of his answers as I did, and sped off to intercept our man.

He'd wanted to avoid attention by slipping out the back door inconspicuously, but as he crossed the sunlit court, we cast a sudden shadow. Having conceded the yellow jersey, he looked stripped of greatness in his lime green and yellow Phonak kit. Apart from the odd clutch of cycling's more informed rubber-neckers, we were the only people to show any interest in him that morning.

The rider spoke in his high-pitched, almost-charismatic voice, explaining what he had in mind for the coming day.

'I'll attack I guess.' He looked to the left, and he looked to the right. He looked at the sky and he looked at the gravel. He looked anywhere but at his interrogator. Me.

'Yeah. I'll have to attack. There's not much else I can do. So we'll see.'

At that point, he did finally turn to look at me, with the twitch of a smile and a truncated nod of the head. It was the kind of perfunctory gesture which is shorthand for, 'That's it. You've got your answer. Now leave me alone.'

But that flicker of a look had been strangely revealing. Would it be revisionist of me to suggest that deep down I knew something was up? Can I be sure that the subsequent years of disgrace and cover-up and deceit haven't led me to think I remember something that wasn't there? Have I fabricated my suspicions in retrospect? I don't think so.

We made our way to the finish line, travelling across the valley floor and up onto the mountainside upon which Morzine perches. We weaved our way through the usual crowds of innocents who had made their wide-eyed way to race day on the Tour. The American cycling groups were out in force still, though not in the great numbers of the previous year, where they'd lined the roadsides with their yellow bracelets and yellow Nike 'Magnificent Seven' T-shirts. We used to wind down the window whenever we spotted a particularly thick clump of them and bellow 'Go Lance!' in as thick an American accent as we could. Often they would whoop and holler their love and support back. This amused us no end.

We sped past a gathering of Discovery Channel-clad Americans, each one dressed perfectly in all the trimmings, and all riding identical Trek bikes. I wondered if their support was transferable. I wondered also if they had invested even half of their passion for Armstrong in Landis. If Lance was bigger than the sport, then now that he was gone, where did that leave any of us really?

I thought idly about the contents of my tape. It was a decent little sound bite, and would sit well at the front of the show, setting up the emerging narrative of the day and moving the story on from last night's programme, which had ended with a shot of a distraught Landis being jostled into his car and driven off wordlessly from La Toussuire. I was pleased to have got in on tape: it satisfied my journalistic brief but, frankly, I didn't believe a word of it. Landis might attack, but there was no way that he would be able to make it stick. The Tour didn't work like that.

It was only when I arrived at the finish line in Morzine several hours later and fought my way to the tiny little sideyard where the Tour had decided our truck should be parked that I realised something was up. I prised open the back door, and peered into the gloom. Gary and Steve were absorbed in what was unfolding in front of them on the monitors.

'He's attacked,' Steve said, 'on the first climb of the day.' He glanced down to see that I had the tape with me.

I'd rung ahead to let Steve know what Landis had said. He afforded himself a rare little grin. It was satisfying that the opening to our show would prove prescient when the big story of the day unfolded. What we didn't realise right then was that it was going to become not only the story of the day, but arguably one of the most extraordinary stories of the hundred-plus years of the Tour itself.

I dropped off the tape, and went outside again to compose my thoughts and write my opening voice-over script. We had a monitor. I kept my eye on the race as I worked.

Landis was on the lower slopes now of La Colombière. He was six minutes ahead of the chasing group, including Carlos Sastre, Denis Menchov and the yellow jersey Pereiro. But still there were some brutal climbs to come, including the Col de Joux-Plane.

Steve, meanwhile, had been online. He popped his head out of the truck. 'You can get 28–1 on Betfair against Landis to win the Tour de France. It was 80–1 this morning.' He grinned. Then he went back in.

I waited a matter of seconds, and then charged after him. I had ten euros in my pocket and gave it to Steve. Would he put in on for me? I didn't have an online account. Steve accepted the money.

'I won't put it on. But I'll offer you those odds myself: 28–1. Against Landis winning this year's Tour de France.' He wasn't smiling now. This was business. Steve's cautious attitude to spending money in France was legendary. And here he was talking about the possibility of losing two hundred and eighty euros. This was no time for flippancy.

I made some ground rules, with Chris Boardman and Gary Imlach as witnesses. 'OK, ten euros at 28–1. But there'll be no Rule 4 on this one. No stewards' inquiry. You'll have to pay first past the post, should you lose.'

We shook. He took my tenner. It was a momentous occasion.

Up in the Alps, Landis was roaring back. His solo attack lasted all day. Neither Pereiro nor any of the rest of the peloton could respond.

After watching Landis winning the stage to return to within thirty seconds of the yellow jersey – a time gap he would surely wipe out on the penultimate stage, the individual time trial – the media assembled en masse in the mixed zone. This was not a day to go AWOL. It was an obligation for each and every outlet that day to get their moment with Landis. The barricaded section, set underneath a plane tree off the main street in Morzine, was stuffed full of expectant microphones, necks craned, and faces turned anxiously in the direction from which it was expected the winner would be chaperoned.

I wasn't among them. For some reason, I had been given special dispensation that day to hurdle the barriers and enter the sacred area just behind the podium. This is normally the preserve of the national broadcaster of the rider who has just won. That day, amazingly, the Americans didn't have a crew to hand. Perhaps their man had got stuck coming up the mountain. It can happen.

Either way, the result was that I was lurking around with my camera crew just where I needed to be, because Landis had been hiding. He'd given a rather sheepish grin from the podium, and then vanished into doping control, swerving his obligations to the international media. In short, he simply hadn't showed up. After an interminable delay, a hundred or so members of the press realised that they weren't going to get anything and turned tetchily on their heels. It was, at the very least, slightly bizarre behaviour.

I, too, had almost given up hope, when I virtually bumped into him. He had come careering down the three little steps that led from the anti-doping caravan, and was on his way out of there.

'Floyd. Just a quick word.' His ASO chaperone seemed not to object, but Landis was having none of it. He reached for his bike that was propped up by a tree. There had been perhaps a million people on the Alps that afternoon, and tens of thousands thronging the streets of Morzine. In fact, outside that penned-off area, you could barely move. But right there, at that moment, it was unnaturally quiet. 'Seriously, Floyd. Just one question. It won't take a second.'

He relented. And squared up for the interview. 'Better be quick, man. One question. I mean it.' A little wrong-footed, I ploughed on.

There is always a hiatus, when the TV reporter has to wait

for the cameraman to shoulder arms, adjust the contrast, white balance, focus up and make sure the picture is stable. The sound recordist too must be sure he is getting what he wants. There is simply no point in starting with the questions unless all this is in place. I often look at newspaper journalists with their notebooks and envy them their fleet-footedness. These are big, heavy complex cameras, and the cacophony of noise at the Tour makes capturing clean sound a perpetual challenge. Sometimes it takes as much as seven or eight seconds. Those seconds can feel like for ever when faced with a reluctant athlete who wants to get away.

I call this the Dead Time.

There are occasions when you fill it with a little small talk. I tend to favour blurting something out; a blast of non sequitur far removed from the matter at hand. 'Russell Brand's really irritating, isn't he?' 'What was your first car?' 'I reckon I've got a wart on my thumb. Do think that looks like a wart?'

This was not such an occasion, however. Even in the heat of a French July afternoon, the ice was thickening with each passing second. Landis was almost twitching with discomfort. And so, frankly, was I. We were all stood there, the unhappy members of our reluctant quartet, simply because we had to. At that given moment, and for a multiplicity of reasons, none of us wanted to be standing on that little square of dusty Alpine earth.

'OK, mate.' John let me know I could start.

'Floyd, an amazing fightback. Has it sunk in with you yet that you've probably won the Tour de France?'

Landis looked away at an oblique angle to both me and the camera lens.

His answer was concise. Something like: 'Oh well, you know, it was an OK day. I've not won anything yet. There's plenty of racing still to come, but I guess I can be pretty happy.' Full stop.

He turned abruptly, hopped on the bike, which had been his sole companion over nearly two hundred kilometres, and was gone.

It was an odd sort of interview for a winner to give. Of course, with the judicious application of hindsight, it is simple enough to interpret. Just yards from where we stood, he had just provided a specimen sample of urine that contained enough synthetic testosterone to ruin his career and his reputation for ever. He was already fretting, dreading perhaps that one day the world would be made aware. There are pictures of his celebratory wave to the crowds. What must he have been thinking?

Later on that day, in the dying heat of a blistering afternoon, I paused to take a swig of water from a bottle and reflect upon a strange day. I had stopped by the side of the road. Here the barriers to keep the public out pushed all the way across the width of the narrow streets. The Tour had engulfed Morzine, swallowed it whole. I was looking vaguely along the line of a side street. In the middle distance, an ornate stone fountain gurgled alpine water. Some kids in the ubiquitous T-Mobile shirts of the era were splashing each other and swearing in treacly Bavarian.

I became aware that Paul Sherwen was standing next to me. He looked his normal clean-cut self, in his US liveried freshly laundered polo shirt, razor-sharp parting separating his faintly oiled hair, and his signature imperial trousers: all beige and crisp.

It is worth explaining that Paul lives in some splendour in Uganda. I imagine fondly that somewhere in the very heart of his house there is a Trouser Gallery. It is almost certainly an oak-panelled room containing hundreds of pairs of perfectly pressed trousers, each pair subtly different from the next, but all conforming to a narrow colour range that starts at magnolia and ends with taupe. His mornings are spent patrolling these

lines of hanging garments, his long shirt-tails covering his modesty, and regimental socks drawn high to the knee, with an enamel mug of redbush tea in his hand, choosing the slacks which would best suit the mood and tenor of the day. Since Paul's mood only has a margin for variation of 0.003 per cent, the need to branch out as far as mustard or ochre is remote.

'What can you tell me, Ned? Some fucking bike race that. Some fucking balls.' Paul likes to swear, harmlessly, aimlessly and often.

In this case, it was understandable too. Phil Liggett and Paul Sherwen are primarily engaged to commentate for whichever US network happens to own the rights to the Tour de France in the North American territories. ITV takes the same feed of their commentary. But Paul was acutely conscious that he was broadcasting the first 'Post-Lance' Tour to an American public, many millions of whom had only become familiar with the race because the Texan kept winning the damn thing. To that extent then, the epic events of Stage 17 were manna from TV heaven. Landis promised to be a new all-American hero. And, unlike the never-in-doubt Rambo certainty of the Armstrong years, he'd done it Rocky Balboa style: he'd been down on the canvas, with the referee counting as far as 'Nine!' and had sprung back up to land the knockout blow.

I don't know what it was that Phil and Paul said in their commentary that day, but they would have been 'digging deep into their suitcases of imagery' to convey the drama of that one. So as we stood in the glow, watching the water splash and listening to the German profanities, Paul's ears must still have been singing with the words and feelings the narrative of the day had forced out of him. He must have been buzzing at Landis's success.

No commentator likes to impart bad news. They like to be able to fulfil the dreams and wishes of their audience, imagined or not.

But a germ, a kernel of a thought had already wheedled its way into my thinking. As yet undefined, but gathering shape and form as I replayed the day's events. The problem was, back in 2006, I had no previous experience of doping on the Tour. Sure, I'd heard Gary and Matt and Steve, as well as a host of others, tut-tutting over certain individuals about whom they had their doubts. But nothing I had seen or heard first hand had ever looked or sounded or tasted like cheating.

I didn't really know what to look for, but I was fairly sure that when I did see it I would know.

What I had just witnessed seemed too gauche to be true. Its very obviousness implied that it couldn't possibly have been achieved by doping. Surely if you cheat, you cheat within the margins of credibility, you don't stretch a point by asking Getafix to sling you a gourd of magic potion under the counter and then stroll through the village gates and start bashing Roman centurions together. That would be ridiculous. It would be to invite scrutiny, to implore detection. Yet, everything I had observed from Landis that day both on and off the bike struck me as unnatural. Not knowing then whether I would be shot down in flames for even suggesting it, I went out on a limb.

'Paul, was that, you know . . . should we take that at face value?' My vocabulary was failing me. 'Or was it, um, bent?'

He looked genuinely affronted. At once I wished I hadn't spoken; I'd clearly misjudged the moment.

'It was just a great ride, you know. Sometimes that's all there is. Just a brilliant ride.' He looked serious enough.

'Fucking brilliant,' he added for extra fucking emphasis.

Paul, of course, has ridden the Tour. He understands the dynamics of the race, is alive to the nuances of the professional peloton, and, most importantly perhaps, was still very closely in touch with a good number of the riders, notably the American contingent. I was just a football hack winging it in a world beyond my ken. So I bowed to his greater knowledge. Nothing that Paul had told me wasn't spoken from the heart. He loved the sport, and I felt bad for having besmirched it.

On 25 July 2006, within a day of our return to England, I received a beautifully hand-written cheque for the sterling equivalent of my winnings. I was amused to discover that Steve writes out cheques in the same orderly fashion that he composes shot-lists or running orders. My name was underlined in red. Being busy with other things, I smiled at my good judgement, dropped it in my in-tray and forgot to cash it.

Two days later, on 27 July, within minutes of the breaking news of Landis's positive 'A' sample, I got a phone call. Literally within minutes.

'Have you cashed it?' The unmistakable tone of a man reprieved. Steve's voice. 'Rip it up. Don't cash it. I'm not paying. He's a bloody cheat. Floyd Bloody Landis.'

For the record, this case is still hugely contentious. Not

the Landis one, that's clear-cut. I mean the dispute over the cheque; the foundation of our disagreement still quite unresolved. I maintain that I struck the bet on the basis of 'first past the post', regardless of any retrospective rulings. At some point it may get litigious. And at that point I will be fancying my chances, given that I have Sir Gary Imlach and Chris Boardman MBE as my witnesses for the prosecution.

Suffice it to say, though as I write this, I still haven't had my money.

Even though I won the bet*.

LEWISHAM HOSPITAL: PART TWO, AUGUST 2003

They'd already tried a different question, but it had proved to be useless.

'Which member of the Royal Family has just got married?'

Charles? Andrew? The other one? Princess Michael? Before my eyes a procession of generic Windsors swam, some tethering horses and dressed in Barbours and headscarves, some galumphing around in helicopter pilot gear, maps visible in see-through pouches over the knees. Bald spots, ears and grins. Harry, Marry, Wills and Testaments. No idea.

'No idea.' I shook my head. More to confirm to myself than anyone else that I had no idea . . . feeling that a visual cue like a shake of the head would help my sliding cognitive powers understand that I could no longer understand what was being asked of me or why it might be being asked.

'I'm sorry', I said. I was.

My hands kept moving to my bike helmet. Flat-spotted at the front, and split. Grazed through to the polystyrene all along the left-hand side. It lay upturned like a condemned turtle on the trolley next to me.

My hands knew too where the Piece of Paper was kept. It lay on the counter, alongside the jug of water with the flip-top lid. They picked it up and held it before my eyes.

The Piece of Paper was read to me. Not for the first time, but for the hundredth, I absorbed its drifting hymn, aware that this was no longer news, but stuff that I did know, but now no longer knew and will need to know again.

'That doesn't mean anything to him. He wouldn't know the answer anyway. Ask him something else.'

'When did you get married?'

On the face of it, this should have been an easy one, too. The trouble is that even now I can't say confidently that I would be able to answer it. Kath and I did indeed get married, after a good decade or so together and with two kids already to show for it. But we'd sloped off to the register office early one autumn afternoon, grilled some sausages back at home for lunch with our witnesses, and then taken off our twenty-pounds-the-pair matching H. Samuel rings, never to be worn again. It wasn't romantic, it was tax-efficient. But it wasn't memorable.

I squinted at my interrogator. A young doctor – Specsaver glasses, striped shirt, white coat, and the inevitable stethoscope draped round her shoulders. Like an extra in Holby City, I was beginning to become aware that I was conforming to an increasingly daft litany of hackneyed one-liners. I closed my eyes, scrunched them shut, as if to summon up more thinking power.

'How did I get here?' I asked, aware by now of the absurdity of the question, yet powerless to avoid asking it. There are few things that impart more anxiety than not understanding why you are where you are. And I didn't.

I looked up. The Holby City doctor was in deep conversation with Kath, who kept a solicitous hold of my grubby palm as I sat cross-legged, like a bruised Buddha on the trolley.

'It sounds daft, but he wouldn't know that either. You see, nor would I. The wedding was nothing special, and we don't celebrate anniversaries,' Kath was explaining. She turned to me. 'This is Lewisham Hospital, Ned. You've had an accident, and you're confused. The doctors are just trying to find out what's going on.'

'Who put these on me?' I looked down at my Lycra shorts.

If Holby City *was real, then it would have flashed back to the accident. The pelican crossing. The girl in the road. Me approaching. The green light.*

As it was, my memory wasn't quite that good. It stuttered back into life every now and again, but flashed back to the wrong bits. Pedalling fast past Dulwich College and turning my head to the left to see someone running up to bowl. Crossing over Tower Bridge, avoiding the strangely corrugated edges of the carriageway where the tarmac has melted and buckled up, its slow-sapping gradient and wind from the west.

A paramedic leaning over me. The white ceiling of the ambulance, and sway of its suspension.

Then nothing more.

'How did I get here?'

CAVENDISH - BEGINNINGS

Châteauroux: 9 July 2008. The sun beats hard on the tarmac. A heat haze rises vertically from the Skoda-sponsored finish line. I squint back along the home straight. Black-and-white signs mark the distances left: 50m, 100m, 150m, 200m, at intervals along the strung-out line of straining faces and flag-waving kids. From this piece of asphalt where I stand rooted, the shimmering of the heat curtain looks like the opposite of refreshing rain – a shower of oven-ready air to greet the first across the line.

A fly lands on my ankle, drawn to the drying sweat. I glance down at him. He's waiting too. We are somewhere in the middle of France, and it's time once again to call home the winner. Only this time, it could be different.

In one hand, I clutch my microphone. I'm breathing a bit

like Darth Vader, as the race draws closer. With my thumb I worry the braille-like raised print that spells out the word Sennhiesser. Woody stands next to me, inscrutable behind the summer's latest designer shades, fingers poised above the mixer strapped round his waist in the style of a cinema usherette, sweat pouring off him. My other hand hovers over the radio-talkback control. I tweak the volume higher in a vain effort to hear Phil and Paul's words.

With just 5km left, and the speed tipping 30mph, I am trying to decipher the turn of events. Has the break been caught?

Of course it has. This is HTC-Columbia. Their train hits the front. From this point, as I loosen the elbow on the microphone arm, there is little room left for doubt.

Mark Cavendish was about to unleash his extraordinary talent on the Tour. And we would be right there to see him do it. Heady days.

In the spring of the previous year, I had asked a simple, innocent question: 'Mark Cavendish, this kid on T-Mobile. Is he actually going to be as good as everyone reckons?'.

To the initiated this was an insultingly simple question. But on the radar screen of my understanding, he'd only just shown up. Other great sprinters were there: Tom Boonen and McEwen, with Petacchi and Hushovd, stacked-up slow-moving dots homing in ever closer to their targets. And then suddenly, there was this new blip. A fragment of something greater, perhaps. A UFO that originated from the Isle of Man. To give it an abbreviated name, we called it 'Cav'.

The signs had been there throughout his development and, to those in the know, Cavendish was a loaded bullet ready to be fired. But I dispute that anyone, except the rider himself (for his self-belief is astounding), knew what the next couple of years would bring. This was before the records and the stunning serial successes, the petulance, the feuds, the daring and the doing of the man. The day on which I asked about Cavendish for the first time dates back to an altogether different age.

In fact, it was a cloudy Thursday in London, two days before the start of the 2007 Tour. We parked up outside the Ramada Jarvis hotel in London's Excel centre, which is the sort of place that defies description. So I won't try.

Careful negotiations had brought us to the position where we had an appointment with T-Mobile's Mark Cavendish. I remember being surprised that things had been that difficult to set up. Fran Millar (Dave's sister and sometime cycling agent) had assisted us, as well as an army of PR people from T-Mobile whose job seemed to be predicated on the understanding that the media, in all their guises, are an untrustworthy rabble, and should be hindered at every opportunity. In the end, though, we'd been given a time and a place when we could sit down to meet Mark Cavendish, face to face. It would be our first encounter.

We had done the usual thing: arriving at a hotel, we had scoured the echoing lobby area for a suitable nook to set up some lights and conduct the interview with sufficient intimacy, protected as much as possible from the off-white noise of bags being dropped, phones ringing, and music playing.

I went off in search of the relevant PR bloke. I think his name was Michael Wagner, but that may be my version of what he should have been called. He had that generic corporate German look, which is best suited to airport departure lounges and trade fairs: grey-suited, with a mobile in one hand and a BlackBerry in the other, he had a face which was loosely based on Michael Stich, but with less identifiable character. Unsmilingly, he greeted me, and told me that I should wait there, and that he would bring in Mark as and when Mark deemed it appropriate for Mark to appear. And with that he disappeared back into the main body of the hotel complex without so much as being nice. It was the first of many such encounters with 'Wagner' that summer. They were uniquely life-sapping experiences, which made me vow never to buy a phone from T-Mobile.

I had a picture of Cavendish in my pocket, which I had printed off the Internet so that I could recognise him when he showed up, but in the end there was no need. It was obvious that the short figure in the regulation Adidas tracksuit coming towards me was the main man. He had a restrained swagger: short-striding and purposeful. As he drew close, he looked shyly at me. I noted his long lashes, plump cheeks and full lips. *This man looks nothing like a racer*, I remember thinking.

When the interview got under way, though, I was struck by his thoughtfulness and his self-belief. Those twin tracks define the margins of every subsequent interview I have conducted with him, and there have been many. He spoke quietly of his own achievements that spring, of winning the Scheldeprijs by a whisker from the great Robbie McEwen to claim his maiden Pro-tour win. This, he recalled, was vindication of his form and ability. It delighted him, but it surprised him not a bit.

Now the Tour loomed. He was frank about the limits of his ambitions, freely admitting that he would ride no further than the foot of the Alps before stepping off. But at the same time he declared firmly his intention of winning a stage or two. He could see no reason why he shouldn't be mixing it with the world's greatest sprinters. After all, he told me, he was one of them.

What you think about Cavendish is ultimately a matter of personal taste. For some, his candour, coupled with unusually high-functioning self-esteem, is a source of genuine irritation. His readiness to acknowledge the efforts of his teammates when celebrating a win is one thing, but the scratchiness of his complaints when fate deals him a slighter hand has caused a few to write the man off as cycling's superbrat. Others may just accept this as part of the necessary psychological land-scape of the winner, and celebrate it. After all, there is much to celebrate.

I shook his hand, and gave him my pre-prepared speech with which I assail every British Tour rider on meeting them for the first time. I spoke to him about the need to bring him close to the audience back home, and apologised in advance for the inevitable badgering that would characterise the end of most stages. Would he please be patient enough to cooperate with my daily attempts to illicit a sound bite from him, however much he may find this to be a dreadful imposi-tion? I thanked him very much in advance and impressed on him that his compliance would make my life a whole lot easier.

Cavendish looked understandably unimpressed, and from his lofty height of several inches shorter than me, cast up a somewhat wary look, then with the faintest of perfunctory smiles, he was off. Loping along at a distance of exactly two paces behind him went 'Wagner'. I watched them round a corner, my broadcaster's grin welded to my face. Then I let it drop, and turned to Woody and Liam to see what they made of it. But they were already busily packing down their kit, and hadn't listened to single word of what was actually being said.

'Weird voice,' offered Woody. 'Needed to boost the levels a bit. But then it all got a bit Billy Joel on the hotel PA system, so I couldn't push it any further. Hope you can hear him OK when you play it back.'

I was left with the vague feeling that talking to Cavendish wasn't going to be the easiest job I'd ever have.

Three days later he skidded on his backside over a stretch of Kent tarmac, and by the time he'd dusted himself down and got back on his bike, Robbie McEwen had claimed the stage. I chased after him along the drab stretch of Canterbury road that Le Tour had decided would be part of this year's route, until there was no longer any point. He wasn't going to stop for me that day.

A day later, on a foul and blustery afternoon on the road to Ghent, he fell off again. Using all the intuitive journalistic brilliance of a Pulitzer Prize winner, we deemed it necessary to interview Cavendish once more. This time, we had to involve 'Wagner'. There followed painstaking negotiations over the phone, which bordered on the baffling:

'He fell off.'

'We know. That's why we want to talk to him.'

'I don't think he'll want to talk to you.'

'Well, could you please ask him?'

'I could ask him.'

'Thank you.'

'But I think he won't want to talk to you because he fell off.'

And so it was finally that the matter-of-fact German curtly instructed us (by T-Mobile text message, naturally) to get to the team hotel and then to wait outside on the balcony. When we arrived at the venue after some circuitous navigation, the Belgian hotel staff barely disguised their suspicion. To make matters worse, it was just beginning to spit with rain. It was nearly nine o'clock at night, and frankly we were fed up. Fed up with the chasing the unfortunate and so far spectacularly unsuccessful Mark Cavendish. Fed up with the raining Belgian days of a Tour that had begun in glorious sunshine and wonderful London crowds. And the prospect of continually hassling the elusive Cavendish wasn't improving our mood much.

Through sliding glass doors we gazed on as, one by one, the T-Mobile team came down the spiral staircase to take their seats at dinner. All in their standard-issue Adidas clobber, they had the languid, slow, satisfied gait of the well exercised and well massaged. And of the about to be well fed.

Cavendish appeared, the last of the nine to take his place. We nudged closer to the glass, trying to catch his eye; Dickensian orphans at the window of a sweet shop. If he would only spot us now, he would no doubt come and talk to us for the requisite three or four minutes so we could push off and finish our shift, and he could resume the intimate, pampered life of the professional cyclist without the attention of the national broadcaster on his doorstep.

But no. He sat for what seemed like an eternity chatting to Linus Gerdemann, before standing up from the table and heading towards the buffet where he spent the longest time imaginable weighing up the comparative merits of coleslaw versus pasta salad. All the time, we could see 'Wagner' sitting at some distance from Cavendish, doing nothing by way of cajoling or persuading. Still, he seemed to be enjoying his glass of red and plate of cold meats, so that was some consolation.

By the time the sliding doors finally parted, and Mark Cavendish emerged onto the balcony, we were so dispirited we'd forgotten why we were there. He was disarmingly good to talk to, though, listening intently to my questions, and responding with bullishness and wit. I asked him about his two or three falls on Tour so far. 'I've got that much puppy fat on me, I reckon I just bounce off the tarmac.' His lips curled into a smile. It was humility and toughness rolled into one very sweet sound bite. It made him tremendously likeable.

When we were done, we thanked him for his time, and he turned to head in again. To our surprise, he stopped abruptly in his tracks, and looking at all three of us, wretchedly still standing there, had the good grace to utter an apology, of sorts. 'Sorry about keeping you lot waiting. You should have said.' And with that, he shot 'Wagner' a bit of a glance, and was gone, back off to the buffet for more Parma ham and olives.

Then it was 'Wagner's' turn to shoot a glance at us. We left, hurriedly.

Two years later, at the home of SV Hamburg football club, I met 'Wagner' again. I was there shooting some preview material for a UEFA Cup match. All afternoon, as we waited around for our various interviewees to show up, 'Wagner' and I sneaked furtive glances at one another; aware that we'd met somewhere, but unable to remember where or when. Eventually, I cracked first.

'*Wir kennen uns doch,*' I offered. Haven't we met?

'*Ja. Tour de France, oder?*' 'Wagner' smiled. 'Cavendish!'

The Pfennig had dropped. I spent a little while chatting to him. He'd quit the sport altogether. That summer he'd seen the writing on the wall and had jumped from T-Mobile, indeed jumped from cycling altogether. The shockwaves that followed Jan Ullrich's tarnished retirement had led their national team sponsor to withdraw, the main TV stations to boycott the Tour, and the Deutschland Tour to be abandoned. 'Wagner' cut a far happier figure in Hamburg, and we were able to laugh about the stress of managing a man who didn't necessarily want to be managed.

During the rest of that 2007 Tour, our pursuit of Cavendish was all about trying to second-guess when he might climb off and retire from the race. We tried to orchestrate a meeting before he disappeared altogether, but failed utterly. Often it's simply a question of logistics, which undoes the best-intentioned plans on the Tour. We might well have been able to get to him, and sit him down to reflect on his Tour debut, had he not decided to abandon on some distant incline on the road to Tignes. As he was being swept up by his magenta team car, and then chauffered off, probably to Geneva airport, we were hurtling in the other direction preparing to call home the winner of Stage 8, and the new race leader: Michael Rasmussen. In short, we were about to disappear into a far bigger crevice, and the Tour was about to morph into another shape, trampling the story of Cavendish's debut underfoot. He managed a couple of top-ten finishes, but nothing more than that. Quickly, we all moved on.

A year later, though, everything was different.

I made my way at some hideously early hour to Birmingham airport on the Wednesday before the 2008 Prologue. A few days after returning from football duties in Austria, it was deemed necessary that I board a flight to Brest in Brittany. I sat rubbing my sleepless eyes and chatting to Liam who'd flown down that morning from Glasgow, wondering where another year had gone. As I spoke, I became peripherally aware that Liam had spotted someone way more interesting than me. He seemed a little distracted, a little less enthralled than he should have been in my seamless blow-by-blow account of Euro 2008. Eventually, he leant forward and whispered, 'Don't look now, but isn't that Cav?'

Laptop under his left arm, his right hand trailing a tiny rolling travel case, and this time dressed in a very non-corporate pair of jeans. He plonked his stuff down, and went up to get himself a coffee.

'Yes. It's Cav.'

A little cynically, I saw this as an opportunity. We were virtually alone in the departure hall that morning. The demand for places on a morning flight to Brest from Birmingham was obviously not quite what the airline would have wished. There was Liam, there was Cavendish, and there was me. To a journalist in my position, this represents a dilemma, a challenge, an opportunity and a problem, all rolled into one. The way in which sport is marketed and managed these days has restrained the once free and easy association between the media and the athletes to such a rigorous extent that encounters such as this seldom happen, even in the much less regulated sport of cycling.

The simplest thing would have been to leave him completely alone. The most invasive would have been to load up the camera and try and grab an interview, guerilla-style. The most productive, and also the most polite and engaging alternative was the one I chose. Go over and have a natter. What harm could possible come of it?

I shook his hand. 'Hi, Mark. You well?'

'Hi. Not bad thanks.' A shy half smile. He glanced down at his laptop once again. I started off with some small talk. We spoke about his hugely successful Giro d'Italia. I asked him for his thoughts on the Tour. We spoke briefly about Brittany and airports and coffee. And that was that. I reckon it couldn't have lasted much more than a minute or two, and for no significant portion of that time did his eyes leave his computer screen. Sensing that I was on borrowed time, I went in for the journalistic kill. The question which we all dread, and which we all have to ask. The question that is the benchmark by which we judge each other.

'Mark, could I scribble down your mobile number?' I thought that the rather cutesy use of the word 'scribble' might somehow diminish the absolute significance of what I had just asked him. I tried to make it sound like I was asking him to pass the sugar, or what he was going to have for tea, when in fact I was asking him to trust me. That was the nub of it. Had I gained his trust?

'Sorry, mate. I don't like handing out my mobile number.'

And that was that. The next issue to present itself was one of social etiquette. For how much longer, after what had amounted to a form of snub, should you hang around? To leave immediately would suggest that it was only ever the mobile number that you were interested in, and that the entire encounter had instantly been rendered meaningless. But staying on too long afterwards would be awkward, too. Hadn't it just been made fairly clear where the parameters had been set? What could possibly be gained from dragging both of us into further discussions about the white chocolate chips in the muffin that sat glowering on a saucer in the middle of the table. Somehow, I fudged my exit and took my leave.

There was nothing about the encounter that had been rude or inappropriate. But it had been surprising, and a little disappointing. It bore the hallmarks of football. Until this point, cycling had seemed to me a happy playground for journalists, where the approachability and availability of the riders had seemed to be inbuilt in the character of the sport. Even Armstrong, although I know of almost no one who's ever claimed to have his mobile number, has been up for a chat now and then in a lift at a hotel or clutching a warm cup of coffee on a chilly morning as the mechanics prepared the bikes.

Yes, the mobile number is the obsession of the modern jobbing hack. By your SIM card's contacts are you measured. Sportsmen have developed many different ways over recent years of not giving it out. Changing their number on a weekly basis is still the favourite means of fending off the outside world. I have even fallen foul of the 'made-up number scam', when a Premier league footballer, whose number I had asked for, amusingly answered, 'Sure. It's 0777 777773.' I got halfway through writing it down before I realised what was going on.

But again, you must return to the issue of trust. I was two weeks into filming a documentary with Steven Gerrard a few years ago at the height of his fame as the swashbuckling captain of Liverpool. The building of trust had been slow and painstaking. It took a long time for me to persuade him that our intentions were benign, our discretion absolute. Then, one hideously wet December afternoon as I left his mansion in Formby after a long day's filming, I forgot I had my outdoor shoes on and trod at least a dozen filthy black footprints in single file across the full extent of the white carpet in his living room. This was not a good moment.

If anything was designed to put our relationship under stress, this was. Despite my offers to get contract cleaners round straight away, he sent me, on my way back down to London, with a scowl and an unconvincing sounding, 'Don't worry about it.' But worry was all I did. I fretted into late that evening, when out of the blue, I received a text message. 'Enjoyed filming today. Hope you got home OK. Don't worry about the carpet. Skipper.' The message was a very welcome relief, but the real prize was that it included his mobile number, of course. An act of trust. Of course, he's changed it a dozen times since.

'I'll ask you again tomorrow about your mobile number, Mark,' I quipped as we disembarked the tiny propeller plane at Brest airport. The faintest grin, and he was on his way.

The first few days of that Tour didn't go well for Cavendish. If his reputation for prickliness is built on anything at all, it's built on the interview that he gave to Matt after Stage 3, when the bunch had failed to chase down a break, and Cavendish had seen another realistic chance of a maiden stage win disappear. Matt collared him just as he crossed the line, and pushed him hard on why the chase had failed. It was something I'm sure that I, too, would have done. It's just that that year, I was somewhere else at the time.

The interview incensed Cavendish to the extent that a forensic analysis of it appears in his autobiography, which came out the following year. Four pages at the start of Chapter 3, to be precise.

There are many things you'd like to do when you've just blown your chance in a stage of the Tour de France, but trust me when I say that giving a television interview is a fair way down your list of priorities.

Mark's just warming up.

'Mark, Mark, can we have a word?'
He must have seen from the look on my face that the prospect didn't exactly fill me with glee, but the guy had a job to do. Anyway, as soon as the camera starts rolling, you're trapped; tell him to stick his microphone where there's never any sun on the forecast, or even put it more politely, and you've just starred in your own version of How to Lose Friends and Alienate People.

I've seen that look on his face. It's a kind of soft-edged threat. It has an intensity that unsettles you. Matt did well to hold on to his train of thought. He concludes:

'Interviewer: 'Mark, so what have you learnt from today?'
Me: 'That journalists sometimes ask some fucking stupid questions.'

Although not actually what he said (Cavendish writes that he only thought of saying this after the interview had been recorded), it has a certain ring of truth to it. It's probably what he thought. And it's probably what he still thinks.

I like Mark Cavendish, almost precisely because of his occasional thinly disguised fury. He may exercise his right to answer monosyllabically, petulantly, with irritation, anger or grievance. He sometimes, again rightly, decides not to talk to the cameras. To walk, or to talk. It's up to him. He can do, or be, whatever he likes. But unless the dumb lens of the television camera is present, he will exist in a vacuum. And, alongside the 'fucking stupid questions', there will be no glory, no adulation, no crowds. There will be no riches. No race. Mark Cavendish is thoughtful enough and clever enough to know all this. At least most of the time.

One afternoon the following spring, after he had stormed to three individual stage wins of the 2009 Giro d'Italia, we spoke at length about this. I had made my way to Bar Italia in Soho where Mark was 'doing' the British media in one fell swoop. His book had just come out, so there was that to plug too. Dressed in his regulation white Columbia shirt, complete with wrinkly unironed collars, Cavendish had set up shop in an upstairs room. One by one, members of the press filed in and out of there, using up every last second of their allocated timeslot. I requested an audience later on in the day with him, figuring that the fewer journalists I had queuing up after me, the less pressure would be exerted by the Columbia press officer to get the thing done.

'Hi, Mark,' I offered as a loosener. Then, brandishing my copy of his book in one hand, 'Won't keep you long. Just got a few fucking stupid questions for you.'

The ploy worked. Cavendish cracked a huge grin, and protested straight away, 'That wasn't you, you know. It wasn't you that did that interview.'

'I know it wasn't. And I want you to go on the record and tell everyone that it wasn't me.' We were enjoying this. The release of a little tension.

With the camera rolling, we then went on to discuss the subject in depth. I wondered whether he thought we had the right to ask such questions on the finish line. His reply astonished me.

'Of course. It's cycling. It's what makes our sport special.' He went on to defend his tormentors in the press.

He noted the differences between cycling and other sports,

he paid homage to the culture of the bike race which flings
its heroes into the sweaty clutches of the people, where they
can see their heroes, 'gladiators', as he referred to them, for
what they are: just men who do a hard job. He paid articulate
tribute to the traditions of covering the Tour; those moments
on the television which had lodged in his memory and framed
his understanding of the sport that had been his childhood
passion.

The moments he recalled were precisely those post-race
shots of triumph or defeat, when the camera is witness,
prosecution, and defence, and the rider is in the dock. He
understood to perfection the nuances that made up the fabric
of my job on the Tour. It was a little humbling to hear him
speak like that. I had always assumed that Cavendish belonged
to a generation that didn't think too deeply about the wider
heritage of their sport. I was quite wrong.

For my part, I willed him not to change. I tried to impress
on him that his occasional awkward moments serve only to
paint a rounder picture of the man, and speak of his fullness
as a character, as a man pushing himself to the limits of his
endeavour. No right-minded person would ever begrudge him
the right to remain honest and authentic.

And so we came to a happy truce. He defended my right
to stick a microphone under his nose; I defended his right to
ignore it. Then the real interview resumed.

'Mark, does it irritate you that your achievements have
gone unappreciated by large sections of the British public?'

'No, but I tell you what does irritate me. It irritates me
that I get asked that question all the time.' Etc., etc. And
straight away, we were back to what we both do best. Fucking
stupid questions and tetchy answers.

To return to the sunshine. To go back to Châteauroux.

My radio blasted into life. 'One rider out the front, but
he'll be caught. One kilometre to go. Columbia on the front.

It's Cav-tastic!' Steve Docherty bellowed his excitement over talkback.

Then the helicopters, the clattering of hands on the advertising boards, the increase in pitch and volume from the loudspeakers . . .

'Cavendish!'

The first of his Tour stage wins came in Châteauroux. It was Wednesday 9 July 2008. I remember little else of the day. But I remember the heat. I remember the result.

MANGE TOUT

Food. However oddly it may be presented, it fills in the gaps in the Tour. With normal life on hold as we hurtle headlong through another July away from home, food compensates for a nagging feeling of dislocation. It's not unreasonable to suggest that it becomes a substitute for happiness and something of an obsession. Luckily we are in France. And they're quite good at cooking.

The 2003 Tour had begun to roll south. By the time my birthday came around, it had reached Lyon and was bracing itself for the famous assault on the Alps, which would leave Beloki in hospital and Armstrong in the yellow jersey. That evening the production company had managed to find us accommodation just outside the city in a tiny hamlet, constructed, to all intents and purposes, along a bypass.

For a country rich in beautiful villages and towns, there are many which are considerably more prosaic. I can remember

little of the two-star auberge in which we found our beds that
night, other than that it conformed to a checklist of depressing
features: yellow wallpaper, brown bedspread, dusty nylon flowers
in a dusty vase in reception, next to a small bowl of ageing
sweets. Shuttered windows were flung open on entering the
room in an attempt to blow away the smell of last night's guest.
The shuddering of traffic sloughing along the Route Nationale
and a toilet, that doesn't flush so much as vibrate and sputter.

There was no question of dinner on-site that night. Our
keys had been laid out on the counter. The landlady was
already in her pyjamas, with the French version of *Temptation
Island* blasting out of a television in her back room.

Once we'd thrown our bags in our rooms, we convened
seconds later, hungry and a little angered by the turn of events
that had left us once again standing in a grisly hotel reception
without a dinner plan. Matt dragged Madame away from the
television for a second time and consulted her. She seemed to
suggest that there would be a chance of getting a bite to eat
about half a mile down the road. This struck us as a little
unlikely, since it was just a busy bypass, and we would be
heading out of town.

To our astonishment though, after a ten-minute walk we
found ourselves in a little square framing a fountain in the
middle, and two restaurants, with tables outside. Where this
had materialised from I have no recollection, and at the time
no understanding. It seemed to make no sense at all. Then,
in a second stroke of good fortune, we made the right choice
between the two restaurants.

What followed was both funny and fabulous. Menus were
handed out. We staggered through them, and made our choices.
When the lady who owned the restaurant came out to take our
orders she simply refused to accept them, telling us instead
that we had made incorrect selections and that she would bring
us something quite different. She did the same with the wine.

She laughed and cajoled and generally bossed us around. But she provided us with a remarkable feast. I ate a rich beef stew. We sat with idiot grins strapped to our faces, soaking it all in. The wine was fine and salty. The night was warm. The Tour felt very good at that particular moment.

Later on that evening the lady's daughter was ordered out to come and talk to us. According to her mother, we would have so much in common. It transpired that she was a rugby correspondent. She knew nothing of cycling and cared even less. We knew little of rugby and cared even less. After a few moments of polite nodding and amused silence, she thanked us and took her leave, shaking her head in irritation at her mother's assumptions.

It was one of those rare nights on the Tour when the race and the clamour and the stress just backed off, and we could breathe and drink and relax. It was also the first of hundreds of places I've visited and loved and of which I have completely failed to make a note. And now it's too late.

It often is on the Tour.

It was very late too when, a year or two later, we descended some creaking staircases into the fusty dining room of the Hostellerie de la Poste somewhere near Tours. By a miracle of compassion, the patron had agreed to keep the chef on if we hurried to the table. So we did.

The place was empty, expect for us. It was stuffed full of reproduction eighteenth-century furniture, all falling gently asleep under the antique electric flickering of a vast reproduction chandelier. One of the floorboards was loose in the middle of the room, and as each of us crossed the open space to reach our table, our footsteps made a tabletop crammed with crystal decanters rattle violently. One by one we took our places.

The food, as I remember was full of butter, and a bit full of itself. The wine, a bottle of Château du Val de Mercy (one of the rare occasions on which I actually committed to memory a memorable bottle of wine) was as beautiful to drink as French wine often is. The outstanding feature of the evening, however, was the menu itself.

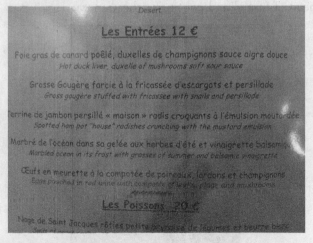

When the moment arrived to order and, even though I didn't want it particularly, I had no other choice than to apologise for my lack of French and in a clear, crisp and slightly over-enunciated voice articulate my wishes.

'I would like the Spotted Ham Pot "House" Radishes Crunching With The Mustard Emulsion, please,' I declared pompously. I wish I'd been able to order the Marbled Ocean

In Its Frost, and the Leeks, Plugs and Mushrooms, too. But embellishment would have been unnecessary.

Already, we were all shamefully overwhelmed with schoolboy giggling, as the poor waiter looked on, clearly disappointed with our attitude and inwardly damning Britain and the British. Later on that evening, Matt tilted his chair too far back, and fell over, making the decanters nearly explode. We paid the bill and left.

It's the aberrations that I remember best.

And one evening in particular. Like the mini-Stonehenge scene in *Spinal Tap*, it's still funny. Often at three o'clock in the morning, when I am beset with the usual anxieties, I will take time out from fretting about my life to analyse once again what exactly it was that went on which left Liam clutching a head of fennel and pouting at the camera.

It was Bastille Day. It often seems to be. And for once, rather than sitting out the French national holiday on the concrete terrace of a Kyriad hotel overlooking the back of a Carrefour car park, it seemed we had lucked out. We were in Aix-en-Provence. The beautiful town has its slightly ugly parts, of course, and before you get the impression that we were staying in some beautifully restored townhouse on the Cours Mirabeau, rest assured that we had located the only one-star hotel in town. Dark, fetid and awful, we dumped our stuff in its gloomy rooms and disappeared into town to eat and watch the French get all dangerous with fireworks.

So there we were, fortunate enough to have found a table outside, despite the crush of people gearing up to party. It was nearly ten o'clock, and the town was only just beginning to fill up. We studied the menu, and ordered starters according to our well-rehearsed customs. Liam requested something challenging, possibly with added cruelty. Woody would have asked for something light. I almost certainly had a gazpacho in mind (the evening was hot). Matt knitted his brow, and then rubbed his temples.

'Do you know what? I think I'm not getting enough vitamins. Too much dairy. I need something good to eat.'

'Have the old *assiette de crudités*,' prompted Liam, not unreasonably. Why anyone would ever want to order a plate of sliced carrots and a raw spring onion I had no idea. Yet, Matt went for it.

'*Et pour moi, je prends l'assiette de crudités. Voilà.*' He finished decisively, flapping the menu shut in the waiter's face for extra flamboyance.

What, then, went on between the request and the execution is anyone's guess. But what was placed in front Matt was either a peculiar joke, a hallucination or the only answer to an over-stacked and overflowing vegetable rack. But it was the biggest bowl of unprepared, huge and raw vegetables I am ever likely to see offered up as a light starter.

Staggeringly, it contained two complete heads of fennel, a clutch of spring onions, a cos lettuce, a red lettuce, a head of cauliflower, at least five large tomatoes, three endives, a green pepper and a red pepper.

Our jaws hit the deck. But we solemnly took to the task, the table pulling together to come to Matt's aid. We're good like that in times of need. After a solid half an hour of unfettered vitamin intake, we gave up. We'd barely scratched the surface of this extraordinary starter.

More often than not, though, it is not the meals served in restaurants with the pretension of being 'gastronomique' that stick in the memory, rather it's the chance encounters, the welcome, simple meals in welcoming, simple places that spread the love, the feeling of well-being. A wide, smile-cracking pleasure it is, to sit in the warmth and be fed.

There are a number of hotel chains that populate the fringes of French towns and their associated industrial zones like barnacles. They differentiate one from the other in one critical way: while Campaniles, Kyriads and Ibis all boast restaurants, Formule 1, Etaps and Balladins leave you high and dry.

The food these budget hotels serve is surprisingly good, and very cheap. Although, since they generally only exist to service France's army of travelling salesmen who trawl the country on a tight budget hawking their various wares, they can often appear quite overwhelmed by the arrival of the Tour's multinational menagerie.

Once about a hundred of us all descended on a Kyriad

hotel in some anonymous part of the country, which was seemingly staffed by only one local teenager. Within minutes of the first wave of Tour workers sitting down and glaring impatiently at her, she was floundering utterly in her attempts to keep up with the tempo of orders coming her way. Her coping mechanism in this instance was to dissolve into giggles at every word uttered in her direction.

It was one of those encounters that leaves the English-speaking world mystified and irritated in equal measure. She appeared on the face of things to be quite incapable of understanding anything said in French to her, if it was nuanced with anything approaching the accent of a non-native speaker.

'*Pour moi, les pâtes, s'il vous plaît,*' I offered, concentrating hard on my diction.

She shrugged her shoulders and giggled.

'*Les pâtes? C'est bon?*'

'*J'en sais rien.*' Shrug. Giggle.

She looked over her shoulder away from us, appealing for help from a solitary Frenchman eating at a table next to us. Could he help her interpret the desires of this collection of idiots from abroad who speak only in disjointed glottal stops and random fricatives?

With a nod of the head in my direction, he translated for her. '*Il veut les pâtes.*'

'*Ah. Alors, pour vous les pâtes.*' She noted down my order with a little giggle.

Later on that evening, the chef, already working with smoke coming out of his ears as well as his little kitchen, was called upon to assist with the taking of orders, his young co-worker having dissolved into a heap of teenaged uselessness.

Then the ice-cream freezer blew its fuse and burst into flames. Which was a good job, because we were struggling to translate 'Magnum White' into perfect enough French to make our order understood.

The food was good, though: my pasta was perfectly prepared and the others had some sort of stuffed quail with complex textures and worrying little bony bits. For no good reason at all, they gave us a free bottle of rosé. We left the table covered in mess and full of good humour.

There are also meals which won't be forgotten because they are homespun or spontaneous affairs, where the owners of auberges, chalets and gites have provided for us from their own fridges. There was the couple in the Carmague who left a plate of cold meats, cheese and bread out for us on the terrace of their beautiful farmhouse. And a bottle of thick, deeply red wine. When we arrived it was nearly midnight and we ate overlooking the little vineyard that had produced the stuff. In the morning we bought a case of their wine for next to nothing, as we sat at their breakfast table overwhelmed by a choice of twenty different home-made jams.

A week after that, we stayed in a chalet in the Pyrenees run by an English couple from the Home Counties. Our midnight arrival was marked by the shattering sound of one of those wine bottles, which fell onto their drive as we opened the car door. But they too had laid on a feast for us. By one o'clock in the morning, we were each clutching a glass and trying not to feel too self-conscious in their hot tub.

The next year, our sat nav let us down badly. We were trying to find an auberge in the countryside near Gap. It was getting late and we were lost. Eventually I realised that I no longer had any choice other than to phone the owners and plead for directions.

This is not an easy proposition if your French is as restricted as mine, mainly because it almost always starts with the unanswerable question from which all solutions and/or mis-directions must follow: 'Where are you at the moment?'

I gazed through the windscreen. We had reached a T-junction. Ahead of me was a clear choice between turning right into a bit of France to the right, and turning left where a further, more left-sided bit of France would open up in front of us. I had no idea where we were. Hence the need for the phone call.

More by luck than linguistics, however, we soon found the place. It stood on its own in a tiny hamlet, next to the post office. We unloaded our gear, and, on approaching the lady sitting outside at a table just about to eat her dinner, we posed the next critical question.

'Est-ce qu'on peut toujours manger ici quelque part?' She shook her head. The restaurant hadn't even opened that day and, besides, there were no other guests. We must have looked as abject as we felt.

Just then, her husband returned in the car from a fruitless search-and-rescue expedition (he'd driven off to find us). But of course, he declared on hearing of our predicament, his family was just about to sit down for a late dinner. If we didn't mind the simplicity of the food, we'd be welcome to join them. We didn't mind, and so we joined them. Within minutes of carrying our stuff to our comfortable little rooms in an annex above the post office, we were sitting down with Norah, Remy and little Enzo to a fresh tomato salad, bread, oven chips and steak. It tasted great. Remy opened a bottle of rosé.

We saw that off in a matter of minutes, and raised the game. Running to the back of the car, Liam returned swiftly bearing a bottle of Bordeaux and Côtes de Bourg. The Renault always clinks suspiciously.

As the wine flowed, so did the chat. Remy wanted to talk about the disintegration of respect for sportsmen, particularly with regard to the French football team who had let themselves down so badly a few weeks prior to that during the World Cup in South Africa. It was, thought Norah, a mirror image of the disrespect eating away at French society. Enzo, a hyper-active seven-year-old who, his parents confided, rarely went to bed before midnight and would often sleep in till midday, was more interested in the free Tour de France stage calendar which Woody magicked from somewhere. It kept him quiet for minutes at a time. In the morning I gave him a vuvuzela, which I had brought with me from South Africa, and we took our leave before our sudden friendship with this splendid family ended, as they faced up to the reality of life with a highly motivated plastic horn blower.

Before driving off, however, we balanced Liam's camera somewhere precarious and took a self-timed picture in which we all managed to smile simultaneously.

But, although dinner is a lottery, and breakfast, no matter how you dress it up, is something to be endured, lunch is a thing of beauty. Ever since the days when Channel 4 used to show the Tour, the same production company has made the programmes. And over those many many years, the same caterers have fed the programme makers. A considerable (and in the interests of commercial confidentiality, undisclosed) portion of the annual production budget goes towards the preparation and presentation of fabulous, hearty, regionally sourced fresh French food.

An extended French family who live, for reasons I have never established, in Forest Hill in south London, have the catering contract for lunch. The day they lose it is the day I resign.

Romain is a pleasant, harmless maniac. In his mid-twenties, no more than five foot seven tall, a little round of physique with a military haircut and a matching beard, he collects free Tour stuff with a passion. Most days, therefore, you will find him wearing some sort of T-shirt, donated to him by an American TV network, in an ever-advancing state of decay as the sauces of a hundred lunches are rubbed into its fabric, and the sweat of a hundred stocks eat into its weave.

He will normally offset this with a baseball cap from a German station, worn at the jaunty angle of a Brooklyn MC. Sometimes, if he is feeling particularly outré, he will wear two. Just because he can. And because he's a maniac.

Romain's mother, Odette, who barely looks a day older than him, works tirelessly loading and unloading the fresh produce from the back of their hired Petit Forestier refrigerated truck, wiping down surfaces, fixing the temperamental coffee machine, and basically ensuring that all the life-sustaining trimmings are in place and in operational order. By the middle of each Tour, Odette begins to turn dark hazelnut-brown, and as her tiredness increases with the murderously demanding schedule, so her low-key, chilled cheerfulness becomes a more and more precious commodity. A simple, ''Allo, Ned' can bring a smile to an otherwise damp and miserable mountain morning. That and the endless supply of apricots, peaches and plums.

Odette is married to Philippe, Romain's stepfather. He towers over the whole enterprise, a bolt-upright, bespectacled pony-tailed giant. Clearly born in the wrong century, Philippe could have enjoyed a passable career as a cameo actor in every series of *Blackadder* other than perhaps the fourth. A medieval knight, an Elizabethan explorer, a Regency fop. He has it all in his compass. As well as making a *tartiflette* that fills you up just by looking at it.

Apart from being a gentle, wry, dependable man, he cooks with great love and significant pride. Philippe sets the day's menu, and while Odette and Romain are detailed to churn out the volume, he whips up the fresh mayonnaise, finesses the *jus* or puts together one of his exceptional cold soups which are served as an amuse-bouche in daily rotating variation. He has a taste for introducing fruit in the most unexpected places, which down the years has taught us all a thing or two. Not for him the pineapple-chunk-on-the-slice-of-ham routine of my seventies British upbringing. He's much more of a post-modern how-about-a-bit-of-grapefruit-in-your-artichoke-salad type.

It's proper cooking. Knocked out every day on gas rings balanced on trestle tables set out under a couple of easy-up marquees in whichever bit of France (or Belgium, Italy or Andorra) we happen to want our lunch served that day.

So, these three characters, accompanied by a supporting cast of peripheral family members and friends who drift in and out of the Tour (Romain has recently married and his wife joined in the fun in 2010), determine to a large extent the mental health and spiritual welfare of a host of Tour operatives. It is a growing congregation, which extends further and further each year, as their reputation for serving up the most outstanding catering the Tour de France has ever known spreads throughout the compound.

You need only look at the expressions of all the others as they wander past our catering tent to sense what deprivation they must feel. While Philippe and Odette look after the needs of the anglophone world, as well as the Scandinavian countries and the upper echelons of ASO, the rest of the world must fend for themselves.

France Télévisions, with their 300 staff, set up a military camp, which more closely resembles a field hospital than a canteen. They seem to eat in well-ordered shifts, but a glance over in their direction normally offers up the impression that they are subsisting on bread and cheese alone. And wine, obviously.

The Germans have a vast presence in the compound, which appears undiminished despite the waning of interest back home. Indeed, in 2008, when they 'weren't covering the race' in protest at the spate of doping offences, they still had four times as many staff on-site as we did. It has to be said, they cater miserably for themselves. Unable to eschew national cliché, they serve up a resolutely German-looking and largely pork-and-starch-based affair every day. It is mostly beige in colour. They don't appear to enjoy it.

I have no idea what the Belgians and the Dutch – or, come to that, the Spanish and the Italians – do to keep themselves fed. I suspect that they forage. I know that the Australians do. Having blown all their budget on getting to France in the first place, they have nothing left over in the kitty for lunch. They dig the compound over for dry tubers and nibble the succulent ends of overhanging branches.

Yet we eat like kings.

Philippe and his team of four live in the smallest caravan on the planet. For a month they try to grab a few hours' kip squeezed up alongside each other like cornichons in a jar, their Union Jack curtains letting in the morning light as the sun breaks out over an alpine ridge.

And when that happens, they know, we know, and the Tour knows: it's time to start peeling the spuds.

THE TOUR EATS ITSELF

Nobody had spoken for a while. It was midnight, and we hadn't eaten since breakfast. The starters had just been plonked down in front of us. Then Liam broke the silence.

'I think he's brilliant.' Liam cracked a wide smile, and then went back to spreading a wedge of hot foie gras onto slice of baguette.

He shook his head, a contented chuckle beginning to spread out within him. As it began to take hold, he looked up again, and spitting a little goose liver towards us, restated his new-found affection for Kazakhstan.

'Vino. I just think he's fucking brilliant.'

He reached for the glass of Madiran in front of him. 'Vinokourov!'

Liam raised his wine, almost religiously, and saluted us across the table with the name of the disgraced Astana rider.

His deeds had been so flagrant that they were almost comical. We could forgive him, now that we were sitting in a restaurant, tucking into a fattened and diseased animal organ.

'Alexandre Vinokourov!' we replied, in the manner of a congregation intoning the Blessing.

A couple of hours prior to that, it'd been a little harder to see the funny side. This was 2007. It was the year when the great race ate itself.

We had woken up in Pau, and resentfully slung our accreditation around our necks.

It was a rest day. But not for us the restorative pleasures of the launderette. We were on our way to a hastily arranged press conference. Michael Rasmussen, the stick-thin Danish climber, had been wearing the yellow jersey for some days after a string of emphatic performances in the mountains. Yet a fug of accusation lay over the Tour all the while that he was in the lead. It all related to Rasmussen's inability to explain his whereabouts in the spring when he had failed to inform the anti-doping authorities of his location. They had tried to contact him, and they had failed.

As the obfuscations grew, so too did the sense that he had deliberately misled the doping controls and, rather than being in Mexico where he lived with his wife, had been in Italy, more specifically Tuscany, getting up to who knows what mischief. Every day we tormented him a little more with our questioning. We did so not on a whim or for fun, but because we believed he'd been systematically selling the entire Tour, and us and the cycling public, a huge lie.

It was getting to everyone. The Danish TV reporter, who had the allotted task of interviewing her home country's newest national hero every day, was going incrementally mad. Because of her particular position, she had to be more careful than others with the tone that she took, and could only soft-pedal the scepticism. After a number of days with Rasmussen wearing the yellow jersey, she was visibly dreading facing up to him, when she knew she had to adopt a tone of phoney congratulation.

During the second week of the Tour, it was made public that Rasmussen had even been sighted in Tuscany in the spring. This was when the clamour for his head passed the point of no return. Every day he was paraded in front of the press in his yellow jersey; every day, the questioning grew more intense. Still more accusations surfaced, some of them quite bizarre. An American rider claimed that Rasmussen had asked him to smuggle some doping products in a shoebox containing new trainers.

ASO, the Tour organisers, eventually lost patience with the Dane. He was embarrassing their race. That afternoon Marieline, their chief media officer, came to me in the TV compound when the race was just a few kilometres away.

'Today, I will bring Rasmussen to you straight away.' This was an unusual thing to say. 'I think he has many questions to answer.' They had seen and heard enough.

I understood that I was not to let him off the hook lightly. It proved to be a painful exchange during which I managed to move him from a position of 'no comment' to an outright denial of the accusation. Often it's not the fact of denial but the manner in which it is delivered that is most revealing. In Rasmussen's case, he could hardly have cut a more evasive and unconvincing figure.

But still it was not satisfactory. In an attempt to quell the growing storm, ASO called a press conference for the rest day. And this was where we now found ourselves. A big hall, looking towards a table encrusted with microphones with cables leading out of the room, onto the street and up onto satellite trucks for instant distribution across the world. Rasmussen, with a lawyer at his side, faced up, shifting in his seat as wave after wave of questions crashed against him. Matt Rendell took his place in the middle of the front row and accused him directly of registering with the Mexican cycling authorities as a means to hiding his location.

By lunchtime, it was finally over. Rasmussen had stuck to his story, had issued denial after denial. He had held firm. We unpicked our cables, packed up our kit, found our car and headed back to the Hotel Bristol, where we were staying.

We sat down on the veranda, where the rest day could really begin.

Instantly the Tour vanished. Talk turned to other things, to life outside the race. We nattered in faltering French to the couple who ran the place: a tidily turned-out boutique hotel in the middle of town on which they had spent huge sums of money renovating. They were curious about our jobs, even though the Tour impacted little on their lives. They were fascinated too to witness the speed and vigour with which we now moved seamlessly on to our second bottle of Sancerre on an empty stomach. The sun was out, the wine was great and the conversation flowed easily.

It must have been about 3 p.m. when the hotelier appeared once more, bringing with him another little bowl of black olives. He put them down and let slip a casual remark, which was to ruin our day for a second time.

'It's interesting what you were telling us about the *maillot jaune*, because they've just said something on the radio about another big-name rider testing positive. Some Russian bloke, I think.'

We put down our glasses. Three Englishmen and a Scot looked across at him, pale with surprise. As if reflecting the shock in our eyes, he looked a little scared himself.

'Alexandre Vinokourov?' I ventured, although the question was rhetorical. I already knew the answer.

A few days earlier, in the shadow of Albi's magnificent cathedral, someone had got to Vinokourov. Perhaps it had happened in the dead of night. Certainly it would have been carefully pre-arranged. The accomplice might have come in through the back, where they carry the rubbish out from the kitchens. Or perhaps Vino had sneaked down the corridor, pushed open a one-way fire exit door, and allowed his courier to slip in from some untended corner of the car park. He might have left the hotel, and gone to a safe house. We will probably never know. But either way, he got his blood.

As he lay there, looking up at the dried little corpses of mosquitoes stuck to the ceiling of his hotel room, he would have had no idea that the refrigerated, centrifugally spun, red-cell-rich blood being siphoned into his system belonged to someone else. Perhaps it was the hidden stash of another, lesser name, a hopeless case, who had chosen this course of action in an effort to save a career that was going nowhere. The theories surrounding the case are outlandish. I've even heard it told that the blood might have come from his own father.

Vinokourov may well have fallen asleep dreaming of derring-do and greatness to come. He might have imagined blasting the time trial to pieces, and then with a tip of his cap and a wink in his eye, evading the law as they hunted for signs of doping. All they would find would be blood. His blood.

He would pass through the border undetected, heading for safety like a POW in *The Great Escape*. Little did he realise that a couple of days later he'd have a Gordon Jackson moment: 'Nice blood, Mr Vinokourov.'

'Thanks very much. It's not mine, you know.'

'Guards, seize him!'

Scarcely fifteen minutes later we arrived at his hotel on the outskirts of Pau to a scene of complete chaos: a dozen police cars and vans, fifty gendarmes, a hundred or so cameramen and journalists, and now us adding to the mix.

We asked around. No one had seen Vino being led away. The feeling was that he was still locked up in the hotel as the cops rifled through everybody's room. We struck a deal with an Australian crew. If they waited outside the front of the hotel, we would stake out the rear. We would share our footage and spread out our resources. So we inched our way through privet hedges and herbaceous borders to the back of the hotel, where, like a not-terribly-well-drilled SAS unit, we took up our position on the far side of a raised section of lawn.

There were a handful of police officers stationed at each rear entrance. Their job was not so much to prevent us from entering the premises, as to stop people escaping. The place was locked down, and although we were stamping all over private property, the police were more than happy for us to carry on our work.

Police raids on the Tour are a curiously public spectacle, which must have something to do with 'justice being seen to be done'. The gendarmes like to look their best for the cameras when they raid a cyclist's hotel. They polish their boots, and they wear their best shirts to match their purposeful briefcases.

I think at some point we may have fallen asleep. At the very least, I cannot guarantee that I was completely alert. It was the Sancerre, you understand. Every now and again, one of us would pop his head above the parapet and scout out the back of the hotel. Woody's boom extended into the air like a periscope, as he lay on his back, cursing the day he ever signed up to cover the Tour de France. Not much happened as the blisteringly hot afternoon wore on. Our empty stomachs and mid-afternoon hangovers were making their presence felt.

Then, suddenly, mayhem descended once again.

Marc Biever, the Swiss directeur sportif of the Astana team, emerged, to everyone's surprise, from the side of the building; the one minor loophole in our otherwise hermetically sealed approach. We joined the party late. By the time we caught up, he was submerged under a tidal wave of microphones and bodies. We had no chance. The bundle was too broad for Woody to extend his boom over the top, and the thicket of people too dense for Liam to snatch even the most obscure of headshots. So, frozen out at the margins of the storm, we waited, and wondered what on earth we could do to rescue the situation.

But then, with a biblical parting of the waves, the mass of reporters split asunder and out popped the beleaguered directeur sportif. Quite by chance, and much to his regret, I should imagine, he walked straight into our frankly unintentional trap. Within a matter of seconds we were on him.

Quick as a flash. 'Marc. Do you feel let down by Alexandre Vinokourov?'

He stopped, adjusted his glasses on his nose, and looked quizzically at me. 'I'm sorry. What do you mean?'

There is nothing worse than asking a hard-hitting question, and then having to ask it again.

'Do you feel let down by him. By Vinokourov?' I asked, a notch louder, inwardly tutting.

'I don't know what you mean,' came the reply.

At this moment, it should have occurred to me that, English not being his mother tongue, Biever might actually not have known what I meant. But through the haze of my wine-soaked reflexes, I took his understandable obtuseness for evasiveness. I pressed home my point.

'I want to know if you feel let down by Alexandre Vinokourov,' I said, once again, and now almost very loud.

Biever looked pained at me. But he stood his ground and shrugged his shoulders. The next day, Woody said I should have 'asked him if he felt disappointed'. It was the first and only time he has ever interfered in my job description. But I think he had a point.

'Did Alexandre Vinokourov let you down?' One final time.

He mumbled some stuff about 'A' and 'B' samples, and with that, he was gone. I couldn't help feeling I might have handled the interview with a little more subtlety.

By the time we eventually settled down to eat that evening, it felt like the Tour was unravelling before us. We wondered separately whether we would have jobs to come back to the following July. We speculated on what might happen next, little knowing that the race itself would trump all our guesses.

The next day, we watched on in amazement as Bradley

Wiggins's Cofidis teammate Christian Moreni was led away in front of all our cameras and bundled into the back of a gendarme's car after he'd ridden to the top of the Col d'Aubisque.

At the same time, Michael Rasmussen was being booed wearing the yellow jersey and on the podium by the small crowd who had gathered there.

That evening the entire Cofidis team endured the indignity of a police escort back to their hotel rooms. Like Astana, they too withdrew from the race.

And then in the dead of night, Rasmussen as well was stuffed in the back of a car, driven away to a secret location, and disappeared from view. All this happened while we stayed in Pau. All this played out while we enjoyed the hospitality of the Hotel Bristol. Whenever the Tour has taken us to Pau since, we have dropped in there for a coffee and to reminisce.

So in 2010, on finding out that Alberto Contador had tested positive, it came as no surprise to me that the incriminating doping control had been taken in Pau. It seems to be the plughole down which reputations disappear.

As a journalist, these stories are thrilling to report. As a cycling fan, they are toxic. And Vinokourov, through his seeming lack of remorse, remains to this day not without a curious fascination.

Liam retains a mystifying, and enduring affection for the taciturn Kazakh. He went as far as inventing a new piece of vocabulary; 'Kourov!' A shorthand version of 'Vino', it simply means wine, and to this day he will shout it out, in a restaurant, as he raises a glass of blood-red claret to the memory of 2007.

Of course, the Astana rider was back in 2010. He won a typical Vinokourov stage, full of defiance and spontaneity. He lapped up the applause. He believed himself absolved.

Liam and I waited in the mixed zone to ambush him.

'What guarantees can you offer that you are now riding clean?' I asked.

'This is a new Vino.'

'Do you regret 2007?'

'I will not talk about 2007,' he offered, with a pained wince. Then he moved on to the next microphone.

I'll talk about it, though. To anyone who'll listen.

THE MOUNTAINS

I drove up to within five kilometres of the summit, on the south side of the mountain. There was a café, and a small car park. I left the hire car there, hiding the key behind the offside front wheel. Then I tightened the laces of my running shoes, took a couple of deep breaths of frozen Provençal air and set off up Mont Ventoux.

It was Christmas 2007. We were visiting friends who had a house at the base of the big mountain. I was thrilled to be staying this close to it, having only otherwise glimpsed its humpbacked form from the motorway, speeding past en route from the Alps to the Pyrenees, or vice versa. There is a helpful road sign, in 'touristique' brown, which points it out, with the words 'Le Géant de Provence'. Despite having five completed Tours under my belt, not one of them had included an ascent of Ventoux. So I was eager to see it for myself. Even if that meant running up it.

It was a crystal-clear, but bitterly cold, winter's day. The gradient was steep, but just reasonable enough for me to sustain a semi-breathless jog. The road snaked upwards, and I was conscious that behind me an expansive view to the south was opening up. I kept my gaze to the tarmac though, concentrating on my rhythm, as the cold air grew a little thinner.

With about a kilometre to go, the tarmac became shrouded in snow. Old snow, which had fallen some time ago, compacted, thawed a little and then refrozen. I scrunched into it, placing my footfalls as firmly as I could so as to avoid slipping. It was becoming hard. My calves were tightening.

I did stop briefly to see the Tom Simpson memorial and read the various tributes and messages from a wide cross section of the British cycling scene. Wolverhampton. Tiverton. Dulwich. It was curious to see such homely place names in that volcanic setting. A concentrated drop of British sentiment, a dot of Blighty on the lunar landscape of Mont Ventoux. How close he'd been to the summit when his heart gave out. I set off again drawn towards the iconic red-and-white striped tower of the meteorological station, which marks the summit.

Eventually I reached the top. Cresting the ridge quite suddenly, I saw what lay on the other side. Looking north, there was an endless panorama of France. Pretty much all of it.

It was a view of immeasurable depth. I had a sense of the whole of the hexagonal shape of the country spread before me, and a little to the east, the colossal icy forest of alpine peaks. With nothing of any size between where I stood and the great mountain range, they were lined up and on display. It's Ventoux's isolation which defines it.

I became aware that I was not alone. I had been joined on the parapet outside the weather station by a cyclist on a heavy, ancient-looking mountain bike. An old boy in his late sixties, he'd ridden up there just for the view, he told me. I could see why. Together we tried to figure out which alp was Mont Blanc, then he gave me a long drink from his water bottle and set off back down the mountain, explaining that '*Pour grimper, il faut boire; pour la descente, il faut manger.*' He grinned, and showed me a slightly bashed-up looking *pain au chocolat* that he presented with a flourish from his kagool. I followed a little while later – and within an hour or so, I was back in the warmth of our friends' house. I jabbered on excitedly about the view from the top. That picture, the Alps.

The Tour de France has always been a month-long commercial for the country; broadcasting images of valleys, fields of sunflowers, medieval villages and aqueducts which are designed to shout out from the TV: '*Visitez La France!* It's brilliant! We've got just about everything!'

Recent years have seen astonishing innovation in the quality of the images on TV. The helicopter has been a key factor in the Tour's ability to market itself as landscape eye candy. Now the advent of high-definition pictures (if there is indeed anyone out there who actually knows how to make their telly receive them) has coincided with a quantum leap in the stability of pictures available from the aerial perch of a helicopter. The cameras are battered by the vibrations that result from being housed underneath a helicopter. But they now sit encased in a shell, which cushions them almost completely. Using baffling hydraulic technology such as 'five-fold axis high bandwidth full stabilisation', cameras can now be fitted with huge, long, heavy lenses that zoom to the full extent of their capacity, right into the distance of the horizon, and maintain a perfectly stable shot that neither jerks nor judders.

One unforgettable image springs to mind in particular. The Tour was trundling over eastern France heading for Bourg-en-Bresse. Not much was happening in the race, so the French director started looking around for shots. Suddenly he cut to a picture of Mont Blanc.

People stopped what they were doing in the TV compound to watch their monitors, hooked in at once by the clarity of the picture. There was the white enormity of the mountain, framed up perfectly against an azure sky. Slowly, slowly, the cameraman, manipulating the airborne lens by remote control, pulled the shot wider and wider until a huge landscape filled the image, the ant-like figures in the peloton racing far below in the foreground, Mont Blanc now just a tiny white detail on the horizon.

The mountain must have been a hundred miles away, maybe more. But the camera brought it right into our living rooms and gave us a pure hit of that thrilling annual sensation: the mountains are here!

There is a moment like this, which marks every Tour: your first glimpse of the great mountain ranges of France. It might be that you nod off on the autoroute, only to find, as the speed slows on the approach to the *péage* at the Grenoble exit shaking you awake, that without your realising it the horizon is now entirely entombed in Alps.

Or, it might be that the Tour has been hammering through Normandy or Brittany, an arc heading ever further south through the rolling country of Limousin and the flatlands of Aquitaine, before heading straight towards the pale jagged shock of the Pyrenees – Spain's over-engineered garden fence.

Up high is where the soul of the big race resides. Through a century of print, cartoonists have always anthropomorphised the mountains in French papers, breathing monstrous life into them and letting them roar. In their drawings they bare vicious sharp teeth, pointy, rocky noses, tufts of snowy hair, and often arms and hands, which pick up smaller mountains and hurl them at the defenceless riders. There is always an enraged storm cloud gathering above them, with Zeus-like bolts of lightning cracking over the summit. The riders have no chance.

The two opposing mountain ranges have their individual characteristics. The Alps are markedly better bred than the Pyrenees: neater, sharper, richer, sunnier. Somehow, in their ozone-depleted, Euro-jet-setting heat, they seem brighter. The Pyrenees, on the other hand, have a less-intense dose of the wooden-chaleted alpine kitsch. Their road surfaces are coarser, their forests gloomier, their villages built from stone, dank with the downpours of Atlantic water dumped angrily over their peaks.

They're just a bit wilder, really. And it doesn't stop with the landscape either. The people on them play their part too. It is no coincidence that it was the Alps which Hannibal crossed with his elephant troops. If he'd tried it over the Pyrenees, his herd would probably have been sliced up, marinated, grilled on a disposable barbecue and slapped between a burger bun. These mountains, and the people who populate them for the Tour, take no prisoners.

One morning, up in the Pyrenees and wrapped chin-high in a pacamac, I trudged off through the chill to find our catering tent. I was after a coffee and a madeleine. It should have been a Marcel Proust experience. In Proust's *In Search of Lost Time*, the narrator has the blocked sink of his memories unplugged by the taste of these buttery little cakes in one of the defining passages of twentieth-century literature. But my mind remained stoically blank. It was that sort of a foggy morning, and I was exhausted by two weeks of following the race.

I allowed the mixture of sweet cake to mingle with the astonishingly bitter coffee. They blended on the tongue. I sat in our tented dining room on the mountainside that we had arrived at overnight, and watched Philippe and Odette prepare lunch. It was good to see them, slicing carrots behind pots belching gouts of aromatic steam. A smell of wine and sage filled the air.

As so often, the weather in the Pyrenees was hard to predict. You might have expected the sun to have got to work on the mountain mist by now, but judging by the gentle patter of drizzle on the canopy, it was actually getting darker. As if to blend in with his surroundings, Philippe was in a foul mood.

He was banging around the coffee machine (which has a habit of running out of both water and coffee at just the minute he has a million other things to attend to), taking out his frustrations on the flimsy bit of kit.

It was surprising to find him angry. Philippe is a big man, but he is remarkably even-tempered on the whole, with a laconic smile and an ability to brush off most of the indignities which touring throws at him. He is not prone to shows of genuine anger. At first, therefore, I thought he was joking. It was only when he showed me his van, parked up alongside his catering truck, that I understood. The windscreen had been shattered, and the van lay wounded on the roadside allowing the wetness of the mountain air to permeate the front cab.

'They're fucking crazy, Ned. You know. Fucking why did they fucking do this?' Let's not forget after all that Philippe lives in south London.

Thousands of Basques, gathered on the mountainside, had rioted the night before. Philippe and Odette had been ambushed.

He removed his glasses and, pinching the bridge of his nose, scrunched his eyes shut. It was the gesture of a weary man with 2,000 kilometres already behind him, lunch to cook for 120 people, and, now, a windscreen to fix. How he managed to get a nice man from the French equivalent of Autowindscreens to drive up a mountain on the day of the Tour and replace his windscreen, I have no idea. But then again, I am never quite able to understand how it is he manages to serve magret de canard in a car park round the back of a provincial rugby ground.

The Basque violence had come as no great surprise to anyone, but its expression that night had taken on a new wildness. Philippe and Odette's was not the only tale of vandalism to emerge. All around the Zone Technique, drivers were waking up in their cabs, reaching for a coffee, or a towel, and bantering with each other as they showered and tried to make light of it all. They began to swap war stories.

Philippe told all. It had been seriously late as he and Odette, propping their tired eyes open, and peering into the gloom as the mountainside unfolded in front of them, finally neared the summit. They were nosing their refrigerated Petit Forestier truck through crowds of Basque cycling fans, conscious all the while that they were steering a valuable, but vulnerable, cargo of cucumbers, cheeses, wines and gateaux round switchback after switchback. But they were old hands at this kind of driving. Estimates of crowd numbers are notoriously implausible, but that night, it felt as if a million people might genuinely be crawling over the side of the mountain. Makeshift bars lit with clattering generators had sprung up in the hollows by the side of sheer cliff walls. Music and laughter simmered in the warm night air at the foot of the climb. But by the time they had taken the truck up closer to the top of the mountain, there was a chill breeze, and they wound up the windows. The further they climbed, the more the mood changed, as if the altitude itself were the intoxicant. Suddenly there was almost no one left who was sober.

Basques with a sense of grievance had congregated on the upper slopes, close to the ski resort itself. They were drawn higher by the promise of witnessing the sharp end of the race the following day, and the promise of an actual bar selling actual beer for them to whet their appetites. Young, mostly, and dressed in the orange of Euskaltel-Euskadi, the Basque national cycling team, with bandanas and flags and scarves, they swarmed around the roadside, singing their allegiances and spitting their distaste for the French and the Spanish. They had come to make a point and here, in the dark night on top of the mountain range that is at the heart of their sense of identity as a people, they had found their voices, roared on by the twin spirits of protest and vodka.

There was barely a single gendarme there that night, although many had predicted what might happen. The convoy of Tour vehicles in which Philippe and Odette had taken their place suddenly became the target. The attackers jumped out in front of the lorries, forcing them to slam on the brakes (probably putting paid to few jars of cornichons at the same time), and pelted the drivers' cabs with beer cans, traffic cones and whatever else came to hand.

All night the action continued. Philippe and Odette managed to park up in the caterers' car park where they tried as best they could to get their heads down while the angry orange picket line continued to create mayhem out on the road. The trucks still came lumbering towards the finish line, their huge gearboxes growling at the stumbling hordes of Basque revellers.

One driver told me the following day how he had watched as the cab of the truck in front of him was stormed. A couple of Basques had taken it upon themselves to open the door and try to get at the driver. The lorry veered a little as the man behind the wheel booted his invaders as hard as he could. He repelled the attack, and, leaning over, somehow managed to slam the heavy door shut in their faces. Sometime after that, all the trucks had reached their destination, many carrying the marks of the ascent. And towards dawn, the mountainside gradually grew quiet, as one by one the army of Basque foot soldiers turned in for the night, or, more accurately, fell into a stupefied sleep. The battle had been a score draw, but the point had been made.

Later the next day, the seething beery mass would form the enduring image of the stage's racing, as the riders pushed through the delirious crowds, parting the sea of huge, orange and green Basque flags flapping in their faces. The night's chaos barely got a mention in the commentary, as the Tour revelled in its revellers.

Basque patriots have a confused attitude to the race. On the one hand they rail against it as a symbol of Francophone cultural imperialism, and an invasion of their mountains. On the other hand, they know their place in its pageantry and they rise to the occasion. They celebrate the passage of the great race with heart and hangover, roaring their support in their rare language, which is itself being pushed into the sea by the allied forces of Spanish and French homogeneity. Their tongue after all, pre-dates pretty much everything. It is descended from Bronze Age languages, and has developed over time entirely separately from the Indo-Germanic roots which dominate Western Europe.

But Basque remains impenetrable. Even Matt, for whom almost no language barrier is impossible to hurdle, throws up his hands in despair when faced with a wall of drunken Basque bonhomie. On my first experience of the Pyrenees, we were dispatched down the climb up the Luz-Ardiden (just hours before Lance Armstrong was to hit the deck and then execute the defining ride of his career). Our task was to 'vox-pop' the

Basques. To extract some content from them which spoke of their aspirations and their passion for the Pyrenees and for the representatives of the team bearing their colours.

Not prone to shirking a challenge, Matt, nonetheless, wore an expression of horror and helplessness.

'But I don't speak Basque. And they don't speak anything but Basque. I won't understand them,' and then he added, 'at all.'

The problem for him that day was that none of us believed him, least of all Steve, whose idea it had been. We were certain that it must be a bit like Spanish. Steve gave a look that ended the conversation. Matt knew resistance was futile. He assumed the grave, saddened air of a man who knows his fate has been sealed.

Only when we got some way down the mountain did I realise the extent of the problem. The Basque fans were riotously pissed, for starters. The camera acted straight away like a lamp to moths, except these moths had ketchup dribbling down their chins and kept dropping their shorts to impress on us just how proud Basque men behave when provoked by the presence of a digital recording device.

And when they weren't singing Lord knows what obscenities, they were laughing at us. Not with us, you understand. At us. Matt valiantly held out a microphone and somehow a question emerged. I forget what language he opted for. I suspect it was Tahitian. The answers came flying back, a crackling firework of sound, featuring more Xs and Ks than Eddy Merckx himself.

'Axxarrankatha. Barraxxakakakaxxaria. Kox. Arax. Xarraka. Ha ha ha ha ha.' And off they would stumble, back to paint more giant orange genitalia on the tarmac, or just to smear more ketchup on themselves.

A few years later, on the 2008 Tour, I was to learn at closer hand what goes on in the collective (un)consciousness of a mountainside gearing up to welcome the Tour. Back in a production meeting in the spring I had wondered out loud if there was any chance that I could shoot a feature about the experience of spending a night camping out on the side of a mountain. The idea presented a logistical nightmare, as most things on the Tour do, given the difficulty of getting around narrow roads stuffed up with official and unofficial traffic.

Nonetheless, we put a date in the diary, and, more significantly, a tent was bought. The production invested £29.99 at Millets in this idea, at which point it became clear there was to be no going back. It had to happen.

The date chosen was the Sunday 13 July, the eve of Bastille day. The mountain was the Hautacam. The next day the Tour would finish there, having climbed into the Pyrenees from Pau. The idea was simple enough. I would be armed with a small camcorder and would film myself, in the well-worn style of a video diary, as I passed the night among the revellers and the international flotsam and jetsam that had scattered itself all the way up the fifteen-kilometre climb. I packed a change of clothes and a toothbrush. I had a sleeping bag, a pop-out one-man tent, and a box of bread, salami, cheese, fruit and wine, which Philippe and Odette had kindly packed for me. I was ready.

The Tour had finished in Bagnères-de-Bigorre that day, and so the first thing we had to do was pick our way through the solid traffic running down the valley road, and then turn off to climb the Hautacam so that I could be dropped off. It would have been a laborious trip at the best of times, but this was the Tour de France, when hundreds of thousands of other people had exactly the same idea.

On the roads, the eventide scramble had begun. Everyone was looking for an ill-suited and uncomfortable bed for the night. Campervans jostled for space on the verges of the road. Tents were popping up next to truck-stops. Chain gangs of American and British cyclo-tourists were grouped around unfolded maps, studying them with wearied tension as the prospect of a hot shower and a hotel meal grew ever more enticing, and ever more remote.

Woody, Liam and Chris Boardman, who were all travelling in my car, also had comfortable hotel rooms booked in Pau, and were yearning for them. The banter had begun.

'No dinner for us then. Oh no. We'll just stick around here in a traffic jam,' Liam began. 'But it'll be worth it, just so that Mr Boulting can craft his brilliant piece of tour cinematography. Just so long as he can fulfil his artistic ambitions, we'll gladly forgo our right to a hot meal.'

I grinned, a little sheepishly. Dinner is an essential pressure valve on the Tour, and theirs was being scraped off the plates and chucked away. I think I'd have felt the same.

'How much further?' ventured Chris, in his matter-of-fact deadpan.

We were already inching our way up the Hautacam. It was about eight o'clock in the evening, and there wasn't much roadside left to colonise. The crowds were vast. I looked out of the window with more interest and attention to detail than usual. Normally these sights simply form part of a moving backdrop to the jerky progression of the Tour. Certainly, it was a grand event, this pilgrimage of devotees, this migrating human herd. But the sea of faces would have lacked definition, and in its vast generality would never have seemed as important as my own individual concerns and frustrations. In the bubble of the Tour the crowd simply constituted the context in which the drama of one's own life was played out. But now I was about to immerse myself into their world, and I would have to pay them closer attention. I felt like Dustin Hoffman's character in *The Graduate*, when he jumps into the pool in the diving suit. There. But not really there.

Eventually, after climbing to within about 3km of the finish line, we rounded a sharp left-handed bend, and I signalled, with the assuredness of a water-diviner, that this was indeed the spot. It was a grassy slope on the inside of the switchback, with a scattering of tents. It was a little exposed, but boasted an extraordinary view of the mountains opposite. They were swathed in a menacing-looking purple cloud against which the dipping sun was fighting a losing battle.

Liam and Woody started filming my preparations, overseen by Chris. I suddenly felt like one of his six children, watching Dad take control of the family holiday. Chris scouted a location for my pitch, flattened the grass, considered the lie of the land and prodded the turf for tent-peg-purchase with scientific intensity. Satisfied with his findings, he pointed to the spot.

He unpopped the tent. It kind of flopped onto the mountainside, looking much like one of those tiny 'fortune-telling' fish you place in the palm of your hand. It curled up at the edges as if it had died from exposure.

Chris cackled with delight. This now genuinely seemed to amuse the former Olympic Champion. 'You going to sleep in there?'

'Yes,' I replied.

'That's funny,' the former world record holder concluded.

But the jealous fuss he made over my box of provisions was completely unnecessary. It was as if Philippe and Odette, in providing me with a few bits and pieces for dinner, had actively denied him something, which was rightly his. He was outraged that I had been given a bottle of Côtes de Bourg. He felt a personal sense of indignation, that I had been given a thick slice of Camembert.

The time came at last for them to leave me on my own. They retreated, filming me as they went; a forlorn figure on a darkening mountainside, clutching a camcorder, with which I filmed them as they went. In the final edited piece, this is the moment when the professionally shot footage hands over to the much shakier and more amateur video-diary footage, which I shot myself.

They drove off back down the mountain, beeping their horn with unconcealed glee. I gazed across at my surroundings. There was a brief break in the traffic, a temporary respite from the noise of the road. Time enough to register the tiny sound of a thousand different souls putting kids to bed and uncorking bottles in a dozen different languages. Their voices melted into the void against the chill of the evening sky that was beginning to bear down on the landscape.

I unpacked my stuff and laid it out as best I could. I fiddled with the camera, and began to grapple with the peculiar demands of the video-diary format. Filming myself going about my ordinary business struck me as a peculiar vanity. Especially when conducted within the privacy of my own one-man tent. I was embarrassed for myself. But as soon as I stepped outside, clutching the damn thing at arm's length, pointing it back at me, my sense of foolishness grew until it bordered on shame. Nevertherless, it had to be done. To go through this experience and not return with anything like a cogent piece of telly would be adding pointlessness to futility.

Armed with my bottle of wine and my video camera, I

yomped down the ten yards of sloping mountainside to meet the neighbours. Within seconds, and without even taking off my shoes, I was standing in their 'front room', balancing a plate of spaghetti, a cup of pastis and a camcorder. They were a warm, kind family from somewhere in France that I had never heard of. Not that I let on. I am sure that I nodded with enthusiastic familiarity as they told me about their journey from Saint-Jean-de-Wherever to find their plot of land next to mine on the side of Hautacam.

They asked me where I was from. Londres. '*Ah oui, oui.*' They had a cousin who'd been to a language school in Eastbourne. Most French people do.

Then they asked me what I thought I was doing. This was trickier. '*Je travaille pour une chaine de télé anglaise.*'

Really? They looked me up and down, a little sceptically. 'BBC?'

'*Oui,*' I lied.

'*Ah, très bon ça.* BBC verrry goood. Ha ha ha.' No one abroad has ever said to me 'Ah, ITV! Ant and Dec! Very good.'

So it was that, with their daughter-in-law now acting as the official BBC camera operator, I passed a very fine hour in their company as the pastis flowed and the night got gradually colder and colder. We talked about the nationalities, the numbers of different countries represented in the tented settlement. We aired prejudices, shared stereotypes. We talked about the racing, the riders, the route. They metaphorically raised their *chapeaux* to Armstrong; not something I was used to seeing the French do. But this was the 2008 Tour, led for a long time by Cadel Evans. It had been uninspiring so far, and even the French were now yearning for a dash of the swashbuckling Texan. If you're going to win the race, then ride like a winner, we generally agreed.

I left them to it, and with darkness now settled on the Hautacam, carried on my rounds of the neighbours, the pastis now emboldening me, and easing my embarrassment with the camera.

I passed by a few grizzly old veterans gathered around a recalcitrant TV set which they were trying to tune in to the Tour highlights show. These two old boys had seen every Tour together for the last twelve years. I suspect that this is what swathes of French middle-aged manhood do to get away from home life. Every nation seems to create a mass participation event for men of a certain age, which involves canvas and flasks. For the British it's fishing. In France it's Le Tour. They planned to drive over to the Alps and climb Alpe D'Huez in a week's time. In 2003, they'd been there the day Armstrong assumed control of the race. We remembered the day. We shared the Côtes de Bourg. And then I stumbled on.

I was down on the road now, strolling past campfires and gas stoves, singing kettles and singing people. But the rural idyll was shortlived. For, as the clock ticked towards midnight, the Tour Proper had started to hit the mountainside. The convoy of articulated trucks containing thousands of tons of metal barriers as well as all the broadcast equipment, the catering, the podium, the commentary tribune, the VIP stand, etc., etc., etc., had begun to grind its way up to the finish line. They flashed their lights and sat on their horns, blasting their way to the top. They roared past tents, missing guy-ropes by inches. On narrow stretches of the road, I had to squash myself flat against the cliff-side while the trucks hammered past me, or hop up precariously onto the parapet on the outside of the road to let them pass, dicing with the bottomless drop on the other side. There seemed no end to the convoy. I was amazed to witness its passage from this perspective. Violent, noisy, triumphant. A terrifying game of chicken had begun. The fittest, boldest and drunkest took turns dashing across the road just in front of the lorries, risking everything for the sake of a pastis-soaked thrill.

Andy, our driver that year, edged our truck past, picking me out in a blast of recognition. I saluted him.

By now I had reached another long switchback. Here, where the road widened slightly to allow for a passing bay, was a temporary nightclub. Lights, dance floor, DJ, bar, everything. There was even a bar-room fight, although it was a pretty half-arsed affair which ended in two Basque students missing each other repeatedly with wide, rangy left hooks before swapping hats and collapsing on the floor convulsed with laughter. All this took place, while their friends were baring their backsides at the passing convoy.

I stopped for a beer, chatted to a couple of Dutch kids who had got the Rabobank team from 2007 to sign their team-issue shirts. They showed me Michael Rasmussen's signature and made the universal sign of the syringe before crying with drunken laughter, draining their beers and turning to order more. I wished them well, and turned for 'home', the lure of my canvas tomb now proving irresistible. As I left the nightclub behind me, I wondered at the logistics of it all. There was a ten-mile stretch of the same scene endlessly self-replicating. Diesel generators discharging into the mountain air, powering the noise, light and beer, and oiling the wheels of mayhem.

Trudging back up the grassy slope towards my tent, I stopped off one last time, drawn to a scene of painterly beauty. A group of a dozen young Basque students had a campfire roaring, kept burning by a constant supply of aromatic bush wood from their well-organised colleagues on a foraging rota. I asked them if I could join them, and then concentrated on filming them as they began to sing. I had no idea what songs they were, but they sounded perfect; the alien, ancient language bellowed with throaty sincerity across the bowl of warm light, which flickered across their faces.

They could have been singing anything. It was wonderful to hear.

I suppose they must have asked themselves who I was and what on earth I thought I was doing filming them. But if they did, they hid their suspicions well. I listened for a while longer, politely declined their offer of a swig from their shared bottle of Metaxa, and then headed home to the wilting dew-speckled accommodation Chris had sorted for me. I opened my front door with that trademark zipping sound, which more than any other noise evokes the chilly privations of the campsite, and clambered in. Climbing into my sleeping bag and chewing on a salami, I lay awake for a while enjoying the mixture of sounds outside.

The holy trinity of a summer's night on Tour in the high Pyrenees: Basque singing, diesel engines and French laughter. I fell sound asleep, and dreamt with frightful intensity that I was in a tent on my own on a mountain.

I awoke an hour or two later to find that I had dissolved into a crumpled heap at the bottom end of the tent. It is one of the great hardships of mountainside camping, a phenomenon that deprives all but the comatose of a decent night's sleep, and I was just about to make its acquaintance.

Because mountains rise steadily, there is an entire absence of anywhere flat. This may sound fairly obvious, but until you've felt the resultant effect, you're in no position to judge its seriousness. Forced to sleep with my head higher than my feet, which faced down the mountain, I had been unaware of what might happen to me. But it is a clear physiological impossibility to gain restful sleep with your calf and thigh muscles gently bracing you against gravity. Eventually they will simply give in, and you'll wake to find yourself curled up in a ball at the foot of your tent. Using a baguette as an improvised ice-pick, I scaled back up the mountain, to the rolled-up ball of jumpers and socks that was making do as a pillow. I lay my head down and closed my eyes again, feeling the gentle insistence of the inevitable crumpling process beginning to take hold even as I drifted off. Outside, it was cold and quiet, the revellers now dotted all across the hillside in their own cocoons, waging their own private wars against the laws of physics.

After what seemed like six hours and thirteen minutes, I gave up pretending to myself that I was sleeping. It was 6.13. I deemed that a respectable-enough time to unzip my tent and get going. Coyly, and with the camera self-consciously nosing through the opening first to get the shot for real, I blinked into the morning air.

Overnight everything had changed. Still, clear air stood high in the valley, and reached from the grass to the stratosphere. Far away, the sun had just burst over the crested ridge of mountaintops that stood guard to the east, making the colours of the various tents on our side glow. It was going to be a beautiful day.

For now, I had the mountain to myself. The various victims of pastis, beer and Metaxa were still sleeping it off, somehow. I filmed a little, turned the camera on myself to complain about the terrible night's sleep, and then set off for a high point on a rock 100 yards further uphill. Here, with the help of a bottle of water to prop the camera against, and a quite inspired eye for cinematography, I framed up a breathtakingly beautiful shot of the Pyrenees. It would have been breathtaking had it not been spoilt a little by the sight of me in silhouette, gargling Evian mixed with Colgate and spitting repeatedly into the fine mountain grasses on an otherwise perfect day for the Tour de France.

After years of pussyfooting around the issue, I had finally seen life from both sides. My night on the Hautacam had taught me a little of what the mountain means to the Tour.

And what the Tour means to the mountain.

WIGGINS AND THE TAX-HAVEN TOUR

I have in my hand a piece of paper. It is yellow and grubby and it used to be folded up so that it would fit snugly into the back pocket of my jeans. Indeed, that's where I found it, nestling shamefully at the bottom of the dirty clothes basket. That's where I had flung the jeans along with other filthy souvenirs from a month on the roads of France. There it had stayed: in the bedrock, deep below the surface, as the shifting sands of soiled socks, shorts and shirts came and went above it. Down at these depths, the jeans kept their secret locked up in their denim tomb, cocooned from the ravages of passing time.

Until now. Gripped by an appalling trouser shortage, I was recently forced to prospect further and further afield. My search unearthed the jeans, and the jeans offered up the yellow piece of paper among other Tour junk: a cracked biro from a hotel room, a two-euro coin, a plastic-wrapped badge from the tourism office of some obscure French town.

These are the provisional results from Stage 15 of the 2009 Tour, produced before the various splintered gruppettos have even crossed the line. They are rushed off the press and distributed to the media by hand. There are, beneath the Tour de France logo and the various sponsors' headers, eleven riders listed, in order of their position in the General Classification.

Carlos Sastre, the defending champion is in eleventh place, three minutes and fifty-two seconds off the pace. Andy Schleck's in fifth. Andreas Klöeden is one place better than him. But the top three names belong to Contador, Armstrong and Wiggins.

In third place: Bradley Wiggins. Three-quarters of the way around only his second full Tour, poised on the shoulders of the seven-time winner and the astonishing Spaniard who, back in 2009, looked destined to eclipse even Armstrong's status. Wiggins, the unlikely lad with the long limbs and the crooked smile.

I look at the typeface and still find it hard to take in.

It's 2009. I am back in the thin air of Verbier, on the Swiss mountaintop. As I fold the paper and tuck it away in its time-vault pocket, I consider with growing excitement the scale of his achievement. I am heading down the slope away from the finish line. The TV trucks have grunted their way up the mountain and into their precarious summit-side parking grid. Massive vehicles are jacked up sideways along the vertiginous mountainside. Dropping down through the tangle of power cables and leaving the metallic blare of the PA system behind me, I head back towards our truck, my earpiece still wirelessly relaying Gary Imlach's closing words as we head towards our off-air time. Soon the programme will be closed off and another defining chapter in British Tour history will, like the sheet of paper in my pocket, be folded away and placed into the past.

He'd warned us, of course. He'd told me a couple of weeks before.

The Columbus Hotel in Monte Carlo had a modern marble-and-leather interior with soft lighting. In a lobby overlooking the entry staircase, Wiggins had sloped over to 'share his thoughts with us' ahead of the 2009 Tour. It was the eve of the race. I leant across the vast expanse of a smoked-glass tabletop towards the sardonic figure of Wiggins, slumped in the Barcelona chair opposite me, his nylon Garmin team tracksuit offered no resistance against the shiny upholstery. He seemed to slip lower and lower, melting downwards to the floor. His Princess Diana eyes were doing their downcast thing and a curious smile played across his mouth. He spoke thoughtfully, softly.

'I'm in the form of my life. I've never felt this good.' This wasn't boastfulness, I thought to myself, but quiet honesty. 'I'm aiming for a top twenty finish. Who knows, maybe even higher.'

It's worth putting this in context. Here was a man who had finished the Tour on only one previous occasion. In 2006, he'd managed 124th place, three hours, twenty-four minutes and thirty-five seconds slower than winner Oscar Pereiro. On the first mountain stage that year Wiggins straight away lost forty minutes on the leaders.

Three years later, even though we had glimpsed him riding alongside the climbing elite in places during that spring's Giro d'Italia, his ambition still seemed preposterous. The target he had set himself from that hotel chair in Monaco was at odds with the formbook.

It is unusual for an athlete to post such a specific, let alone ambitious, target. The fear of falling short normally modifies outward shows of bravado, distilling any act of prediction to the equivalent of the footballer's 'take each game as it comes'.

The next day the 2009 Tour started. We had rigged up our set and, unusually for us, had such a fine view of Monaco harbour behind us that we were able to dispose of the central panel, which is normally used to mask the sight of a row of generators or the likes of a German catering truck. This time Gary Imlach, in his finest Monte Carlo polo shirt, and Chris Boardman, standing alongside him wearing his best pair of Rohan slacks, were framed by a ghastly forest of masts in the Port Hercule. The ensigns of a hundred tax havens fluttered bad-temperedly in the sultry air.

Woody and Liam and I lugged our heavy kit around in sapping humidity, meandering up and down the clogged-up embankment of Quai Antoine, ducking and diving through crowds of Americans and Brits and the occasional Frenchman. We stood for a while, waiting for Fabian Cancellara to appear outside the Saxobank Team bus, all three of us absorbed by the sight of a vast gin palace shamelessly emptying litre after litre of human excrement from its septic tank straight into the port.

It stank. In fact, Monaco stank. In the cool of his team's bus, Wiggins was probably listening to The Jam. Not long now before the 2009 Tour would get under way.

The Prologue route ran from the port up into the hills, then turned sharply and steeply and headed back down the Avenue Princess Grace to the waterfront again. Fifteen and a half kilometres, but featuring some sharp climbs, and some technical descending to rejoin the Formula One circuit.

It was not, in other words, a circuit designed with Bradley Wiggins's long frame in mind. But, as was widely predicted, it suited Cancellara. He tore into it, and into the yellow jersey. He put eighteen seconds into Alberto Contador, who in turn edged out Wiggins by just a single second; the Londoner managing a third place finish to improve on the fourth place he'd ridden in London two years previously.

A short time after he'd finished, Matt was dispatched to fetch Wiggins to join us on the set. He found him warming down on some rollers outside the Garmin team bus. Would it be possible for him to join the ITV team on the set for a few minutes?

'ITV can fuck off,' Matt was told from underneath Wiggins's towel. This was a Wiggins joke, it seemed. He has a love of heavy-handed dead-weight wit, which can leave you wondering what it is you might have done to upset him.

Yet his demeanour a little later, when he stood on the set dwarfing Gary and Chris, was different. Clutching a microphone as he spoke, with the sweat of his efforts slowly crystallising into salt, the view of the port behind him was crowded out by a few dozen British cycling fans who had made their way through the chaos of the media compound to where the ITV truck stood. While many might still have been smarting from a deflating sense that his chance of winning a stage had passed him by, Wiggins was clearly thinking and believing in a much longer game, a grander objective. His disappointment wasn't so much well disguised. It just wasn't there at all.

When the show went off the air, Wiggins shook hands and turned to leave, and the crowd broke into spontaneous applause, cheering and shouting his name. This was something I had previously only ever witnessed happening to French riders in front of French crowds. Yet the Brits had arrived that year in large numbers in Monaco. Middle-aged couples from Swindon, wiry old boys from Cumbria, kids from the Isle of Wight in replica kits. Our presence was swelling. Something was in the air.

Wiggins rode off alone through the crowded streets of Monte Carlo towards the aptly named Columbus hotel. A new world was calling him.

The next time I had occasion to deal with Wiggins came three days later in Montpellier at the finish line of the team time trial. Wiggins's Garmin team finished in second place. This in itself should have been enough to catapult him into the yellow jersey, had he not lost forty-one seconds the previous day when the peloton was split by Columbia's sudden acceleration on the approach to La Grande Motte. If Wiggins been the right side of that divide, he would now have led the Tour de France by three seconds.

This time, the 'ITV can fuck off' moment was laced with sincerity. It was not verbalised, but it didn't need to be. I am not sure, at the time, that I realised the depth of his disappointment.

Parked up in the shade by the side of a road near the rugby stadium, Garmin had set out a row of nine chairs for their riders to collapse into after forty kilometres of agony. Around this strangely haphazard chill-out zone, their staff had roped off a private area, to keep press and public at bay. I stood there, the sweaty T-shirt clinging to my back, waiting to catch Wiggins's eye, microphone handy. I called his name imploringly a few times. He saw me, winced, stood up, and moved to the far side of the pen. We upped sticks and moved with him, shadowing his every move. Minutes later he saw me again, and waved me away again. And so it went on. I was humiliated. He was irritated. But we were locked into our behaviours: I needed the sound bite, he needed me to vanish. There would inevitably only be one winner. It wasn't me.

After what seemed like an age, but must only have been twenty minutes or so, Wiggins ducked under a rope, grabbed his bike and started to ride off, heading back down towards the finish line and away to his hotel. Like a team of parents in a three-legged race, Woody, Liam and I galloped after him, cabled together and looking every inch the idiots that we were. Ahead the crowds were still dense. His slight figure snaked through the pack of faces, but in the end Wiggins had to slow down. We caught up with him, and I fired in a last desperate attempt.

'Brad, give us a word. Just one question.' He rode on, stony-faced, without so much as a flicker. This was Bradley Wiggins lost in private frustration.

My role is not to be the riders' friend. It's to bring home the sights and sounds, character and soul of a race that places immense demands on its protagonists. Often, in their silence, their unwillingness to talk, or even in a flash of anger or contempt directed towards us, they articulate the brutal pressures more accurately than any manicured words might achieve.

In such circumstances, I understand my job to be the lightning conductor.

For the next two days, Wiggins's race went quiet, while we ploughed onwards and, generally speaking, south-westwards. Hidden safely in the bunch, he will have buried his thoughts while Thomas Voeckler stole a march on Mark Cavendish into Perpignan, and then listened to team radio with his heart in his mouth the following day as teammate Dave Millar, with 10km to run, nearly outwitted the chasers through the rain-soaked avenues of Barcelona.

Then came Andorra. I remember it well because it was the day before my fortieth birthday. With the deluge of Barcelona behind us, we had climbed up and away from the clouds in Spain and into tax haven number two of the 2009 Tour. The skies had cleared overnight. In the morning, the usual grinding ascent towards the finish line seemed to sparkle. Knowing that I had some time before the race arrived, I had laced my running shoes and slipped on a vest. We laboured up the steep climb towards Arcalis, a tidy ski-station surrounded by the jagged teeth of a Pyrenean horseshoe. I asked to be let out of the car with 6km to go, and I ran up towards the finish line.

I passed campers firing up stoves. An army of middle-aged Frenchmen soaked up the morning sun in Speedos and un-buttoned checked shirts, their idling daughters looking vacant and traumatised in equal measure. I passed cheerful Luxembourgers on Schleck-watch, their medieval blue flags catching what little breeze picked at the mountainside. Along the road cheap radios and chatter, the white noise of a morning on the Tour.

It was a short climb, no more than twelve kilometres in total to the summit. But it was steep in places, the gradient never seeming to settle. Finally I reached the top, red-faced, and with my accreditation flapping at my chest, I came to a breathless halt, apologising as I hop-scotched past the guys whose job it was every day to stencil the giant letters SKODA on the tarmac just next to the finish line.

The first summit finish on the Tour, I thought. This was where the race would really start.

I was not, however, thinking about Bradley Wiggins. Nor, I should imagine, were at least half the peloton. Especially not when, within the closing kilometres of the climb, and still riding strongly, Wiggins starting shouting, 'That's what I'm talking about!'

Amazed at what I had seen on the monitors, I went on Brad-watch. Brice Feillu won the stage. Rinaldo Nocentini rode himself into a surprise yellow jersey. But I disregarded completely the need to go chasing the main men. Armstrong could wait for another day. Contador? Well, Matt would grab a word with him, if we bothered at all.

All alone in my particular mission, I had waited for Wiggins to come over the line. He was in a group of eleven riders containing all the main contenders. As the hordes descended on Armstrong, we spotted Wiggins, sneaking through the pack and continuing up the hill at speed, heading for his Garmin team vehicles parked a few hundred yards away in a grassy compound on the steep mountainside.

Breathlessly we caught him up, just as he reached a van in the Garmin livery. It was locked. There wasn't a sign of anyone. The morning sunshine had been replaced by a chilling grey cloud cover. Where were his soigneurs?

We started filming, as Wiggins's long shaky legs stalked around the outside of the van, a stream of expletives leaving him all the while as he tried with increasing exasperation every locked door handle. He just wanted a drink, a towel and privacy. He banged his fist against the side of the van and cursed. It gave a deep metallic thud whose reverberations were soon lost in the continuing din of motor horns and excitable commotion drifting up on the cool mountain air from the finish line.

There we all stood: Wiggins teetering around on cycling shoes. At two paces distant was Liam, his eye welded to the viewfinder and the heavy camera loaded onto his shoulder. Woody, one eye on Wiggins, the other looking down at the mixer, his microphone boom reaching across the gap like a hand outstretched for an unwanted handshake. And me, head bowed and hand mic dipped down, held by hands folded in front of me in the manner of a schoolboy in the headmaster's office. I felt guilty witnessing his discomfort, yet knew it would make revealing viewing. Also, as I still did not know exactly where I stood with Wiggins, I felt quite unable to offer him my congratulations. It was a curious stand-off.

Minutes later, help arrived in the form of a Garmin soigneur. He guided Wiggins over to an estate car, opened up the boot, and finally thrust a cold drink in his hands. He collapsed down, perching on the opened rear end of the vehicle. He ripped the can open, and drank heavily. He emptied it, in fact. I watched his Adam's apple bouncing up and down in his long neck as he gulped.

This is the type of detail you have little choice but to end up observing minutely as you wait for the athlete to be obliging. He knows what you want, but will rightly only answer when he's good and ready. You feel a little like a faithful family pet waiting for its owner to go walkies. The same imploring eyes and unfathomable patience. The same dumb behaviour.

By now we had been joined by the Britpack. Writers from the *Guardian*, the *Telegraph*, Reuters and *Cycling Weekly* as well as a microphone from the BBC had appeared. We formed a respectful semi-circle. This was a car-boot sale with a difference. Time stood still. Wiggins cracked open his second can. He threw his neck back and drank again. We watched, fascinated and irritable. Deadlines were closing in on us. This story was a little too thirsty for our liking.

Eventually, Wiggins signalled his readiness with the trace of a smile and a beckoning flick of the head. He started to talk into our bunched microphones.

'I knew I could do this. I've been confident, ever since this spring when I changed things a little. I've lost weight but kept my power. It's just nice to be able to show to myself what I know I've been working towards.'

And then the sober assessment: 'You know, this was just the first day in the mountains and I got through it fine. But there's a hell of long way to Paris and a whole load more mountains to get over. This is a great start, but it doesn't mean much just yet.'

As he rolled the words out, we drank them in. Nodding dogs. Egging him on to speak in prouder, louder terms of his achievements. But Wiggins was utterly in control of the messages he was sending the public, and at the same time of the messages he was sending back into the peloton and back through his own ears and into his heart.

Andorra had been special. But as the race rumbled out of the Pyrenees, and attention returned to the sprinters, we all became a little obsessed with weight. Wiggins and his missing kilos kept us fascinated from day to day.

We ambushed him at the start village. We ambushed him at the finish line. We spoke to him whenever and wherever we could to talk pounds and ounces. He offered simple explanations where we demanded complex ones. He'd simply been on a sort of diet. With loads of exercise. There was really nothing more to it than that.

He'd always been thin, but in a peloton made up of men whose BMI is so low it'd double if they ate a cheese sandwich, Wiggins stood out in particular.

And yet, it seemed that for many people outside of the bright British bubble of enthusiasm, there were plenty of unanswered questions. To most of the rest of the world, he had appeared from nowhere on the leaderboard. So during that middle week, people from all over the international media compound made the trek across to our modest truck. German TV wanted to know if we had any footage of him playing the guitar. The Danes wanted pictures of him from his childhood.

But there were those who felt differently. A few of the Dutch and some of the French wanted to know what he was on.

This came as a shock to me when I first perceived the depth of their cynicism. It felt as if some outsider had just gatecrashed a private party and set about insulting your family. But, more than that, I was nagged by worry. Had I missed something? Had I neglected my duty somehow?

I had prided myself on going about my business on the Tour with my eyes and ears wide open, live to any insinuation, receptive to rumour. I had become better with each passing year at filtering the wheat from the chaff. I really should have stopped and thought more deeply about the Wiggins case. It was true that in the ultra-suspicious world of cycling journalism his transformation would automatically have raised eyebrows.

And yet, as I finally set about unpicking his past dealings and thinking about those who'd had influence on him and his upbringing as a rider, I found nothing to provoke alarm. The bad vibes simply never chimed. My conviction in his innocence became clearer. Nonetheless, I reproached myself a little for not having thought to ask the question earlier.

One day on the 2009 Tour, somewhere near Tarbes, Wiggins must have read my mind. Or he must have been reading too many message boards on continental cycling websites. We stopped him just before he got away at the end of a nothing sort of a stage.

He was wearing a pair of extraordinarily large white plastic sunglasses. This fascinated me, particularly since, when I looked him in the eye, all I got back was a stereoscopic vision of two identical earnest-looking ITV Sport reporters. It quite put me off my stride.

But that day, without me even raising the subject, he acknowledged his detractors. He offered up the oxygen of recognition to the murmurs and mumbles of discontent. I was astonished. Standing by the side of a field, hemmed into the side of the road by a slow-moving line of Tour vehicles, with one leg mostly falling off down a drainage ditch, Wiggins told it like it was.

'I know they'll talk of doping and that people won't believe that I can do all this clean. But that's it, that's cycling, that's where we're at. What else can I say? I know it's sad.'

That phrase cut through. It dragged back into the hot French air all the ghastly baggage of 2007, when Wiggins had been escorted back to his hotel room by the gendarmerie. One of his Cofidis teammates had been busted. The entire team withdrew from the race. After two weeks of appalling effort, Wiggins had found his Tour prematurely and ingloriously ended.

A day or two later back in Manchester, Wiggins called a press conference to discuss his enforced withdrawal. It was a stinging assessment of the Tour. His languid delivery betrayed some emotion. Not for him any more the nest of vipers of the continental pro-racing scene. He painted a picture of a peloton rotten to the core. It was an articulate rebuke to the corruption in which his sport was steeped. Instead, he declared, he would now dedicate himself to the pure, clean aesthetics and ethics of the track, in pursuit of the perfect pursuit. I was struck by the coherence of his attack on road racing.

His words made my surroundings seem temporarily a little tawdry: the as-far-as-the-eye-can-see array of Tour vehicles, awnings and branded marquees mushrooming up in each gap between the trucks. The self-important accredited chosen ones scurried from one duty to another, in and out of edit-suites, satellite feed points, ad hoc radio studios, all filing stories for consumption back home that told only half the story. We had all bought into the cheating. We were all part of the problem. The truth didn't matter so much that it should stand in the way of good fiction.

So in 2009, it was uncomfortable to hear Wiggins evoke the ghosts of 2007, as this time the finger of suspicion rounded on him. I applauded him for facing down the issue, and not scurrying away. In effect, he answered the questions, before we'd even asked them.

The next summit finish on Verbier could not come soon enough for those of us who wanted to know just how good he might prove to be. We feared its arrival and craved the certainty it would impart. It was judgement day for Wiggins's Tour.

What happened, then, on that Swiss mountain top? Of all the days on my eight Tours, no other single stage has been replayed in my memory as often as this.

That day, Alberto Contador won. His attack had been widely predicted. It was the day he rode himself into the yellow jersey, and effectively dispensed with any notion that Lance Armstrong might be capable of winning an eighth Tour de France. Behind him the race spread out. Nibali, the Schlecks, none could live with him.

Yet as that small clutch of elite riders spilled over the top, the French media pack remained largely unmoved. Their sights were set on Nicolas Sarkozy, who had dropped in for the day. He was the showbiz draw, the darling of the crowds, the small man with the pulling power, and quite possibly the politics, of Peter Stringfellow. Because of his presence on the race, we were being chaperoned by half a dozen of the hardest-looking shaven-headed secret service guys it's possible to imagine. In the glaring sun, Liam, briefly taking the weight of the camera off his shoulder, had the temerity to park his tired backside on the bonnet of an unfamiliar-looking, unmarked, black limousine. A tap on the shoulder from one of the highly trained assassin types was enough to send him jumping up.

Then Sarkozy's official car finally arrived and screamed to a frantic halt. All hell broke loose. It provoked a whirlwind of cameras, guards and fanatical crowds, all trying to snatch a glimpse of the little great man. You could have been forgiven for forgetting there was a bike race on.

For the rest of us, the race was the only thing that mattered.

One minute and twenty-six seconds further down the mountain, and flanked by former Tour winner Carlos Sastre and world champion-to-be Cadel Evans, Bradley Wiggins was doing battle with the boundary of the British believability. A further nine seconds back, Lance Armstrong had cracked, and was digging in, unable quite to hold the wheel of the grimacing East German, Andreas Klöden.

On tiptoes, peering over the shoulders of the hundreds of people who stood in the way, I strained for a view of the TV pictures.

Wiggins looked fluent, almost comfortable. What right did he have to be tapping out the rhythm of the mountains along-side men who'd lived at this rarefied altitude all their cycling lives? Wiggins, a man of the aerohelmet and the time-trial bike. A man for pure sustained speed over flat terrain, a track man. He was the lung-busting long-legged champion of the pursuit. He had come from a world of pure speed in the particle accelerator environment of the velodrome, where the passage of bike through air was uninterrupted by either contour or switchback.

None of that bore even a passing resemblance to the slopes of Verbier: pocked and scored tarmac, crumbling in places from last winter's frost, with its accelerations and slacking-off of pace, the road unsettled and unsettling, as sometimes imperceptibly, sometimes violently, the mountain lifted and lowered its gradient like a treadmill set madly to shuffle. It was the sharp end of a Grand Tour in the high mountains and Wiggins was looking at the finishing line.

Suddenly, and with the thrill of recognition, I got it. The noise of the race flying up the mountain was the breaking of a barrier. I had seen, of course, with bewilderment and delight, the emerging domination of Mark Cavendish. I had watched, in Armstrong, the most systematic winner come and go, but this was different. It was possible to identify with this elongated figure suffering his way up into Switzerland. Wiggins spoke a language we understood.

So I stared at the finish line, and closed my eyes briefly as I listened to the commentary. I had a notion of what it might be like back at home, among those who care for the sport, watching on in the front rooms of Mansfield and Morecambe, Welwyn Garden City and Dundee, as ponderous midsummer, post-Wimbledon weather scudded over rows of houses.

We invested, that summer, a little of our pent-up Britishness in Wiggins. A kindling of frustration, a maggot of self-doubt, a chip on the shoulder with a dab of HP Sauce. This was the baggage he bore on our behalf. He carried with him decades of our pressing noses against the shop window of the Tour de France, watching a perfectly oiled, deeply tanned procession of the more-or-less trustworthy step hard upon their pedals and accelerate away from the rest. The Basques, the Belgians, the Americans, the Italians, the Spanish and even, now and again, the French. They were all players in a game to which we had been invited, but knew from the outset we had not a chance of winning. But now suddenly, and from nowhere, we had Wiggins.

I peered harder still to get a glimpse of the action on the screens. A trio of riders were now closing in on the finish line: Sastre, Evans, Wiggins.

He'd dropped Armstrong.

Suddenly the pictures on the TV cut to a shot of a French reporter starting to conduct an interview with Nicolas Sarkozy. There were howls of anguish from the truck, as Steve realised that we were about to miss the moment we'd been waiting for. In the confusion that followed, the Wiggins group crossed the finish line together, without anyone even bothering to show them.

It had been an astonishing arrogance, a remarkably ill-judged decision. French television had assumed that an interview with their premier would trump anything offered up by the Tour. The most extraordinary part of all of this was that they flicked the switch not just for their own viewers, but across all the networks around the world taking live pictures. Broadcasters who host an event are obliged to supply what is known as a 'world feed', in which items of parochial interest are excluded and the action is covered in a neutral and non-editorialised way. By and large this is diligently observed by France Télévisions for the duration of the Tour. But this was an unprecedented breach in their code of conduct. It had probably been a mistake, but the fact that it had happened to a Brit flung us onto a moral high horse, from which it took us days to dismount.

The run-out zone in Verbier was tiny. Barely a hundred

yards of tarmac. Wiggins came over the line, rode to the side, almost fell off his bike, but just managed to step off it before collapsing to the ground.

There he sat, while all hell broke loose around him. Eventually he was offered a drink, a towel and a way out. He got to his feet again, like Bambi on ice, and clambered over a railing into an enclosure reserved entirely for Vittel, the mineral water company. He stumbled towards a patch of tarmac in the shadow of their truck. There was an industrial fridge, full of cold water bottles, and two French students on a summer job handing them out. But, rather than making sure that Wiggins was offered a bottle, they started berating him instead for simply being there. I gazed at the scene, wondering if they even knew who he was.

We got ready to do a live interview as soon as he had composed himself. While he sat wrapped in towels and slumped in a canvas fold-out chair, Woody started rethreading hundreds of metres of cable from the truck through all the chaos to the tiny corner of Switzerland where Bradley Wiggins sat, after the greatest ride of his life.

To recall in detail what he said wouldn't do it justice. I held the microphone and he spoke. It was as simple as that. I prompted, and he spoke again, fully, frankly, and with great pride. He managed, even at that rarefied height and so close to the event, to make clear his understanding of his achievement. Of all the interviews I've ever been fortunate enough to conduct, this gripped me the most. It was a rare privilege.

'Just wait for the time trial in Annecy. It's Wiggo-Time!'

The tone of his voice, the look in his eye. That all came back to me when I found that crumpled-up piece of paper, still grimy from the finish line in Verbier.

However, third place overall was to be his high-water mark. A week later, he spoke to us again, on the cobbles of the

Champs-Elysées. This time it was a matter of seconds after finishing the Tour in fourth place in Paris. He was reunited with his wife Cath and his two young children and, after the briefest of hugs with them, he did his duty once more to ITV. His face was lined with smuts from the exhaust pipes of the Parisian streets.

He looked, more than anything else, knackered.

'I am aware of what I've achieved. To equal the great Robert Millar. To go better than the even greater Tom Simpson. I know what I've done.'

His words came slowly. I imagined that the eight victorious laps of the cobbled Champs-Elysées had given him time enough to judge the sentiment correctly.

It was life-changing for Wiggins. Even if he did know what he had achieved, I doubt very much if he knew what was about to happen to him.

The following year was another story altogether, whose telling would contrast in every imaginable way from the innocent pleasure of 2009. That's for another day.

Those three weeks are the ones I choose to remember. They made him a millionaire. They gave him considerable fame. They bestowed on him a pressure, that proved to be a bit corrosive. And they gave me my finest memories of the Tour. Remember what the piece of paper said.

Contador. Armstrong. Wiggins.

REST DAYS

There are two rest days on the Tour de France. The first comes after nine straight days of racing and travelling. The second, seven days later. They are loved, craved and abused; the Tour's release valves. Never mind the riders: rest days are sacred for all of us.

Sometimes they can catch you unawares. The pace and the intensity of the Tour carries you blindly and unknowingly over a precipice of work and into the thin air of a day off, like a cartoon character chased off the edge of a cliff to find his legs still whirring madly beneath him. It can be odd adjusting to the sudden need to do nothing much.

Generally speaking, rest days are for strolling, chatting, drinking and sweating in a launderette. They are characterised by one consistent feature, no matter whether they happen to take place up a mountain or in an industrial estate: you can take your accreditation off.

It comes as a shock to realise that it is possible to walk the planet, drink coffee, go shopping, and converse with other members of the human race without the need to be accredited. Anyone who has ever needed to be accredited for any length of time longer than a week will never again vote for a politician who believes in the introduction of compulsory ID cards. It is the slow death of the soul, brought about by a small square of laminated card with a blurred photo.

Unencumbered, then, by the need to prove the validity of your existence at every turn, the day stretches before you, unruffled, peaceful, empty. Empty, that is, except for the need to find a launderette. This is as much a part of our Tour de France as a ride up the Champs-Elysées is to the real one. Although we are pretty well versed nowadays in how to operate the machines, dispense soap powder and fold the tumble-dried clothes, it is still vital to get there early. A sizeable town, like Tarbes, for example, at the feet of the Pyrenees, may have 80,000 inhabitants, but it might only boast three or four launderettes. Not enough for the armies of Tour people about to descend on them, each with a black bin bag full of malodorous clothing slung over their back like a sack of coal.

The best part of a morning can sometimes pass while you wait for the staff of the PMU caravan float to wash their green jumpsuits. And while you wait, you have to sit tight in the sauna of the launderette for fear of losing your place in the queue. The hours pass with idle chat among the international hodge-podge of half-familiar faces. People pop in, who you know you should know, but know equally well that you don't. After bantering briefly about the hilariously long nature of the Tour de France, and cracking the usual half-serious joke about the riders having it easy, an uneasy silence often settles on the surroundings. Gradually you become aware that the only thing you really have in common is the fact of your accreditation. Take that away, and a strange disconnection takes over. It's like seeing your workmates naked. It can be a little awkward.

Sometimes, though, it works differently. I remember once sitting on the terrace of a very humble little bar in Grenoble while my laundry gyrated itself into health. I was sharing a mid-morning beer with one of the army of Tour de France media officials who police our activities on the Tour. Yet, he was off duty. It was one of those situations where the beer, the sunshine and the soothing realisation that no finish line had been drawn anywhere on the tarmac that day plunged us instantly into a conversation far deeper and more intimate than the situation warranted. The act of non-accreditation-wearing released us both from our regular professional inhibitions.

He confided in me his distaste for the Tour, his loathing of cycling, his passion for music and desire to travel to Africa to escape from the general spiritual decay of modern France. A virtual stranger to me before I set down a *pression* in front of him, he was now opening up in unexpected ways. A glance at his watch halfway through our second beer, as he was showing me photos of his girlfriend who was at art school in Rome, told him that his spin cycle was through. And that was that.

We were soldiers from opposing trenches of the First World War playing football at Christmas. The next day, he was back in his uniform, looking angrily at me and signalling to me that I could ask just one question in the interview zone.

The next year, he never reappeared. Perhaps now he's propping up a bar in Mozambique. But without the rest day's spiritual blessing, I might never have known that he was just a thoughtful young lad doing a job. And now I have totally forgotten his name.

Drying requires extreme ingenuity, since the passage of the clothes through the launderette invariably bottlenecks after the washing machines. It astonishes me every year how long it can take to dry a pair of denim jeans. The simplest option is sometimes to spread them out in the sunshine, although this can get a little edgy at times. Once in a run-down area of Toulouse, we commandeered the street furniture outside the washing salon, and when that wasn't enough, our pants and socks and shorts started to spread down the street until they almost completely eclipsed the front of the café next door, which was still closed. Sadly for us, the patron's brother owned the *tabac* across the road, and got on the phone straight away. We watched him, as he reported our disrespectful drying.

'Hey listen up. Some English journalists have hidden your café from view with their pants . . . yes, you heard me correctly, their pants. I think it will reflect badly on your establishment for years to come, and may affect your turnover in the long-term. Shall I have them shot?'

And with that, he threatened to have us shot. And the pants.

Another time, on a ridiculously long transfer on the 2009 Tour, we stopped to enjoy a rest day in the middle of nowhere. It was a tidy little guest house in a miniature village some-where not that far from Brive. It was run by a fussy Yorkshire couple who made us laugh by barking angry instructions at their staff in the kind of French that sounds as if it's a very specific dialect of Wetherby. With no launderette within a thousand kilometres in any direction, our host offered us the chance to use the guest house's own facility, a snip at ten euros per wash per head.

The problem was, once again, drying. So for a while his sunny little breakfast terrace drew admiring glances from all passing motorists as it lay festooned with a kind of sock-based bunting. It gave the impression that a colossal marital dispute had taken place, which had only been resolved when the husband's entire wardrobe had been tipped out of a first-floor window.

People passed by on foot and stared. We shrugged apologetically, and pointed at the shadowy figures inside of the man from Yorkshire and his wife going about their business of snapping at each other.

Eventually, and to protect the good name of his establishment, our host lent us a drying rack. We disappeared soon after that, our jeans still damp around the waistline, and beginning to poach in our suitcases as we drove.

Nonetheless, the washing of clothes is a ritual I have come to love. This is partly because it brings me into contact with a different France: one which is not putting on a show for tourists. Launderettes, in common with railway stations and kebab shops, seem to be a kind of town-planner's shorthand for Crap Part of Town. Once the machines are loaded up, there is often a thirty-two-minute wait, perfectly designed for a stroll around the local amenities. Occasionally, for a heavier soil, or an older model of washing machine, this can be as much as a forty-six-minute wait. This represents an ideal opportunity to have a nose around the dodgy-looking betting shop next door. Or perhaps to get your hair cut by friendly Algerian barbers who delight in burning off ear hair with cigarette lighters. You can even be a little more adventurous, and, as Liam once did, buy a ukelele.

Sometimes, there is nothing to admire in a place. Instead of kebab shops we are served up a panorama of wild, jagged Alpine peaks. Of what possible use are they?

Disappointingly, in 2009, we spent the second rest day in a high-altitude cluster of wooden hotels and silly clothes shops, known to people who like that sort of thing as Verbier. After Monaco and Andorra it was the third tax haven we visited that year. If we'd hopped over to Jersey, we'd have had the full set, and could have started developing it with houses and hotels of our own.

Verbier is the kind of place that makes you want to pay high levels of taxation as a simple gesture of open defiance at the prevailing culture. I call it a 'place', although it's not actually a place, except in the most narrow, GPS, Google Earth sort of a way. It is located in Switzerland, but that's about it. Neither the place nor the people seem to be genuine, in any conventional sense.

The Swiss may boast Italian, French and German as their national languages, yet in Verbier, a weird hybrid of English holds sway. From one minute to the next, as we wandered around the pine-clad hell-hole, we seemed to confront a wall of Hilfiger-clad clones who spoke the kind of English that doesn't differentiate between idiocy and marketing.

We were staying in a huge chalet, which was run by a Swedish family. The staff consisted of about seven generations of ostensibly bohemian Swedes, loosely affiliated to the same family, and all with serious investment portfolios. They seemed to hover around every corner, merrily swapping advice in a plethora of different languages on which restaurants served the best melted cheese. That's about all it is possible to eat in the Alps, it seems. A smell of paraffin and dairy farming hangs gloomily in the air.

The place was so booked out that parking was the biggest issue of the evening. With so many cars trying to squeeze onto such a small stretch of alp, risks were being taken. Some other French residents of our chalet, in their desperation, had dropped the front wheels of their car over the edge of the road, so that they hung uselessly in mid-air. The car was propped on its underbelly. This was adventurous parking indeed, even by Tour standards.

In the morning, miraculously, the car was gone. I guess it must have been towed away. Or they just let it drop.

Crash!

'What was that?'

'The Mercedes. We'll get another one.'

We weren't the only ones staying in Verbier that evening. Large sections of the fund management and banking communities of Western Europe and the USA had fled there too. Presumably on the run from the chaos they had left behind them on Wall Street. Team Saxo Bank were in their corporate element, annexing a posh chalet into which they had packed as many white, middle-aged, middle managers as they could fit. They stood in tight clumps juggling finger food and talking to each other in braying hybrid English about their heroic attempts to ride up to the summit on their team replica bikes. They were wearing out their iPhones as they flicked through souvenir photos of their deeds. I saw Fabian Cancellara, in his après-ski leisurewear, riding down to do his PR bit at the party on his bike. It can't have been more than 200 yards from their hotel, yet he felt the need to ride there. Perhaps he'd simply forgotten how to walk.

Columbia, along with Mark Cavendish, two-thirds of the way through his six-stage haul of 2009, were lodged just opposite. Their hotel was a jagged wooden cliff face staring across a car park at more timber-clad nightmare constructions in the charmless ski resort. Outside the front entrance, where the team vehicles were parked up, a swarm of the curious and the obsessive were gazing with loving, jealous eyes at Columbia's team of German mechanics hosing down the riders' bikes. One fan stooped to take a picture of a track pump, and then picked up an empty water bottle to assess its weight.

In this way, the Tour was winding down before a rest day. A chill was closing in on the mountaintop as Woody, Liam and I snaked our way down through the dregs of the afternoon's entertainment. Hordes of Danish and Norwegian bike fans in their early twenties stumbled around the place in various states of disarray and undress, bellowing ribald songs in Scandinavian tongues, which sounded belligerent but which were almost certainly charmingly innocent. One of them, an ear-splitting chorus in support of Thor Hoshovd's campaign for the green jersey, ended with the stirring refrain, 'Mark Cavendish is a fish.' It was passionate stuff.

Cavendish himself was spotted walking back up the mountain from their hotel arm in arm with his freshly acquired girlfriend, Fiorella Migliore, former Miss Italy. He was dressed, as riders are contractually obliged to do, even when not on active duty, in the team's liveried shell suit. He looked like he'd just finished a shift at the local leisure centre. But he smiled the relaxed smile of a man whose life was getting better by the hour. George Hincapie, in the role of gooseberry that night, walked alongside them, towering above the young couple and looking three times as old.

We had eaten somewhere forgettable, played pool somewhere irritating, and were now looking to join up with our friends from the Organisation. The urbane and charming Olivier, and the unreconstructed stubbled, chain-smoking Mathieu, had vaguely indicated that we should meet them at the only bar still open in town. A place with an uber-prosaic name, such as The Room, or The Place, I forget.

Inside, the pub was heaving. Euro beats kept everybody pinned to their seats or against the wall of the stifling cellar. People stood three deep at the bar. I volunteered to get the beers. After a twenty-minute wait to get served, I was to be next. I watched as the man in front of me, an olive-skinned young hedge-fund manager with a jumper over his shoulders, ordered precisely what I was about to order.

'I'll get three beers.' It was more of a statement than a request.

They were plonked in front of him, the tops flipped off by expert Swiss hands, 'OK, that's twenty-five francs.'

I could see the mental arithmetic pass over my neighbour at the bar like a cloud. Why, that was about fifteen pounds for three small bottles of Becks. Oh well, so be it.

He passed over a luridly coloured note. The hand remained outstretched. 'Each. They're twenty-five each.'

He turned and left. So did I.

I later established that the queue for the bar consisted entirely of people like us; an endless procession of drinkers reaching the front, and turning straight around, beerless. Within fifteen minutes I was tucked up in bed, back in my chalet.

Woody and Liam had less luck. They stayed a little longer out of politeness, but then, on their way back up the hill, they had the great misfortune to stumble across a 200-Swiss-franc note lying in the street. Presumably it'd been dropped by someone rifling through their chinos in search of their

BlackBerry. My colleagues were soon bounding happily back to the bar, fully intending to hand the lost money straight in to the nearest barman. Which is what they did, in exchange for beer. They returned very late indeed.

The Verbier rest day dawned along with the realisation that Bradley Wiggins, who had just ridden himself into a podium position, had decided to hold a press conference. We should probably cover it, even though it was technically our day off too. He was staying some sixty kilometres away, down in the valley below. Wearily, Liam and I drove to Wiggins's hotel, only to find out that he'd taken a helicopter to Lake Annecy to ride a bit of the time trial course. But he would indeed be back later to hold a press conference in the early afternoon.

We returned to Verbier, irritated beyond measure by the sudden removal of the word Rest from our Rest Day. We just had time to dump our stinking washing at the World's Most Expensive Launderette for a service wash, where the lady behind the counter nearly called the police at the sight of Liam's favourite pale blue Fred Perry polo.

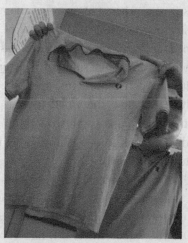

She had a point. The smell released when Tour bags are peeled open is indescribably bad. On the 2010 Tour we arrived in the most beautiful little boutique hotel in Bagnères-de-Bigorre on a rest day. After a string of soulless chain hotels in industrial estates, this was a place so immaculate, tasteful and welcoming that it made us want to weep.

But instead of crying, we unzipped our suitcases in the perfect sweet-smelling foyer and began to stuff dirty washing into black plastic bags to take to the launderette. We could have done this in the privacy of our own rooms, but instead chose to transfer our washing in full view of the charming lady who owned and designed this jewel of a hotel. Our hostess, still holding on to her smile of welcome, backed off visibly and, with one deft movement, opened a set of French doors at the back to allow the smell to dissipate a little. I hope we had the good grace to blush. I think we did.

Back in Verbier though, our washing safely under way, we had an issue to grapple with.

I had failed to mention to Woody the possibility that we might have to work on our rest day. So he'd taken advantage of the chance of a proper lie-in, by getting to bed at 6.30 a.m., about 100,000 Swiss francs worse off, no doubt. The trouble was, we needed him to come with us to the press conference. It was already midday.

We needed him to wake up. We had to wake him. Liam had to wake him.

I waited in the car outside the chalet, the kit loaded up, and ready to go. Liam reappeared to tell me how badly the news had been received. It seems I was not popular. It was just as he was relaying the extent and exact nature of the abuse heaped on my head by my loyal friend and sound recordist that we caught sight of a figure pressed up against a window on the third floor. Woody, it seemed, quite unaware that his shower looked directly over the street, was scrubbing himself into life under the running water, quite naked, and quite visible to anyone walking by.

Wonderfully, the shower seemed to last for ever. After three or four minutes, I had stopped crying with laughter, and simply sat gazing up at the window in delight.

He appeared a little while later, clutching his sound kit, and shades on. The act of telling him what we'd seen from the street set us off laughing again. Woody, it has to be said, didn't enjoy the joke.

'Let's go.' We drove the rest of the way in silence.

One of these days he'll see the funny side of it. Probably when he reads this book and sees that I've included the picture.

CONCLUDING ARMSTRONG

I went to a branch of Radio Shack last July, mysteriously drawn in by the logo, the big round 'R'.

Radio Shack, the US equivalent of Tandy, was the headline sponsor for Lance Armstrong's last ever team. But to me, and to millions around the world, the big round 'R' was simply a visual shorthand for Armstrong.

I have a curious response to 'out of context' sightings of things I associate with the Tour de France. For example, recently I was thrilled to discover how many UK hardware retailers now stock Quick Step laminate flooring, the main sponsor of the Belgian national team. Each time I come across it in a store, I stop momentarily and consider laying some parquet wholly unnecessarily over my floorboards at home. I

gravitate needlessly to branches of Caisse d'Epargne to withdraw money in France, and I would always favour Liquigas
for all my Italian-based propane needs.

All right, I might have made that last one up, but the sight
of a Norbert Dentressangle truck on the M40 is enough to
send me careering into the central reservation. I simply forget
that these products and services have a life outside their
sponsorship of the Tour de France.

The 2010 Tour was scarcely five days dead, and here I was,
in a small ugly town called North Conway at the foot of the
White Mountains of New Hampshire, staring at the bland
exterior of a branch of America's favourite electrical accessories
retailer. I sat in my car, gazing at the store. What impulse had
brought me here?

Primarily it was the need to purchase an audio jack lead.
But also, I was curious. My last meeting with Armstrong
had not gone well. I felt like he and I had a little unfinished
business to resolve.

He would have been blissfully unaware of this, but as I
sat and watched as the Radio Shack branch manager unlocked
the doors at exactly nine o'clock (I was the first customer of
the day), I was filled with the compulsion to make contact
with him one more time, and settle so many conflicting issues
once and for all. I guess a little bit of me hoped to find him
there, beavering away in the storeroom, or dusting the digital
camera display.

I flipped back the days of the calendar, imagined my drive
back to Boston. Mentally, I reboarded the plane, before arriving
back at Heathrow the day after the Tour de France had
finished. I rattled back in time on the Eurostar, chatting to
Woody and Gary Imlach, before finding myself in the late
warmth of an otherwise dull afternoon on the Champs-Elysées.
The podium ceremonials were reaching their conclusion. I
was waiting for a last chance to interview Lance Armstrong.

The occasion was unusual from start to finish. Armstrong, who for so many years had annexed the top spot on the big yellow stage, and who only the previous year, 2009, had stood alongside Contador and Schleck in third place overall, had finished the Tour de France in twenty-third place. His presence on the podium was only required because his Radio Shack team had won the Overall Classification in the Teams Competition, a consolation prize so neglected, so meaningless in the grander schemes of the Tour de France, that even Armstrong looked a little sheepish in accepting it. He trudged off the stage one last time, and, allowing his teammates to slip ahead of him, turned to the waiting press cortege, and with a weary half-smile presented himself for his final duties; one last flourish in front of a cluster of microphones.

As ever, it was Frankie Andreu, his former teammate, who led off the questioning. With the weight of corporate middle America bearing down on his network, and therefore on him, his questioning wasn't exactly probing. 'You gonna miss all this, Lance?' was about the gist of it.

I allowed for Andreu to get three questions away. Then I threw one in.

I wanted to know if his head had been right. It was plain to see that his body was no longer willing. I wanted to find out from Armstrong if he had been distracted by the growing threat from the FBI investigation into doping on his former team. It sounded implausibly melodramatic, but that was the sub-story. That summer they were after him. The stakes got higher every day.

'Lance . . . !'

He turned ninety degrees and looked. He narrowed his light blue eyes minutely: a glance that I knew well, a balance of anger and disappointment. A muscle flinched at the base of his jaw as he clamped his mouth tight shut. Then he turned through ninety more, and was gone.

I watched him go. He looked old to me. I have always been appalled and amazed that I am a couple of years his senior. He seems old enough to be my dad.

He walked barely five paces before he disappeared from view and was engulfed by a wave of The Accredited, those myriad officials whose function on the Tour is indeterminate but whose presence in large numbers always suggests the proximity of Armstrong. A flash of yellow on the trim of his cycling jersey, and he was gone from the Tour.

I dropped my microphone down by my side. That was it then. The closest I would get to him now, and for the rest of time, would be Twitter.

Ever since Lance Armstrong started to 'tweet', he's been a mild disappointment to me. A man who used to inspire with his mental acuity, resolve and finesse now seems to have revealed himself as a banal kind of bloke. On reading his postings, I am often left with a feeling of deflation on finding that a man whose feral intensity so defined his aura drinks lager, insults enemies, toadies up to friends, waves the Stars and Stripes, guzzles chilli con carne and claims that digitally remastered American rock 'kicks ass'. It's almost like a mid-life crisis hooked up to the World Wide Web.

I need, then, to return to an age before Twitter, an innocent bygone age. I need to return to 2003 to recall my first impressions on being confronted by the rider whose myth was about to outgrow the race that had spawned it.

Lance Armstrong's name was the only one to have crossed the divide from the Initiated to the Ignorant. He had done it in a way that neither Indurain nor Hinault had managed before him. Perhaps only Eddy Merckx, in the modern era, had jumped out of the acres of newsprint in a similar fashion to emboss his name in the totality of public consciousness. In short, and it's a test I often apply as a gauge of someone's celebrity: My Mum Had Heard of Him.

And so had I. I hold my colleague and friend Simon Brotherton responsible. Afternoons spent listening to BBC radio in July would be characterised by an interruption to the Wimbledon rain interruptions, so that we could cross over to some anonymous town in France for the 'closing kilometres of today's stage in the Tour de France'. Simon, in his excellent straightforward way, would then call home the winner of the day: Cipollini, Zabel, whoever, before briefly being invited to explain how come the stage winner of the day wasn't going to win the overall race.

Once that misconception had been dealt with, talk would inevitably turn to Lance Armstrong, and Simon would be forced for the umpteenth time that summer to trot out the barest bones of the man's amazing biography; the Texan cancer survivor, now stamping all over the verge of greatness.

I am dealing with the past. I return to the moment when I first saw him. A small man on a vast stage, his presence saturated with meaning and importance. To get there I have to peel away the layers of ambiguity that have settled on my understanding of Armstrong. I have observed him at close quarters at the height of his powers, and I am no clearer in what I understand him to be.

I have been cynic and celebrant, sometimes both within the few seconds it takes to articulate a thought about Lance Armstrong. But, as sportsmen go, and they can be an appallingly anodyne bunch, his proximity, as an athlete and a spokesman for his own enterprise, is compelling. From my first encounters with him, he has drawn me in. When he talks, he has an extraordinary ability to listen carefully to the content of your question, grapple with the inevitable connotations, and shape it into a finely considered answer, full of nuance and conviction. In the midst of the chaos that accompanies the man through France he has the capacity to hone in on one point of focus.

There are those who feel very differently. Paul Kimmage, for one. He is the author of the outstanding *Rough Ride*, a book that talks candidly about doping in the peloton during the early 1990s when Kimmage himself was a professional cyclist. Kimmage is a man with rock-solid convictions. He quite pointedly uses the word 'cancer' when describing the Texan's influence on cycling. He has confronted Armstrong face to face, using just those terms. That takes some courage. For Kimmage, nothing moves independently of the Armstrong issue: it demands a resolution, and in so doing, it damns those who fail reach one. For Kimmage it is killing cycling.

He may be right.

There are others, too, who have soldiered on in search of the silver bullet, the single fact that will finally condemn Armstrong retrospectively in the analysis of history. David Walsh is one such man. The author of *L.A. Confidentiel* and *From Lance to Landis* has made it part of his life's work to accumulate evidence that will drag Armstrong down. It may be that British libel laws discourage its publication in the UK. In France, it sold a quarter of a million copies.

Walsh and I met in Johannesburg, where we were both covering the 2010 World Cup; he for the *Sunday Times*, I for ITV. I told him that I wanted to write this book, and that it would include a chapter about Armstrong. His only advice was this: 'Don't regret what you write, Ned. Don't look back at your words in later life, and regret the position you took.'

I let the door slide open in front of me, and walked into 'The Shack'. The air-conditioning nearly knocked me over, a frosty blast that made my eyes water. I made my way to an aisle filled to bursting with cables and leads, SCART, DIN, audio, mini-jacks, everything. I gazed blankly at them, as I listened to the hum of the air-conditioning housed somewhere in the rafters. I imagined the water draining off the unit into some hot dusty gully round the back of the building.

I thought about the hours of my life I had spent pressed up against the baking steel sides of Armstrong's team bus, watching as the air-con unit dripped an unrelenting flow of water onto the gritty earth beneath it before it ran away in a trickle under the bus.

Behind the tinted glass windows, of the bus I would imagine Armstrong sitting in super-cooled comfort, thinking about the race and drinking one last Coke before his shower. Perhaps he would have seen us outside, a phalanx of unmoving flesh, forced into a ridiculous tableau of clinches as our sweating bodies overlapped, and intertwined.

He was always on the inside.

I was on a beach when I heard the news that I assumed would wreck Lance Armstrong. It was the late summer of

2005. Just a few weeks earlier, he had won his seventh Tour and retired. I was staying in Valencia for Everton's Champions League qualifier up the road against Villarreal. By some coincidence, Simon Brotherton, the BBC's cycling commentator who also covers football, had joined me. Along with some football colleagues, we were enjoying an afternoon off on the beach, when I received a call from home.

'Have you read it?'

'Hello, Matt.' It was Matt. 'Read what?'

'This changes everything. This is the biggest moment in cycling history.' He went on to tell me of the headline in that day's *L'Equipe*. '*Le mensonge Armstrong.*' The Armstrong lie.

L'Equipe had revealed that frozen urine samples, voluntarily given, from the 1999 Tour had been unfrozen and retrospectively tested for the presence of EPO, the blood-booster. Two of Armstrong's had tested positive. These tests had been conducted for scientific research purposes, and not under the auspices of the anti-doping authorities. Nonetheless, this was the first time that EPO and Armstrong had appeared in the same sample. It felt important. Actually it felt like the point of no return.

Simon was wallowing in the waves, a little way out. I turned to my left and told the astounding news to the first person I could find. This person turned out to be Jim Beglin, ITV's football co-commentator and former Liverpool full-back. The politest man in television wasn't about to tell me he couldn't have cared less. But I could tell he couldn't have cared less.

I jogged down the beach, and swam out to where Simon was, unable to contain myself. I gabbled my news at him. He chose his words carefully.

'Well, if it's true, it's not good. In fact, it's probably the end of our summers. Cycling is the Tour de France and the Tour is Armstrong.' He stood up to reveal that the sea was actually only waist high.

Then, he concluded. 'He'll say it's not true, though. You know that he reckons the French would do anything to ruin him.'

And so it came to pass. The *L'Equipe* warhead fell short, dropped into the sea detonating somewhere off the coast of Spain, and only splashed its intended target. Armstrong's denials stood up in court and against the scrutiny of public opinion, although that depends on which side of the Atlantic you draw your poll sample.

His defence seemed to amount, just as Simon Brotherton has presaged, to 'probably not true, you know the French'. He accused the French laboratories of tampering with his samples. Armstrong's image remained intact, and international reaction amounted to little more than a raised eyebrow. What seemed at first a devastating accusation just melted away.

Besides, back in America, the man was about to file his application for sainthood. It was an application that had some merit. I do not have the facts and figures to hand, but the monies raised in his name, or rather, its catchily adapted cousin 'Livestrong', are truly vast. His name and his cause now constitute a global phenomenon.

More pertinently, the inspiration (and that is not a word one uses lightly) of Armstrong's personal battle has helped countless cancer sufferers to fight their illness. That is a remarkable achievement, which, in the eyes of many, constricts the room for criticism.

I think of Geoff Thomas, the footballer, who I met briefly in 2001 at the fag end of his long and very accomplished playing career. A couple of years later I met him again, this time as he was recovering from leukaemia. His discovery was Armstrong's book. His passion became cycling. He rode the route of the Tour de France twice. He went on to set up his own charity, which in turn has raised millions of pounds. Wonderfully, Geoff is now in roaring good health. Such things are not there to be sniffed at.

Yet, here's the thing, and it has to do with Venn diagrams.

For me, Armstrong has two sets. Set A: Lance, Seven Times Tour de France Winner. Set B. Lance, Cancer Survivor, Cancer Research Fundraiser.

In the minds of marketing men, the two sit on top of each other, to the extent that you are no longer sure which is a subset of which. They are inseparable.

Yet, that is not how it should be. While Set B can be enhanced and aided by Set A, the same should not apply in reverse. Armstrong's record as an athlete stands and falls by the things he did on a bike, and the things he did to win bike races. There is no subset. They exist independently of one another.

I was honing in now on what I wanted. I scrutinised the box. Audio cable. Mini-jack to mini-jack. Three-foot long. Perfect.

At the cash desk a man in his early sixties was already smiling as I approached from the far end of the store, and extending his hand to receive the goods.

'How're you going?' he asked, with a pleasant, shy grin.

'I'm very well, thanks' – I glanced at his name badge – 'Mike.'

Then I was seized by a sudden idea. Perhaps Mike could help me clarify my thoughts about Armstrong. He might be able to sum it all up, to put an end to my feelings of ambivalence with a pithy one-liner.

'Did you watch the Tour de France?' He looked up from the till. 'I mean, you've got loads of TV sets here. Were you showing the cycling? Did you watch Team Radio Shack?'

'Sure. We had it on most days. I guess I watched it pretty much all.'

'And Armstrong?'

'Well.' He handed me my cable. 'He's kinda done, I guess. He looks cooked to me.'

I had to agree. I said goodbye to Mike, and walked back to my car, clutching my Radio Shack receipt.

BLOKES ON BIKES

There's a strange thing going on with cycling. It permeates the sport at all levels. And despite the best efforts of the big-brand, big-time marketers, it's never managed to shake off the inconvenient truth: it's actually just a bunch of blokes on their bikes. That's all.

There's no getting away from it. Despite the valour, and the mythology. Despite the global media frenzy, the heroism and the Wagnerian settings, cycling remains a sport which is contested by a bunch of blokes riding bikes really fast.

I used to ride my bike really fast, too. Well, ish. I think back to my blue Raleigh Olympus on which I used to trundle around Bedford, from the park to the school to the swimming pool. I am painfully reminded of my awkward twelve-year-old alter-ego. Pudding-bowled, in a blue zip-up pacamac, I was as dull and predictable as an episode of *Wogan* on a wet Tuesday night. But on my bike, I enacted a wordless and naïve narrative, which involved heroes and villains and derring-do, as well as plenty of kerb-jumping and the odd half-arsed wheelie. I was King. A Man among Men.

There was a particular fantasy, which I enacted, where I imagined that, in some bizarre and unspecified way, I was chauffeuring the Prime Minister around, on my Raleigh Olympus. I had been handpicked for the job clearly on the understanding that I was the best, the very best there was at negotiating the smoothest passage through the suburban streets of Bedford. I could provide a seamlessly gentle ride along Stanley Street, avoiding all the well-known potholes, as well as the more subtle variations in road surface of which a lesser rider might fail to be aware. I could negotiate passage through the pedestrianised area that linked Tavistock Road to Chandos Court. I drew praise for this ability from the highest quarters of government. I drew on the personal gratitude of the imaginary statesmen. I would chastise myself remorselessly for any unnecessary jolting, however accidental. At the end of each ride, I awarded myself points out of ten. It was never a perfect ten, but it was never much worse than a seven, either.

Of course this all neatly avoided the fact that actually it was the early eighties and I was an average sort of boy in an average sort of town. But my bike, at least to me, gave me my otherness. It bore me in vertiginous repeating figures of eight around the bandstand in the middle of the Bedford park. It fed my imagination, and gave me the space to lose myself in fiercely real trains of thought, mind games for the mild-mannered.

When I rediscovered the desire to hop on a bike and push off on my own, I was in my mid-thirties, and had started to grow a little soft around the edges. It was on returning from covering the 2003 Tour de France that I went to the nearest bike shop and got myself a second-hand road bike. To my amazement though, the act of pedalling and feeling the tarmac skitter along underneath you instantly flicked on a switch that had been dormant for decades. Straight away, I was off again. I was not so much lost in thought as not quite there, somewhere else. A connection had been made across fields of my life, which I never thought possible. I was riding in a paceline with my twelve-year-old self, taking turns to pull at the front.

I am, in this respect, making no claims to uniqueness. In fact, I would suggest that cycling's huge appeal to the middle-aged man is based on precisely this desire, whether witting or unconscious, to connect with a time in which his life seemed a simpler, more harmless kind of existence. The MAMIL (Middle-Aged Man In Lycra) leaves it so late in life to hop back on his bike because he first of all has to build up enough things in his life that he needs to escape. And that can take time.

Sadly, now, I cannot fully engage with the chauffering game. Something has clearly withered within me, possibly my soul. But that hasn't stopped the recessive twelve-year-old gene inside me from inventing more age-appropriate nonsense to lend my cycling a meaning and a purpose and a pleasure, which still makes even the most banal ride a private thrill.

Can I maintain an average of 15 mph even on a commute through central London, with its many red lights? A glance at my computer tells me I've dipped to 14.7 mph. This is a disaster.

Can I beat the number 180 bus from Woolwich to Greenwich? (Easy.) Shall I deliberately ride on the thick white lines even when it's drizzling? (Not a safe thing to do, but quite exhilarating.) Shall I stick to the inside of the traffic as they queue through Deptford, or shall I be Mr Outside, the fearless firebrand of the middle of the road?

There it is. I am just a Bloke on a Bike.

Which brings me back to professional bike racing. However much it is obscured by the scale of the event, there is something a little bit ridiculous about it all. We have constructed a pedestal on which we place the finest Twelve-Year-Old Boy that humanity can produce. Even Lance Armstrong at the age of thirty-eight, standing on this pedestal that we have called the podium, cannot be immune from the nagging feeling, very, very deeply hidden, that he too is just a small boy in black socks with his knees showing.

Can I beat Jan Ullrich from Bourg d'Oisans to Alpe d'Huez? (Easy.) Shall I pick up my bike and run across the fields on the descent into Gap? (Not a safe thing to do, but quite exhilarating.)

So it is then that cycling occupies two different spaces in our understanding. It is both the realm of the incredible, and the ordinary. And in this respect it is unique.

Football is a sport that offends many a cycling purist. Do not listen to such prejudice. At best, it is born of jealousy, and at worst, class snobbery. Football, even at a very 'average' level, is a game of tremendous skill and courage. It works emotionally and aesthetically as a game because of the tension between the controllable and the chaotic which runs through it.

It is founded on a flawed premise, which lends it the beauty and the passion it can inspire, and that premise is simple: it's almost impossible to master a ball without using your hands. A foot coming into controlled contact with a ball is fundamentally a nonsense. Like using a carrot for a chisel, or a sock as a bucket, it's designed to madden. That's why those rare moments when a player connects cleanly with the ball thrill in the way they do. Wayne Rooney's overhead kick in the Manchester Derby will only happen once in his career.

I have never been anything other than awful at football. And not once have I either sat in the press box, or stood on the terrace, and even fleetingly thought to myself, 'I could do that.'

But here's the difference. We can all ride a bike. And, to the untutored eye, the way that I ride a bike, and that you ride a bike, and Andy Schleck rides a bike, is much of a muchness. He might just be a bit quicker.

So when we watch these acts of greatness from the Tour, for all our *chapeau*-doffing deification of the riders, there is in all of us a little voice, muffled into muteness for the most part, which is wondering, 'What if, instead of Contador, that was me? How would I have reacted when Schleck attacked? I would have gone with him, I reckon. Then, as I caught him, I would have accelerated again, just where the gradient gets steeper. Then I would have time-trialled to the finish, and gained fifty seconds on him. That's what I would have done.'

How many times, rooting for the underdog perhaps, or simply hoping for a more competitive spectacle, have we railed against a rider who has reached the limits of his power and can respond no more when a rider attacks? If it had been us, we'd have been up on our pedals and back at 'em. It's the equivalent of shouting 'Slog out!' from the margins of a tedious cricket match.

Watching the Tour from afar is one thing. Working alongside the riders allows for this sense of ambiguity to breed and replicate: the slightly destabilising perception of unremarkable men doing remarkable things. Or even remarkable men doing unremarkable things. This is the confusion, which arises from the fact that we come face to face with these extraordinary men, in all their perplexing ordinariness.

And so it is, that I take you, rather bumpily, to Stage 10 of the 2003 Tour. It was one of those breathless days in Marseille when the thermometer threatens forty, and the humidity means that any effort of more than token exertion brings about a beading of the forehead.

It was the middle eight of the Tour. The week between mountain ranges, when the race leaders hide in the pack. Normally, of course, this is a chance for the sprinters to reach for more stage wins, but occasionally a breakaway will form which gets away. On this particular day, they left it late. It wasn't until the race was blasting along the shimmering Marseille seafront that two riders broke clear. There was Fabio Sacchi, riding for Mario Cipollini's Saeco team. And there was a Dane called Jakob Piil.

He and I were about to be brought into very close proximity. But first of all he had to win the race.

Once that pair realised that they were clear of the bunch, and that one or other of them was going to win the stage, their cooperation turned to competition. They briefly sat up and shook hands. Sacchi said something to Piil, who later confessed, 'I don't speak Italian. I have no idea what he said. I guess he wished me luck, but who knows.'

I often suspect that the Italian took the opportunity, like the dastardly Marco Materazzi to Zidane, to curse Piil, Piil's sister and Mrs Piil, his mother.

After the handshake, the serious cat-and-mouse game started. Both riders eyed each other closely, unwilling to be the first to go, trying to time their effort. In the end, it was Piil's track nous that won the day, as he picked his moment perfectly and out-sprinted Sacchi to the line.

And there he met me.

I was suffering the blurred vision and fatigued thinking of a man who's been squinting down the Avenue du Prado for half an hour, trying to pick out any sign of a bike race, as the sweat trickled into my eyes. And I was finding it hard to concentrate on anything at all, especially the race.

This was still my first Tour. In fact, my entire cycling experience was less than a fortnight old. I was still giddy with Alpine drama, gulping in deep lungfuls of Tour history with each passing day: Alpe d'Huez, Armstrong, Ullrich. Only a matter of hours before, I had been doorstepping a distraught Manuel Saiz, the directeur sportif of Team Once, the morning after his prize asset Joseba Beloki had smashed himself to pieces on a patch of melting asphalt.

There was more drama in a day of this great race than I had known in some entire football seasons.

Now, though, I was confronted with this. A stalemate. A day of sleepy nothing. Armstrong and Ullrich invisible, and the race so uninterested in expending effort that it allowed these two nobodies to bore us all with their footling little victory. A marginal achievement, surely.

I didn't know then what I know now. There is great emotion attached to these days. They are moments of grace, really, when an individual's efforts, instead of vanishing into an uninterested peloton, are rewarded with the defining second in a decade-long career. I don't know Jakob Piil, but I suspect, somewhere in his house, maybe upstairs in his study, or in a games room in the cellar, he has hung a framed photograph. Piil, riding to the right of Sacchi, his arms bent to the task, the skin on his knuckles stretched taut. There is a look on his face of the most complete delight, given its potency by a wide-eyed surprise that has forced his mouth open as he screams into the cacophonous Marseille air.

Me? I'd never heard of him.

The two men were riding at seventy kilometres per hour towards us. We were positioned, along with the whole of the rest of the vast press pack, at a minimum safety distance of some 150 metres away. So it would have taken 7.71 seconds before he arrived at my feet.

He flew at me, as if guided by the some PR-conscious God, as if he had no choice. He might have aimed for my impeccably turned-out Danish counterpart. He might have ridden right past us all and vanished to leave us chasing along behind him. He might have done any number of things, but instead, at the zenith of his chosen profession, at the moment of his greatest triumph, where all things came together for him and he scored his name in the history of the sport, he came to rest inches from Ned Boulting, ITV Sport's bewildered and unprepared reporter, whose eyebrows were bleaching in the sun, and whose sunburnt ears were now beginning to pulse.

As Piil fumbled for the clasp of his helmet dangling under his chin and fell dizzily onto his crossbars, I had time to note the fevered rise and fall of his ribcage. Each breath in, seen from his back, forced the bumps of his vertebrae apart. They collapsed back together again. You could almost hear them clattering. I felt a pressure building behind me. Within seconds, within the space of half a dozen shudders from the gasping athlete, the bundle had begun. A hundred people perhaps, dozens of microphones, cameramen, sound recordists, journalists, the usual madness of men and women. All of us now crowded into Jakob Piil's private world. I leant hard back on my heels pushing against the encroaching wall of hardware and flesh to avoid being spreadeagled across the diminutive Dane.

And then, equally suddenly, the realisation hit me that everyone was waiting for me to speak. Even Piil. I was the chosen one. The fates had thrown me to his feet, or rather he to mine, and now I would have to oblige them. The code of honour, such as it exists among the press corps, held firm: this was my interview, I must lead the way.

I looked at Piil, and cleared my throat. He had his helmet off now, and turned to face me with bloodshot, staring pie-eyes. They were wild with his triumph.

I drew the microphone towards me and fired. 'Jakob,' I said. 'You won!'

To this day I have no idea what he replied. For in that instant I realised the complete inadequacy of my effort, and I felt keenly the absurdity of our position. Leaning back at sixty degrees, with arms and wires and poles jabbing through me and across me and under me, I wore the simpleton journalist's expression of smiling absorption as Piil provided us with the sound bite we required. A sizeable chunk of the world's media had descended on this man and this spot on this Marseille street to gather this information. And yet, I swear, none of us could have cared less. We weren't even listening to what he was saying. I started to suppress a terrible desire to giggle.

Back in the truck, Gary and Steve had no need to hide their mirth. They were watching a locked-off aerial shot of the finish line provided by France Télévisions. They could see it all unfolding before them on their monitors. It was a bizarre sight: all these people, a hurricane of press and me and Jakob at the eye.

I can't remember how it all dispersed. I suspect that Piil was manhandled away from all of us by the Tour heavies so that he could ready himself for presentation on the podium. Or perhaps the main field came in, and drew friendly fire. Yes, that would have been in it, I suspect. As the yellow jersey and the rest crossed the line, the perfect storm of pressmen would have dissolved as quickly as it formed, leaving Jakob talking into thin air, his moment of glory already, even now, starting to wear thin. A straw fire.

I saw him a few days later, and we spoke again, briefly. I was at Jan Ullrich's T-Mobile hotel, waiting for the surly German to come out and not give me an interview. It just so happened that CSC, Piil's team, were billeted in the same Campanile hotel. The door to one of the first-floor rooms opened onto a wooden balcony overlooking the central courtyard. A small, blond figure emerged in a CSC tracksuit, and began to make his way downstairs to the dining room.

I couldn't quite place him. Nor, I could tell, could the few dozen cycling fans who were stalking the T-Mobile team. Only when he approached where we were lurking with a meek smile of recognition playing over his lips, did I realise it was Piil. I said hello and congratulated him again. He thanked me and went in for dinner, passing lines of autograph hunters who paid no attention to him.

He had been the centre of the cycling world some three days prior. Now, no one knew him. He was thirty years old then. He rode on for a year or two more before packing it in. He had a good, but ordinary sort of career.

He seemed like an ordinary sort of man; a bloke on a bike, in fact, who, on 15 July 2003, did something extraordinary.

I wish I'd had a better question lined up for him.

ABOVE US ONLY SKY

When I first found out about the birth of Team Sky, I was out on a run with Chris Boardman. It was during the Tour of 2008. We had absented ourselves from the rest of the production team one morning, and set off in search of ten kilometres of release.

But it was one of those frustrating routes, and we never quite got going. We were forever running into cul-de-sacs, into roundabouts, or up dual carriageway slip roads. The conversation was much more fluent.

Chris was only working with us at the weekends that year, and had just flown back in to join us. During the week, he had been party to the ongoing negotiations between Dave Brailsford, the head of British Cycling, and a few potential sponsors, as the idea for the British pro team began to take concrete shape. I was fascinated, and wanted to find out more.

'Go on, Chris. Where's the money coming from? What's the team going to be called?' I tried to persuade him to give me the inside track as we vaulted a central reservation and dashed across the fast lane of a dual carriageway.

'I couldn't possibly tell you. I'd have to shoot you. And I don't have a firearms licence.'

'You could tell me and then just break my neck,' I panted. 'Or you could just carry on running at this bloody pace. That'll probably get the job done.' Chris had run the London Marathon that year, and was still racing fit.

'Well. One's a supermarket . . .'

'Londis?' I quipped, simply because it was a short word and I didn't have enough puff to get 'Morrisons' out.

'. . . and the other one isn't,' Chris added, cryptically.

I waited. It's often the best way with Chris. He may tell you stuff. In fact he probably will. But sometimes you have to wait. We ran on, aware of the sound our trainers made slapping against the tarmac.

'I'm not sure how much longer the Tour will be shown on ITV,' he continued mysteriously.

'What do you mean?' I shouted at his back as he put in an unaccountable little injection of pace.

'Someone else will want to show it. Because they will want to show their own team.' He slowed a fraction. I caught up. 'Let me just say, a leading supplier of satellite dishes,' Chris revealed.

'Sky?' I deduced, brilliantly.

Sky! It almost stopped me in my tracks. My first thought, I am ashamed to say, was selfish. It suddenly occurred to me that Chris might be right. I might be working on my penultimate Tour de France. The TV rights, as of 2010, were up for renewal, and it was by no means certain that ITV would retain them. The prospect of losing the gig was unsettling. I gazed at Boardman's briskly retreating form, and put in a middle-aged sprint to try and catch him up. He was loping along the hard shoulder towards a motorway bridge.

For the next twelve months, through to the following summer, I was disturbed by the introduction of Team Sky. TV is a fiercely parochial business sometimes, and I was proud and protective of the little fiefdom that ITV4 had annexed for the Tour de France. Frankly I didn't want the big boys muscling in. After all, I knew a little about Sky.

From 1997 to 2001, I was training up as a reporter for Sky Sports, working with Jeff Stelling on the iconic 'men-watching-football-on-a-telly' show *Soccer Saturday*. It was a good place to learn. I owe my career to the people there who encouraged me.

But it was also a brash, tough environment and, good though my grounding was, I was pleased in the end to move on. Sky, as a corporation, can be a lean, mean place. A former member of the BSkyB board, whom I have got to know very well down the years, has often told me that the reason for their success is that they are a retailer, first and foremost. Not a broadcaster. They sell satellite dishes. They are extremely good at it, too.

I considered it to be inevitable that they would acquire the TV rights to the Tour. It would not be uncomplicated, but I was sure that they would find a way of pushing aside both British Eurosport and ITV, the subscription and free-to-air rights holders respectively. The cost of buying the race would be piffling compared to the investment they were about to make in Dave Brailsford's team.

Yet some months later, and much to my amazement, ITV re-signed the Tour de France for another four years, from 2010 through to and including the 2013 Tour. While I was delighted, I was also puzzled, and curious to see how it would feel to be 'calling home' a British team that bore the name of a rival broadcaster.

I decided from the outset to try and get as involved as I could with the new team. I met with a delegation from Sky in Monaco for the start of the 2009 Tour. I shook hands with the marketing men who were the financial engine room of the whole project, and we agreed that I would start to make a film about the birth of the team.

It was not without its complications. My intention was to shoot a fly-on-the-wall documentary. But the problem was access. Too often, we found ourselves on the exterior wall, while all the interesting stuff was happening inside. All autumn, and into the winter, Sky were negotiating with Garmin to liberate Bradley Wiggins from his contract. All along, I knew that they were close to signing him, and yet I couldn't get any of the main players in the drama to talk frankly about the situation in front of rolling cameras, such was their fear of litigation and counter-litigation.

Instead, I was steered towards expending valuable filming days shooting the design elements of the team, from their Pinarello bikes and the endless quest for the right kit, to the all-important team bus. It was interesting, glossy stuff, but it didn't make for great drama. Finally, we politely agreed to go our separate ways and forget the project. I believe, in the end, that Dave Brailsford had gone cool on the idea, and it was quietly shelved.

Along the way, though, I got a good feel for how the team might work. We were privy to the first team meet-up in Manchester in November 2009. All the riders (minus Wiggins, who was still a matter of weeks away from signing) were there. It was a big 'get-to-know-you' session, really. And it was a little overwhelming for some of the riders. The team was just showered with stuff.

Beautiful new Pinarellos, MacBooks and iPhones (the Apple image chimes in perfectly with Dave Brailsford's minimalist aesthetic), Adidas kits and leisurewear, and Marks & Spencer suits. I listened to Geraint Thomas in the foyer wondering aloud what he was supposed to do with two iPhones. The management team was equipped with crisp white shirts and dark tank tops.

Overnight more goodies would appear in the riders' bedrooms. On their first night they found a little bag of bespoke M&M's on their pillows, bright blue and printed perfectly with the Sky logo. They'd been imported from somewhere in Canada, at undisclosed expense. The next evening they found their pillowcases had been swapped for special custom-made designs featuring a thin blue embroidered line; the same one that adorned their kits and their bikes. They were now to rest their sleeping heads on Sky's branded embroidery. Corporate dreams. Another evening they found especially acquired toothpaste in their rooms. Blue stripes, naturally.

Downstairs, the team had taken over the hotel. Two rooms had been converted into photo studios where moody mugshots were being banked up for future use by the website. Another room was occupied by a TV crew. It was the same one that Sky Sports use to film their team line-up graphics on their football coverage. Shot against a green-screen background, which would later be cut out, the riders were each asked to take three or four portentous steps towards the camera and then come to a halt, arms folded and staring edgily into the lens.

Nigel, the team's ebullient nutritionist, was floating around the place, pulling riders to one side, one by one, and talking to them about the science of eating right. I watched him patiently explaining the word 'mitochondria' to an attentive Kurt Asle Arvesen.

Brailsford and his management team occupied the most important area of all. A dozen of them in their identical tank tops sat all day for two days in a conference room, around a big table surrounded by notes. Each rider was called in to discuss their season's targets, and how the coaching staff might best help to achieve them. We were allowed in briefly to witness Edvald Boasson Hagen shyly suggest that he wanted to concentrate on winning Paris–Roubaix and then secure his place on the team for the Tour de France.

No cycling team had ever been prepared in this way. The riders who had joined from more conventional continental set-ups, such as the Frenchman Nicolas Portal, could scarcely believe what they were seeing. That sense of incredulity would scarcely have been lessened by the glitzy team launch, which drew hundreds of people to Millbank on a freezing cold January morning.

The kits were printed, the bus was buff, and Wiggins was signed; declarations of ambition were dropping into sound bites all over the airwaves.

So when the 2010 Tour came along the following summer, it was all a bit of an anticlimax.

I joined the race late. The World Cup in South Africa delayed my arrival until the first rest day. On 11 July, just as Andrés Iniesta was scoring the only goal of the World Cup final, I boarded a plane from Johannesburg to Heathrow, where I changed to Geneva. By two o'clock the following afternoon, I was swinging around in the back of a car being driven in typically unpredictable fashion by Liam. We ate dinner in a village near Avoriaz in the French Alps, and went back to the chalet where we were being put up. Instantly I felt at home, even though I was staying somewhere I'd never been before.

The following morning, we rose early and chatted to our English hostess over breakfast. Running the pleasant chalet where we had spent the night was just a sideline for her, it seemed. She and her husband actually ran a company which, to put it simply, made giant stickers.

A few days prior to our arrival in the Alps, their company had, purely by chance, been contacted by Team Sky. The cycling team wanted to know if they could print and apply a new logo to the side of their bus during the rest day. You should not underestimate how important logos are to Sky. I was present back in September of the previous year when they test-filmed six different designs for the team kit to see what the jerseys looked like in 'race conditions' on TV. Some of the of the logos were blue, some white, some transparent, like their poster campaigns on billboards which allow the 'content to shine through'. They had started the 2010 Tour in Rotterdam with a straightforward silver logo on the side of their bus. Then, when Geraint Thomas had briefly, brilliantly, worn the white jersey, they had changed the logo to white. Now that he was no longer in white, they flipped once again, this time settling on a blue metallic number.

So our hostess had spent the Monday applying the latest version to the bus. The third design in just over a week. It was a high-pressure sticker, no doubt about that. I dread to think what might have happened to her if she'd left any bubbles in it.

The stickers worked. The bus worked. The Jaguar team cars worked a treat, as did the personalised number plates.

The huge satellite dish that unfolded from the top of the bus roof worked, too.

On a couple of occasions I knocked on the curtain (if such a thing were possible) that divided the cool air-conditioned interior of the bus from the baking rest of France, and popped my head inside. Dave Brailsford, Rod Ellingworth and few others would be sitting in the front few seats of the extravagantly equipped coach, watching the Tour on a huge pull-down HD projector TV.

That all worked fine. The only problem was the rest of it. The actual race. Geraint Thomas's gutsy ride across the cobbles aside, it was a pretty damp squib for the world's best-equipped cycling outfit. No stage wins.

And no challenge from Wiggins.

Having been so captivated by 2009, this was the biggest disappointment of all. Watching on from South Africa during that first week, I had a hollow feeling as I absorbed how he fared on the climbs. I watched him fall off the pace on the climb up to Avoriaz. Even from that distance of several thousand miles, it was abundantly clear that he was not the same rider as he'd been the previous year. I knew that I was heading to France the next day. I wasn't particularly looking forward to our first encounter.

Our paths didn't cross for a good few days, and when we did meet, it was a relief. Wiggins had finally got it off his chest, deciding that a little frankness would loosen the pent-up pressure that had so far stifled his Tour.

'I have to confess, last year was a bit of a fluke,' he told us, dramatically understating his considerable achievement of 2009.

We stood in front of the team bus, Wiggins talking humbly and sensibly. Then the Sky press officer gave me the traditional 'off camera' guillotine sign, and I thanked him for his time.

He sloped away and, aside from a cluster of British cycling fans, no one seemed to take much notice. Dave Millar summed it up when he spoke of the difficulty in matching up the expectations not just of his huge salary but also of the fact that he now had a team solely built around propelling him up the General Classification ladder.

Perhaps Team Sky's stated aim to produce a British Tour de France winner within the next four to five years was never really going to be about Wiggins. There are a number of much younger home-grown talents who were supposed to sit on his metaphorical wheel over the next few years, before themselves assuming the mantle of team leader. That ambition seems some way off right now. And who knows how many logos they might have gone through by then.

Much has changed in the landscape since I was first introduced to this race. The British have arrived, the American has gone and, even though the Devil may still be jumping up and down in his red leotard, the race has shape-shifted year on year into something else.

The arrival of Team Sky has moved it on again. In September their much-loved team bus parked up in rainy, windswept car parks up and down the country during the Tour of Britain.

Wherever it went, from Blackpool to Colchester, the fans besieged it, the clamour for autographs equal to almost anything you are likely to see on the Tour de France. And that probably tells you all you need to know about what might happen should they ever win the big one.

Team Sky has given the growing ranks of British cycling fans a point of focus, a spiritual home. One day soon, I am sure, it will graduate again to give them a point of genuine pride.

But, as far as I'm concerned, Sky, as a broadcaster, can keep the cricket, rugby, golf, speedway and boxing. As long as they leave the Tour to us. Please?

CAVENDISH – THE FINISH LINES

That hot afternoon in Châteauroux in 2007, Mark Cavendish won his first stage on the Tour de France. I caught a glimpse of him as he shot past me.

Three images: he is bent double over the handlebars, mouth suddenly gaping hugely at the realisation he's won. Then a split second later, sitting up and holding his two fists to his helmet, a gesture of incredulity, with something of the devil in it. Then he whacks the air, catching it with a violent right hook, keeping his arm extended. Somewhere in between these flash frames, he blurred past me, unfolding upright. A wild smudge of blue.

That moment blew to pieces all my assumptions about British racing on the Tour. The noise as it burst and fell around me was the sound of a glass ceiling shattering. This was suddenly a different game.

The first sign that everything was not quite as it was came when Mathieu Perez sought me out. In recent years, Mathieu has risen to prominence in ASO. He is the unshaven, unslept, pastis-guzzling chain-smoking doyen of the press. If he cared enough about his ambitions, I suspect he would have all it takes to rise through the organisation and one day become the race director. Only he's far too laid-back. Students of Tour coverage will recognise him. He's often to be glimpsed hanging on the left or right shoulder of the *maillot jaune*, holding an umbrella to keep the sun or rain off the shoulders of the anointed one, or simply coordinating things with a nod and a wink, like an understated auctioneer. He's the guy you see edging closer when the questioner has taken too long, placing a hand on the outstretched arm that holds the microphone, or grimacing displeasure when one too many questions are fired in. He's the conductor. We're the orchestra, albeit a multinational and unwashed one. And if the French, American and German media are the first violins, brass and percussion, we the Brits are accustomed to being the bassoons.

Yet it was the bassoons who got the nod that day. Mathieu indicated with film-noir nonchalance that we should make our way around the back to the inner sanctum, the holy of holies, the area directly behind the podium that teems with cycling's chosen few: podium girls, former champions, directeurs sportifs, stage winners and jersey wearers. We negotiated our way past the security, our passage eased by Mathieu's calm authority.

My first task was to conduct what is known as the 'Eurovision' interview. This is the first interview the winner gives and is broadcast by all the TV channels worldwide who either don't have a reporter on-site, or who don't have the airtime to wait for their own exclusive. I was handed a microphone by a smiling French floor manager. A cameraman arrived. A shining aluminium and leather stool was placed in front of me, and behind that one of those hideous and ubiquitous advertisers boards that bore the logo of a dozen different companies. But no Mark Cavendish.

And then all of a sudden there was. Hobbling in on his cleats and grinning widely, his progress hampered by waves of well-wishers and peers throwing their arms around his neck in congratulation. He was finally guided onto to the stool in front of me. He shot me a brief look of acknowledgement, and then drew long and hard on a tin of something cold and fizzy as he waited for me to start the questioning.

So where to start? This is the question: what is the question? A win is a win, surely.

What we want now, what TV demands to know, is the stuff that has remained hidden to this point, the stuff the blank stare of the lens cannot hope to unearth. The joy goes without saying; the delight is self-evident. TV wants to find out what the rider has within him: the hidden agenda, the feud resolved, maybe, the personal motivation born from some sense of grief or injustice or anger. Can the rider blurt this emotion out? Can he paint words for us all, which bring back the thrill of watching the win unfold? What can he say to make a good feeling better? And, I return to my initial question: where do I start?

I refuse to ask, 'How does it feel?' It's tempting, but I know that reporters who ask that are a pet hate of my dad, and the last thing I want to be aware of is an image of him sitting at home cursing the inadequacy of the question.

No, 'How does it feel?' is taboo. It's off the table. But actually it's the question most closely related to the answer you want to hear. You want to hear precisely that: 'Oi! Superman! How does it feel to save the world?' These athletes, these 'gladiators', do things that none of us will ever experience. *How* must that feel? How does it *feel* to win a stage of the Tour de France? How *does* it feel?

'Mark. Congratulations. What a victory.'

With my BAFTA for incisive journalism firmly tucked away in my back pocket, I sat back and listened to Cavendish relive the race with a minutely detailed memory. He was wide-eyed with pleasure.

Later that night we found ourselves at the Campanile hotel in Châteauroux. The sun was just beginning to dip as Mark Cavendish made his way, post shower and massage, across a lawn towards us. If you could ignore the drone of traffic moving along the bypass the other side of a threadbare hedge, then it was a very special place. We sat down under a pine tree, and he talked again of his win, the relative quiet of our situation intensifying his thoughtful words. The shrill clamour of the finish line must still have been ringing in his ears, but I guessed the noise was fading.

His phone rang, mid-interview. It was his mum. 'Just doing the telly, Mum. I'll call you back.'

An hour or so later, we watched on and waited to film. We felt like unwanted guests at a private function, while team Columbia sat at their dinner table quietly delighted with themselves and their new star. Cavendish sat in the middle of the lot of them. He was flanked by George Hincapie and Kim Kirchen. A strip of late evening light fell horizontally into the dining room making him squint, as he, along with the rest of the team, raised a glass of red to the win.

Standing in a corner of the room, just a few feet away from this quiet, satisfied scene, I don't think I have ever felt more removed from the riders, nor felt as keenly the distance between those who can and those who can't, those who talk and those who act. I've drunk plenty of wine, but never, I would hazard a guess, a glass to rival how good that must have tasted to Mark Cavendish that night.

And then there came Toulouse. It was a day so wet that I walked two kilometres beyond the finish line to find a shoe shop, bought a new pair, left the old sodden pair there, and by the time I had got back to our truck, I had ruined the new pair too.

We did the post-race routine once more. Cavendish said much the same things, just as eloquently. This time we decided to leave him in peace at his hotel in the evening. Kristy, his PR rep, looked positively delighted.

After that, came the Pyrenees. Every day, we expected him to climb off. We asked him every day if it was going to be his last. But still he kept going.

He won again in Narbonne. Again the next day in Nîmes. Astonishingly, a sense of normality had established itself. I would hang back at the trucks for as long as I could, long enough to see the break caught, and Columbia hit the front, then saunter over to the podium, with one ear on what was going on. 'Get yourself over to the podium now, Ned, it's going to be Cav-tastic!'

Cav-tastic. An awkward phrase, more school playground than Tour de France, but it was rich with the curious pride we were taking in every winning ride. Cavendish was our man. He might not have known that, and he might have cared even less, but that was neither here nor there. We'd claimed him.

'Cavendish,' a breath from Liggett, 'wins again!'

The jolly French floor manager. His three fingers held out horizontally. Then two. Then one. Cavendish would know exactly when to drop the fizzy drink out of shot. When the red light flashed up on the front of the camera, we were off again.

'Mark. Congratulations. Three/four wins now.' I too was piling up the BAFTAs.

And then, suddenly, he left the race. And he left us wondering what we were going to talk about for the rest of the Tour. I got news that he was on his way to Lyon airport and heading home.

I rang up some contacts at Granada in Manchester, suggesting they send a crew straight away to the airport. A returning hero was on his way. But they hadn't quite grasped the full weight of his achievement.

'Oh, the cyclist fella. OK. So, is the Tour de France over then?'

My contact couldn't have sounded more underwhelmed if he'd tried. I think he would have preferred to send a crew to cover a chip-pan fire in Oldham than waste any time with this little Cavendish story.

'Still a week to go? Well, why's he coming home, then? Doesn't he want to try and win the Tour?'

I tried to explain the significance of what Cavendish had achieved. 'Isn't he from the Isle of Man, though?'

'Yes, he is.'

'Oh well.' I sensed he'd figured out his get-out clause. 'You're best off talking to Border TV. That's their patch. We don't cover the Isle of Man.'

We live in a bubble on the Tour. For a month it consumes us wholly. I was astonished to discover that the rest of the country didn't feel the same way as we did.

At last the 2008 Tour came to an end. It was the year in which we went from plucky patriots to all-conquering cock-a-hoop serial winners. And Mark Cavendish had blazed the trail for us. In the intervening eleven months I thought much about the man. I followed from afar his failure to secure a medal in the Madison at the Beijing Olympics, and was struck by how peculiarly low-key track cycling looked compared to the grandeur of the Tour.

Before long he was sweeping most before him again in the

Tour of Ireland, and in the Tour of Missouri, a race he chose in preference, and for the second year running, to the Tour of Britain. The thing that takes some understanding about Mark Cavendish is that he is, on the one hand, the archetypal pugnacious British scrapper, carrying into battle with him much of the raw aggression of Wayne Rooney, and some of the spirit of adventure of Daley Thompson. But on the other hand, he's a guy who buys into the world, every bit as much as the world has bought into him.

The life of a pro-rider is, to this day, an itinerant one. Cavendish is no different. He has travelled far and wide, and seen plenty. His horizons are as rich in texture as the bespoke BOSE sound system he's had installed in his Tuscan flat. It's here, in Quarata, with his boys, toys and hills, that the man seems truly at home. It's where he learnt his craft. It's where he served his time in the British Academy. It's how he wants to remain, among friends from home, but far from home.

I visited the little town for the first time in October 2009, a few months after Cavendish's astonishing six stage wins on the Tour. I was filming for my documentary about Team Sky. Dave Brailsford was there to speak to some of his riders, Ian Stannard, Geraint Thomas, Ben Swift, and Steve Cummings. Wherever we turned were British riders, all dressed from head to toe in the garish colours of the teams they were about to leave. They'd all been out on a training ride that morning, and now they were lolling about town, enjoying the rest, and the chat. They all had battered little Vespas, which they drove about the place. Espressos, gelato, mopeds. They were enjoying the whole Italian vibe.

Cavendish suddenly appeared, dressed from head to toe in Columbia canary yellow, astride a beautifully reconditioned 1950s Lambretta. He took his helmet off, slowly, as we came near, then with minimal eye contact, he simply asked, 'How long are you here for?' When we told him we would be gone in a couple of hours, he seemed to be satisfied. Our presence was an uncomfortable reminder to Cavendish, I suspect, of the country back home that claims him but doesn't really understand him.

If 2008 altered the shape of things for him, then 2009 cast them in iron.

In Monaco that year, at the Columbia team presentation, in a big hall near the famous switchback corner of Formula One fame, I sat to the side in the front row of the auditorium. As the lights dimmed and the hall grew quiet, they ran a video montage of Columbia's most recent triumphs on big screens scattered around the auditorium. I suddenly became aware, that at the stage door to the side, Mark Cavendish had appeared, alongside the legendary Erik Zabel, Columbia's new coach. There, in the darkness of the wings, they looked on. Cavendish, watching the film through the back of the projected screens, gazed up at his own achievements, his own image in reverse. He looked thoroughly unimpressed, and when it came to that time when the riders have to stand on a brightly lit stage with their hands behind their backs in tight-fitting clothes designed for riding bikes in, he could hardly have looked more ill at ease. All this was so much nonsense. He knew what he was capable of, and what he was about to deliver.

He won the first of his six stages in 2009 at the very first opportunity, Stage 1 into Brignoles. Job done. We might not have anticipated such instant success. He had.

The next morning at his hotel as we buzzed around making nuisances of ourselves, Liam noticed the appearance of a Second World War-style sticker on the fuselage of his bike to denote one target hit. That morning, he was particularly short with us. He was irritated that his bespoke green shorts and green shoes had not been delivered in time. He had a moan to his staff about it, and then posed reluctantly alongside Tony Martin and George Hincapie outside the team bus, sniping at the photographers for wasting seconds of his time.

That afternoon his team went on to produce the defining show of strength and skill of one of the great sprinters' trains. Columbia's team split the bunch on the run in to La Grande Motte (quite incidentally leaving Armstrong to pull clear of his team leader Alberto Contador), and setting up Cavendish for his second win.

'Cav-tastic'.

By the time of his third win, it was becoming so routine that my presence wasn't even deemed necessary. I was sent ahead of the race to film a piece in the town that would host the finish the following day. This time it was up a steep climb over the final 500m, the kind of finish that the pundits said wouldn't suit him. I made the mistake of putting this to him, after he had duly won number four.

'They reckoned the run-in wouldn't suit you today, Mark.'

'Who said that?' he squinted back.

'Well, plenty of people were saying that the uphill finish might not be ideal for you.' I hedged my bets, temporarily completely unable to remember who it was who'd actually said it, if indeed anyone had at all.

'What? Internet forum people?' He looked genuinely offended that anyone might have doubted this one particular weapon in his armoury. Even as he spoke, I thought how strange it was that this keen sense of vindication somehow needed verbalising. After all, he'd just delivered the most stunning rebuke to his doubters, by winning another stage; a fourth in a Tour that was barely halfway through.

Then a thought occurred to me, which explained a lot. He googles himself. He searches mentions of his name online. In a stroke it made him more human.

The fact that it mattered enough to him what Internet Forum People (IFPs) thought about his sprinting capacity was an expression to me of the fact that he had not quite left the human race. He was still made of the same DNA as the rest of us.

Anyone who dips their toes even slightly into the public realm has to make their peace at some point with IFPs. They lurk at the margin of your self-confidence, taking potshots. If you take out a pair of binoculars and scour the horizon, you will see clearly that the hedges and woods are filled with assassins, all out to get you. It's best to ignore them, before the paranoia overwhelms you and you end up like Diego Maradona, with a double-nostril-barrelled noseful of cocaine, aiming shots at the media camped outside your house.

But at this stage, and on into the spring of the following year, Cavendish's demons were still out to get him.

On Stage 3 of the 2010 Tour of Romandie, he notched up his third win of a stuttering early season that had been beset with internal political problems at HTC-Columbia, as well as some turbulence in his home life, a loss of form and dental problems in the winter. Instead of punching the air with delight to celebrate his return to winning ways, Cavendish chose to stab an emphatic 'V' sign skywards: a peculiarly British insult aimed squarely at the media, and, hiding behind them, the IFPs.

It was, if nothing else, amusing. In the past, Cavendish has spoken with eloquence and understanding of the fiscal contracts involved in professional road racing. He has often explained his obligations to his sponsors, talking in particular about how it is his team's job to get him to the point where he can launch his attack, and cross the winning line displaying his sponsor's logo to the widest possible audience. That's how it works; that's what's made him a millionaire. So, as the world's photo agencies pinged their wares around the ethernet, the images of Cavendish fully eclipsing the HTC logo on his chest with an act of playground profanity provoked mirth and censure in equal measure. It was, after all, pure Cavendish.

Back in 2009, and with that fourth win, he equalled the record held by Barry Hoban for the most stage wins accrued on the Tour de France by any British rider. I had been in phone contact with Barry for a week or so, anticipating the moment, and setting up the possibility of linking them together for a telephone interview should the moment happen. Hoban, a silver-tongued smoothie with a keen sense of perspective and a penchant for good PR, commissioned me over the phone to get a 'bloody good' bottle of champagne on his behalf, and to have it ready to give to Cavendish as and when the inevitable moment arose.

We couldn't quite stretch to 'bloody good', so settled for 'half decent', figuring that Barry probably wouldn't be able to tell the difference from the comfort of his living room. And so it was that the champagne was carted around, slowly getting warmer and fizzier as the great convoy passed through a drenching in the Vosges mountains and a heatwave in the Alps. It sat in the back of our Espace, winking its single gold-foiled eye and threatening to explode at any moment as we swung around switchbacks on our circuitous route to the foot of Mont Ventoux.

We nearly cracked it open in Besançon. But instead Cavendish lost the green jersey and the moral high ground by opening up a petty feud with Thor Hushovd, who he had appeared to impede in the final metres of a messy, ragged stage. He went on the following morning to accuse Hushovd of wearing a 'tainted' green jersey. Then, thankfully, he let the matter drop.

Five days later, we pulled up in a dusty car park in the middle of a forgettable little town called Bourgoin-Jallieu. Outside the HTC-Columbia team bus, there was a clutch of British cycling fans. Held back by barriers from getting too close, they were keen to get a glimpse of the little sprinter. Maybe to shake his hand, grab an autograph, or pose for a photo to SMS to their friends. They, like us, stared at the closed hydraulic door at the side of the bus, the livid yellow uncomfortably bright in the morning sun.

'Will he stop and talk to us, Ned?' they asked me. It was a reasonable question.

'I'd have thought so. You've come a long way.' I tried to

sound confident. 'Just stay as close to us as possible. We're going to grab a quick word.'

In fact, that morning we didn't want an interview. I was there simply to warn him of Hoban's gift, to explain the significance of the gesture, and to allow him some time to prepare an appropriate response. For a week I had been worried at the prospect of springing the bubbly on him unannounced, and getting a nonplussed reaction.

He emerged, looking stiff and awkward on his cycling shoes, but spent plenty of time signing stuff and smiling. He was patient and generous with his time. He didn't move on, in fact, until every item had been signed and every photo posed for. He and I briefly talked records and bottles, and then we hit the road.

A few hours later, it was complete. The win in Aubenas was the clincher. His ninth win in two years. And, to misuse a phrase, he still had Paris. When I handed over the champagne, he smiled humbly, and turning to the camera, he addressed Hoban directly, according him respect and talking of honour. It was the gesture of a practised diplomat, made all the more remarkable by the fact that just a few seconds earlier he had been threatening to decapitate a French rigger whose TV cable had nearly upended him. Such adaptability is Cavendish, too.

We never saw him to speak to in Paris. Replaying the footage of that 2009 final stage win still takes the breath away. At the crucial moment, the director cuts to the moto camera riding alongside him, on the other side of the central reservation. Suddenly the speed becomes unreal, and the margin of victory almost unnatural. Five, ten bike lengths and still pulling away from his rivals. He sits up early, the race won, and coasts across the line open-mouthed, with teammate Mark Renshaw sailing along in his wake, mirroring the arms-wide victory salute of the winner.

As he passed me, positioned just yards behind the finishing line, I knew already that the moment had passed. The curse of the history-maker fell like a shadow across the cobbles. With all that already done, what on earth could he possibly do next?

The answer, of course, was clear. On the 2010 Tour Mark Cavendish faltered briefly, when he lost out to a superannuated Alessandro Petacchi, but then imposed his will on the race once more. And he did this despite losing the services of his blue-chip leadout man Mark Renshaw, after Renshaw's extraordinary head-butting antics on Stage 11.

That day I had to interview Cavendish three times. Once for the 'world feed', then again after he had come down from the podium just for ITV. Shortly after that, I caught sight of the race director Jean-François Pescheux holding court to the francophone media. I went to eavesdrop.

I was astonished to hear that he was explaining the Tour's decision to expel Renshaw forthwith. I glanced back at Cavendish, still conducting interviews a few yards away, and beaming from ear to ear. Pescheux was telling the media, before anyone had bothered to tell Cavendish. Eventually, a Columbia soigneur whispered in his ear. He took a visible step back, and looked up in shock. Such things are public property on the Tour. Dealings and rulings, which in other sports take place behind closed doors, are routinely carried out under the unfeeling gaze of the TV cameras.

I had to interview Cav again, with the updated news. He was monosyllabic. Not rude. He was just quiet, holding it in and picking his words with care.

He went on that summer to win two more stages. Five in total, making it fifteen stage wins already on the Tour de France. More will follow. And as the records pile up, the fascination grows.

So there I'll leave Cavendish for now. His career stretches

ahead of us all. His domination as unfathomable as his mobile number appears unknowable (at least to me). He is a thoughtful braggart, a cultured man of the world, an islander with a continental understanding.

He's the most un-British Brit you could summon into existence. Yet, at the same time, British to his bones.

OH, THE TOILETTE

The Tour turns molehills into mountains and makes neurotics of us all. We absorb the shocks, ride out the bumpy road, as the race throws the unpredictable in our way. Braced then as we are for events to drag us away from what we thought would happen, we cling to those fragments of routine which keep us sane, and without which we would lose all grip. They are the snags of rock just big enough to gain a fingerhold and prevent us from slipping off the sheer rock face of the Tour de France: regularity, security, dependability, toilets.

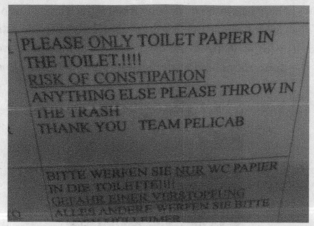

Next to the cordoned-off area known as the Zone Technique, which houses the fleets of broadcasters' trucks, is the cutely named Zone de Vie. This is a tented village to which the actual inhabitants of the town have no access and which is there to sustain life among those of us lucky enough to wear the lanyard around our necks. Although it bears the title Zone de Vie, that would imply a fairly narrow philosophical understanding of what is needed to sustain life. This is a no-frills environment, its sole function to allow the Tour's mobile army to attend to their bodily functions.

Although washing is a priority, so too are toilets. If this is a word that makes you flinch inwardly, it might be worth skipping to the next chapter.

The Tour does its best with the circumstances that prevail, but there are a lot of people to provide for and the heat of July in the south of France is intense. There is only so much time you can endure inside a chemical toilet, with the midday sun bearing down on you. I would go further than that: I suspect there are only a certain number of visits you can reasonably be expected to perform over a lifetime, before the bleached air impairs your vision and leaves you with a blistered bronchial tract. But they serve a purpose, and there have been times when I have been deeply grateful for their presence.

They are, of course, the result of carefully planned logistics, and, as with so many of the other feats of human endeavour on the Tour, they come at the cost of great personal effort.

On my first few Tours, the man in charge of the toilet operation was a prodigious, instantly recognisable operator. He was among the hardest working of anyone following the race, and I include the riders in that. Yet he guarded his fiefdom zealously, a Tsar of Ablutions who would do his darndest to make sure that your visit was as untraumatic as it could be under the circumstances.

He drove a distinctive open-backed truck round France marked 'Pelicab'. It was festooned with a logo of a diligent pelican, its gullet worryingly full-looking, wearing blue overalls and carrying a broom. Each day he would unload half a dozen telephone-box-sized toilets, which he then dispersed around the place. At the end of the day he'd round them all up, empty them of their contents and drive off, presumably via a sewer.

He closely resembled Abel Xavier, the former Everton and Portugal defender whose dark skin was offset by a bottle-blond head of hair with matching beard. But while Xavier affected this look voluntarily, I have a suspicion Monsieur Pelicab acquired it in the course of his duties, being exposed to dangerous levels of industrial-strength Harpic. His beard must have acted like a CO_2 indicator on the side of a boiler. When the hair went totally white, he knew it was time to move on, career wise. I can only hope he's got his feet up somewhere nice, and that someone else is cleaning his toilet for him. I wonder if his hair has returned to its natural colour.

There is a different man who does his job now. One searingly hot afternoon in 2010, when he was enjoying a well-deserved fag break, I introduced myself to the new Abel Xavier, and was amazed to find out that he wasn't French. I'd have thought that a job as prestigious as Toilet Keeper to the Tour would have been a reserved occupation only to be made accessible to French citizens. But no, Rudiger is from Dortmund, in the Ruhr valley, the industrial heart of Germany. He is a tanned, wiry, quick-witted man in his early fifties, who has an astonishing grasp of almost every mainstream European language, so long as you are talking about flushing, showering or generally sluicing.

I caught him on a bad day. There is a truck that houses six shower units. It is used principally by the army of lorry drivers, who drive through the night to park up in the small hours. They sleep in their cabs, by and large, and then expect to shower at Rudi's place in the late morning.

But the showers had stopped working and the patient German plumber was having to deal with a constant stream of complaints in a number of different languages from poorly slept truck drivers. Later on that day, I passed by his workplace once again. The problem with the showers was fixed, but something catastrophic had happened to one of the toilets. I glimpsed Rudi, down on his knees, pumping some blue effluent out of a tank into buckets as if he were single-handedly trying to save the *Titanic* from going under. I remembered him telling me that he had only accepted the job in order to help his son through college in Cologne. Quite a price to pay. I hope the boy appreciates it.

The experience of a few weeks on the Tour will teach you that the chemical toilet is really only there in extremis. Explore every other avenue first.

The matter is best dealt with in the relative comfort of the hotel that morning before embarking on the day's work. If necessary, any further opportunities to take advantage of more permanent facilities should be exploited, however unexpectedly they arise. Even if this means keeping Raymond Poulidor waiting in the foyer of his 4-star hotel while you attend to your needs. What you don't want to do is find yourself with no choice other than Plan B, even though it's inevitable that over the course of a three-week stage race that this will be, at some point, the only course of action open to you.

Another curiosity of the Tour's voracious appetite for toilet facilities is the 'mushroom'. Although they bear a passing resemblance to an upturned mushroom, I like to think that they really get their name because they sprout up overnight. Tour debutants, on seeing them for the first time, consider them to be so wildly decadent that they could only come from France, frankly (if that isn't tautologous).

France is, of course, famous for pushing the envelope in terms of micturition technology, having been the last major

European power to simply not bother with anything much except a hole in the ground, which scarred a few generations of visitors from the British Isles more than they would like to admit.

Then two factors collided to create a big bang in the field, although not literally: the advent of mouldable plastics and the growing internationalisation of the Tour de France.

When these two fuses were lit, and fanned by the winds of climate change that over the latter half of the twentieth century have raised summer temperatures in southern France to levels that require Tour workers to drink constantly from readily available sponsored water bottles, the invention of this particular type of *pissoir* was only a matter of time.

Women would rightly argue that they have been overlooked in this headlong charge towards an easier future. This is undeniably true, and while I can offer nothing compelling in defence of the Tour's toilet allocation policy, I should point out this one, irreducible fact. Everyone can watch you having a pee.

To return to the image of the upturned mushroom, three people can balance on the 'head', facing centrally, and peeing against the 'stem'. The great joy is that they can be plonked anywhere, and, simply drained off every now and again when their capacity has been reached. The physics, though, are a little precarious. At the beginning of the day, particularly if the mushroom has been placed on a patch of bumpy or uneven ground, there is not quite enough ballast to prevent the whole thing from developing an unsettling wobble. However, this improves with each subsequent visit.

I discovered early on that it is really only the English-speaking crews who find the 'mushroom' a source of mirth and mortification. To the French it's probably a source of pride. To the Germans it's just a neat solution to a potentially thorny problem. But to the British, Australians and Americans,

it's a ribald source of fun, unrelentingly humorous and not a
little titillating. It's the first question asked on arrival at the
Zone Technique every day ('Anyone seen a mushroom?' 'Over
there, just behind the Danes'), and it's the last thing visited
at the end of the day too, before jumping in the car and
resuming the endless travel.

The curious thing is the word 'mushroom'. The more
enlightened among us, like US cycling commentator Bob Roll,
tend to pay our host country the respect of calling them
'*Champignons verts*'. But don't for a minute think that this
translates into Actual French. I have tried it, on more than
one occasion, only to be met with a bemused frown from an
Actual French Person and, on repeating my question, been
fobbed off with a dismissive wave directed roughly towards
the local supermarket.

Other than that, there is the demanding matter of etiquette.

The mushrooms often appear in very popular thoroughfares between trucks, used by hundreds of co-workers every hour of the day. This poses a particular set of dilemmas. Is it, for example, acceptable to shout an unabashed 'Hello!' at friends and colleagues, while continuing to go about your business as if this was nothing remotely unusual? Is there any form of legitimate conversation which can continue without hesitation under such circumstances? Sometimes, other veterans of many Tours, quite senior in their own right and respective areas of responsibility, will engage you in high-level editorial discussions about the day's agenda, disregarding the fact that all the while you are urinating down a length of green plastic. It's not easy talking to a Swabian TV executive about Gerolsteiner's form in such a context.

On the 2010 Tour, in the shade of a plane tree which had miraculously sprouted out from within the TV compound (or could it have been vice versa?), I was engaged by Phil Liggett in a longish debate about the morality of Alberto Contador's opportunistic attack on the slopes of the Porte de Bales.

'What do you think, Neil? Should he have waited?'

The silver-haired commentator unzipped himself and started peeing, peering round the side of the mushroom to listen to my reaction.

'I don't know, Phil. On the one hand . . .' I grew distracted. 'Phil?'

'Yes?'

'Can we continue this conversation another time when you are not holding your penis?'

And yet mostly, and with people I feel less inclined to joke with, it would feel churlish to suggest reconvening at another point and starting the conversation from scratch when, perhaps, I wasn't emptying my bladder. I am, I suppose, too British to object really. After all, if you come on the Tour, then by default you are buying into a 'citizen of the world' set of values, in which nothing as trivial as a toilet should upset your equilibrium.

The weekend in 2007 when the Tour de France came to London provoked a seismic culture clash. The minute the Tour plonked its mushrooms down on the Mall, it introduced another layer of socio-political complexity to the issue, which touched on our competing notions of republicanism versus the monarchy.

Public peeing was one thing. But in sight of Buckingham Palace?

Actually it was quite liberating. It was an almost cathartic procedure for anyone of an anti-monarchist hue. Perhaps if the French aristocracy had simply installed *pissoirs* in front of Versailles, nothing would have kicked off; all revolutionary zeal would have been poured out in angry torrents, which would have dissipated before reaching the gates. All that republican fury neutralised in one simple gesture.

No French Revolution. No Bastille Day! No Richard Virenque! All because of a simple mushroom.

CONTADOR – AN EPILOGUE

I was perched uncomfortably on the front of a rather over-engineered modernist chair in an Utrecht hotel room. It was, as hotels often tend to be, right next to a railway station. Through the double-glazed and unopenable window I was aware of the rumblings of Holland's garishly coloured rolling stock as it set about its task for the day, moving the Dutch back and forth across their watery land. The trains crunched over the points, grinding and slipping on steel still damp from the morning mist. It was a northern European sort of noise to set your teeth on edge. One that hinted ominously of greater forces being set in motion.

That was where I was when, one late September morning in 2010, and just when I was least expecting it, everything changed again.

These days I rarely bother switching on TV sets in hotel rooms. The landscape of channels grows bleaker by the year; a parody of itself morphing and evolving across cultural and linguistic borders till eventually nothing is left which is distinguishable from anything else.

But on this occasion, there was a race on somewhere in the world and I wanted to watch it. So I made an exception.

I had waded through endless German language business news channels before finding Sporza, the brash and cycling-obsessed Belgian sports network. It's knowledgeable Flemish-speaking commentators had a flair for dipping into every major European language ('Ooh la la. Fabian Cancellara. Wat een man. History in the making!'). It was the men's time trial at the 2010 World Championships. The pictures were coming live from Australia.

I watched the familiar hunched figure of David Millar, his head snapping up, and then sinking, rising and falling with extreme effort.

The mute cursor blinked at me on the computer screen. But I was glad of a distraction from the job of writing and was at once gripped by the action. At one point the graphics on the TV, based on live GPS readings from motorbikes on the course, suggested that Cancellara and Millar were locked together, tussling for pre-eminence. There was a chance that Millar might prevail, repositioning again the moral compass from 2003, when, with blood artificially enriched by EPO, he had won the thing once before.

Wearing a cobbled-together-looking GB skinsuit with his cobbled-together-looking Garmin aerohelmet atop his cobbled-together-looking body, he was simply tearing into the race. This was a late, unexpected flowering. Even though I knew in my heart he would ultimately not have the beating of the almost superhuman Cancellara, he was giving him a run for his money. I said a heathen little four-lettered prayer for him, and left him to it.

It was with about 15km to go that I returned my gaze to the job in hand and spotted a message on my laptop screen: Contador positive.

'Alberto Contador today confirmed that a sample taken on 21 July 2010 had produced a positive test result for the presence of clenbuterol.'

It was one of those moments again. Millar. Landis. Hamilton. Vinokourov. Schumacher. Ricco. Riis. Basso. Beltran. Rasmussen. I was well enough versed in these stories to understand straight away the sequence of events that would now doubtless unfold.

The shock. The denials. The protestations. Then the support of colleagues and rivals. The sniping from the sidelines of former riders. The accusations of cover-ups. The elimination. The suspension. The comeback.

The rewriting of the history books, and the tearing up of the future. The incomprehension, disgust and anger of the public. The whole emptiness of it all.

I thought of Contador. And immediately I was at a loss. It is not just the fact that I do not speak Spanish, and that he is too unsure of his English to risk answering me in anything other than his native tongue, but I have simply never been able to gain an access point into Contador. His character, both as a rider and a man, seems to repel interest. He holds at bay the curiosity which he attracts. Like two negatively charged magnets, the rider and his public skirt around one another, holding their distance.

I thought of the day in Luchon when I had asked him if he was proud of his tactics. It was the day he had attacked Andy Schleck when his young rival's chain had come adrift. I pictured his passive face, and big round brown eyes no more than a foot from mine, as he strained to hear my words above the cacophony of the finish-line announcer. He had an interpreter alongside him to translate into Spanish any question he didn't understand. This one he got immediately, and launched into his mealy mouthed half-truth of an explanation before the translation had even begun.

I let the Spanish wash over me, and watched him instead blandly justifying his actions. He looked unruffled. Later, when shown a full transcription of his words, I was struck by their lack of expression. Contador, the accountant. That's what his name means in Spanish.

Bertie, we nicknamed him, lending him a geniality he scarcely merits. In some ways he is a champion for our age:

professional, conservative, but there it ends. He had survived the storm called Operación Puerto, the drugs scandal that implicated a sizeable number of athletes in Spain. Although his name had been linked to the inquiry nothing stuck. But now, finally, he had a positive to explain away.

He should have been great. He should have been the greatest. And he should have been worshipped as such.

A Dutch train sounded its mournful and slightly underwhelming horn. The double-decker inter-city to Schiphol airport slid into view outside my window, the passengers on the top level passing by at head height to me. A man wearing a silver suit glanced across from his paper and caught my eye as I looked up from my computer. We exchanged a small smile, at the strangeness of the encounter.

As his train gathered speed and pulled away, I looked back at the TV.

Cancellara had pulled clear on the final split times. Millar was now just 5km out, but he was now riding flat out for second place. The rest of the contenders were nowhere. I watched for a while, as the laptop fizzed with theories and counter-theories about Contador. Like a thunderhead on a summer day, the hot air was getting funnelled into a monster storm cloud. The cataclysms, the nightmare scenarios, the endgames for the sport were being touted all across the Internet: Contador – The Winner of the 2010 Tour de France?

On the final time trial of the Tour, Contador had been pushed surprisingly hard over the first half of the course by Andy Schleck. Indeed, for a period of ten minutes or so, the split times suggested that the entire Tour was in the balance. The virtual yellow jersey swung between them, a second either way. Then, as Schleck's effort fell away, Contador's steadied, and in the end the Spaniard rode out his win by just thirty-nine seconds, crossing the line in Paulliac straight into a seething melee of camera crews. I have a video on my phone of the moment he crosses the line. It has a Buster Keaton-like comedy about it. First a blur of Contador, hurtling from left to right. Then, half a second later, a phalanx of sprinting media operatives, clutching Dictaphones, and cameras, and microphone booms, like a horde of topless women chasing inexplicably after a British comedian.

Somewhere in the midst of all the pushing and shoving that followed, Contador's shades were knocked from his head. As the crowd dispersed, our cameraman John Tinetti, sharp-eyed as ever, noticed them lying on the tarmac and, with entrepreneurial ingenuity, picked them up and hurried round to the mixed zone. There he handed them over to me, along with a marker pen, so that I could get the new Tour champion to sign them. What a prize.

Such relics can be laced with significance. The sweat-stained shirt, the stump, the hat-trick ball, the token of the genius. I have a colleague who reports on boxing who once swiped the corner stool Mike Tyson had sat on in between the rounds of an epic world title defence. His daughter now sits on it to do her homework.

These things have meaning. Yet, as I glanced down at this pair of slightly scratched, green-tinted glasses, I couldn't see much. They seemed as empty as the impassive eyes they were designed to shade.

What was it about Contador that lacked an appropriate sense of importance? When he turned up in Monaco for the start of his 2009 Tour win alongside the returning Lance Armstrong, he was like a little note in the margin compared to the big man. Shunned by his Texan teammate, and frozen out by his coterie of cronies, Contador cut a lonely figure. An air of abandonment clung to him.

The day before the race got under way, in the car park outside the Fairmont hotel, Armstrong held an impromptu press conference, pinned up against a team car by dozens of reporters. The rest of his team, meanwhile, milled around with their bikes, waiting for Armstrong to finish. Right on the periphery, occasionally glancing at his watch, was Alberto Contador, the soon to be two-time winner of the Tour de France, who had it within him, given his age and superiority over the rest, to challenge the legacy of Armstrong himself. He was looking bored and a little impatient. But most of all, he looked ignored.

'That's Alberto Contador over there.' I nudged a colleague who like me was only half listening on the outer rings of the Armstrong throng. 'He's going to win the Tour.'

'Housekeeping!' There was a double knock on the door. I kept quiet. And then I heard the footsteps retreat down the corridor and away from my room.

Over in Australia, and still booming out from the speakers, the Sporza commentator was heading for his dramatic final flourish. It was time for him to refer to his prepared notes. This was the climax of the race '. . . the undisputed, and still undefeated four-times champion of the world, Fabiaaaaan Cancellaaara!' He let rip in English suddenly, apeing a boxing commentary.

I watched the usual thing unfold. Cycling has a way of producing great champions, immense rides, colossal achievements. But it doesn't always provide them with the trimmings befitting greatness. Every other sport culminates in an arena fit for purpose; the more giant the occasion, the more monolithic the backdrop. Fabian Cancellara's record-breaking fourth world title was being celebrated in front of a row of suburban Australian retirement homes. He was embraced and feted in front of a picket fence with a sneaky view into someone's front room. I carried on watching, trying to muster a proportionate sense of celebration.

Some time later, David Millar was called upon by television to pass comment on the Contador case. His status as reformed doper allowed him no respite, even in the afterglow of one of his most full-hearted rides. I watched him from the other side of the world. He looked a little pained, but not at all reluctant. He spoke of the need for certainty, he called for calm, he appealed to people's better natures and trusted, hoped, that all would be explained away. Without diminishing the seriousness of the accusation, he tried to call off the dogs of war.

But the dogs had long since left their kennels, and were tearing down the online alleyways, salivating at the scent of transfused blood. Just as all this was happening at the World

Championships, news broke that two more Spaniards, including the second-placed rider on the 2010 Vuelta d'Espana, had returned an initial positive test, subject to later confirmation. Minutes afterwards, and at about the same time, the Italian police revealed that they had raided the house of the confirmed doper Ricardo Ricco, and confiscated some mysterious tablets.

And on and on and on.

I switched off the TV, and snapped shut the lid of my laptop. I stared out of the window and contemplated heading out into the Thursday morning drizzle for a run.

Another bright yellow train came to a noisy, grinding standstill just outside. I drew the curtain, plunging the room into an even more profound gloom, and I composed a text message congratulating Millar. I hit send, then, a little reluctantly, started to change into my running gear.

Months later, and after a wearyingly long procedure, Alberto Contador was cleared by the Spanish Cycling Federation of deliberate doping. They upheld his assertion that he had unwittingly eaten meat contaminated with clenbuterol. That exoneration paved the way for Contador to ride on. As this book goes to print, the best guess is that he will almost certainly head for the Vendee, where the 2011 Tour starts.

All that, though, was still to come. The news I had just heard was merely the starting pistol, announcing the beginning of a battle of accusation and denial. Back then, I only had one bald fact to contend with: Alberto Contador had tested positive for a banned substance.

I was lacing my running shoes, when my phone beeped at me. It was David Millar, texting from Australia.

'Thanks, Ned. What a joy to rip that first lap. D.'

What a joy, indeed.

LEWISHAM HOSPITAL: PART THREE, AUGUST 2003

Hours wore on. Or perhaps minutes. As awareness crept in, I was seized by the very mildest form of panic, which is really only one level up from fascination. My dysfunction had become apparent to me. Which isn't to say that I could actually do anything about it.

With each attempt to address the turn of events that had dumped me in this curtained chamber deep in Lewisham Hospital, I displayed the attention span of a gnat coupled with the memory of a goldfish. Trying to remember was like purposefully flinging open the door to a room, striding in, and then instantly forgetting why I had entered it. A moment's confusion, then I flung the door open anew. It was tiring.

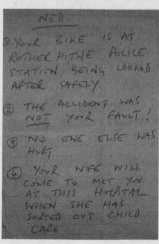

This is where the Piece of Paper came into its own. Hand-written in black rollerball, it listed the chain of events in bullet points.

It wasn't exactly a Buddhist mantra, but I intoned it internally with all the earnest devotion of a monk perched on a Tibetan mountainside reciting Om Mani Padma Hum. In a world which had become chaotic, it at least made coherent sense. The problem was that no sooner had I read it, than I had forgotten it all over again.

Kath, to take her mind off my insanely repetitive line of questioning, had started to scrape away the bits of Jamaica Road still embedded in a deep cut to my right elbow. I watched her with fascination as she fiddled away with a gauze swab dipped in sterile water, flicking grains of tarmac out from a wound close to my elbow bone. I didn't feel a thing.

More evidence that all was not well. The tiniest scratch would, on any other given day, have me swearing blue filth and screwing my face into the shape and flavour of a tightly squeezed lemon. Here I felt nothing.

The curtains whipped smartly to one side and the Holby City doctor was back.

'How is he?'

'How are you?' Kath threw the question on to me like a hand grenade.

'Fantastically well,' I ventured, unsure of what the correct response should be, but wishing not to appear morose.

There followed a discussion between medical professionals (Kath is a qualified nurse) about how best to stitch together my unsightly elbow flap. Then there was a fair amount of rotating my arm to the left and right. Of course, there were also plenty of torches to be shone directly into my eyes. Then the questioning began again in earnest. Clipboards with charts were readied to record the calibre and quality and implications of the replies.

Kath seemed by now, in her frustration, to be driving the agenda.

'Ask him something he'll definitely know the answer to. He's just come back from a month on the Tour de France. Ask him who won the Tour de France.'

'OK. Who won the Tour de France?'

Deeply hidden in my memory, a sudden thrill. A sudden taste at the back of my mouth. I tasted delight, pride and shock.

I thought for a long time. I was reasoning. I was aware that it sounded oddly triumphalist, but I was also desperate to say the right thing. And the right answer appeared within my grasp.

I glanced for the last time at my battered bike helmet and the tear in my Lycra. It was all the confirmation I needed.

'Was it me?'

HOW CAV WON THE GREEN JERSEY

HOW CAV WON THE GREEN JERSEY

Mark Cavendish was under pressure, as I had witnessed a couple of weeks before I left for France. There was nothing new in this. After all, he always was. But it was with some irritation that he challenged a roomful of journalists.

'Who won the last three green jerseys? Don't think about it. Just tell me.'

There had been an uncomfortable shuffling noise. It reminded me of those awful moments in echoing classrooms at school when it becomes apparent that absolutely no one has the answer. I looked at my notepad and pretended to be deep in thought. In fact, I was drawing a picture of a swordfish piercing a football, for some reason.

Silhouetted against the bright Soho Street beyond the window behind him, Mark Cavendish sat forward in his chair, injecting a little urgency into his enquiry. For years, he'd been besieged by hapless hacks asking him if he was frustrated never to have won the green jersey.

'See?' He leant towards the cluster of microphones, when it became obvious that no one could answer him straight away. 'You can't remember, can you? That's the point.'

As points go, it was quite sharp.

I have a confession to make. Covering the Tour, I run and I eat. The running is fine, nothing more than a protracted mid-life crisis. But the eating is more of an issue. Philippe and Odette, who cater extravagantly for the ITV crew, have an on-going love affair with butter and olive oil. Because of their exquisite cooking, and because I run myself most days into a state of insatiable hunger, I tend to overeat at lunchtime. It's no longer something I can control.

There are consequences. Being forty-two years old, and consequently a bit crapper than I was at the age of forty-one, I have a propensity to fall asleep. When it's 30 degrees in the shade, and there's cycling on the telly, I don't just *tend* to fall asleep, I *always* fall asleep. Dozing off after a full-fat French lunch is as inevitable as a Michael Rasmussen time trial crash. I'm not the only one to succumb, I hasten to add. Chris Boardman, a year my senior, has been known to drift off, his chin heading south with his masterful head supported by the palm of his left hand. But, being a freak of nature, he is capable of maintaining full 360 degrees sensory perception even while he's dreaming of scuba diving in the Mersey, setting new hour records, selling more bikes, or whatever it is that he dreams of nowadays. That means it's very difficult to get a clandestine snap of him snoring. Just as you're framing up your camera phone, one eye will snap open. 'Oi!'

On most days, on most Tours, I fashion for myself a restorative ten-minute window in which to nod off. The morning's scripts have been written, the voiceover sent back to London, and all that remains for the working day is to watch the race and mop up the interviews afterwards. Normally the peloton is something like seventy-three kilometres out from the finish line, holding the breakaway at 4'26'. Or they are still rumbling along the valley floor, thirty-two kilometres from the foot of the final climb of the day. This is just the perfect time for a power nap, drifting off while Paul talks about Huguenot castles and Phil chunters along with lines like 'Leopard Trek then, tapping out a rhythm. There's Big Jens Voigt . . .'

I mention this by way of admitting that not everything about the Tour de France is always thrilling. Except 2011. Last summer, I remember falling asleep only once. In Montpellier. For about five minutes.

The race was that good.

How do you calibrate Tours? How, empirically, do you separate the good from the great? The humdrum from the heroic? By what measure can we determine the place each annual chapter will occupy in the century-long heritage of the Tour de France?

The statistics alone will only tell you a fraction of the story. Average speeds on the 2011 Tour, in this increasingly clean era, were nothing to write home about. The lead changed hands an unremarkable number of times. The overall winner himself, Cadel Evans, failed either to win a mountain stage or a time trial. He defended his way to the win. Brilliantly, arguably, but demonstrably short of panache.

So why are we all left with the memory of an immense race?

Here are a few reasons: Jérémy Roy, Thomas Voeckler, Thor Hushovd, Geraint Thomas, Pierre Rolland, Edvald Boasson Hagen, Mark Cavendish, Philippe Gilbert, Juan Antonio Flecha, Johnny Hoogerland. Stick a pin in the list of names and draw out a hero.

Even my convoluted journey to the start line in the Vendée felt epic. It wasn't, of course, but to me these days, any car journey of over 200 miles feels epic. Again, I suspect this may have something to do with being forty-two. A journey feels especially awe-inspiring if it involves driving onto a boat.

My trip would start by driving from my home in London down to Plymouth, where I would catch the overnight ferry to Roscoff. Then I would pass by my friend Judi's campsite near Morlaix, in Brittany, where I would disconnect the battery and leave the car to go gradually rusty under a beech tree in the corner of a field (I planned to return a month later to start a camping holiday with my family). Having dropped off the motor, I then needed to catch a series of progressively smaller and sillier district trains, till Woody and Liam would pick me up from a railway station at a location near somewhere I'd never heard of in the west of France. That was the plan, at least.

What a pilgrimage! I packed a book to read.

I didn't have to wait long, either, for my first sniff of Tour de Franceness. Amid the humming engines and seagulls of Plymouth docks, a flash of red, and the familiar curves of their deliciously eighties' logo. The cycling bit of my heart skipped a beat. It was a truck, yes, but so much more than that. It was a Norbert Dentressangle lorry. Contracted by the Tour to carry out its daily grind, these beasts are the oily soul of the race. And as such they are dear.

O canvas awning of blood red! O humble truck, workhorse of the French motorway network! What dormant longing your sudden presence quickens on this damp evening dockside! *Mon semblable, mon frère!*

I was quoting Baudelaire to myself. I was feeling pompous. I was off to cover the Tour de France. I think I should be forgiven.

The 2011 race looked great on paper. At least that's the impression it made as I gazed at its curves and contours. They lurched and jumped across the folded creases of the official Tour map, spread flat against the plastic table top of the ferry's bistro. The channel was in full swell.

The features swayed in and out of vision; those teasing uphill finishes, and the prospect of a well-proportioned wind in the north-west to blow holes in the race. Then there was the surprising scale and dangerous potential of the mountains of the Massif Central, before the Tour would throw itself at the mercy of the Plateau de Beille, the Galibier (twice!), Alpe d'Huez, and then a final time trial to seal everybody's fates.

And after that, Paris, perhaps with Cavendish in green? That seemed a long way off. Water to be crossed.

With a black marker pen, I ringed the stages I believed he could win. There were seven of them. Then I pushed the map to one side and wolfed down a ferry meal, made palatable only because of the wine decanted from a series of plastic mini-bottles. I found my cabin in the windowless bowels of the ferry, took off my shoes, dropped onto the bunk and fell sound asleep.

It was strange how his story unfolded over the summer. Mark Cavendish, I have always understood, feels closest to those targets that are, well, closest to him. There is a certain remorseless pragmatism to his assembly line of honours. For a long time, I had known only his thirst for stage wins. It was absorbing to watch the growing dominance of the outstanding HTC team that had been assembled around him: their one stated aim being to shepherd the purest, most explosive sprinter in the history of the sport to his launch point. And time and time and time and time again, he had repaid their faith.

The bunch sprint had become his signature. The Tour de France, his parchment. Or if that sounds too precious, his spread sheet, for he understood well the fiscal relationship between winning and reward, between celebrating and sponsorship.

But what of his relationship with the green jersey? That was less clear-cut. He had ridden recent Tours with self-evident irritation in the face of an evolving Thor Hushovd, who had the presence of mind to throw his hands up in defeat when it came to outsprinting Cavendish, and decided to reset his targets by attacking the sorts of intermediate sprints where riders who looked only for stage wins dared not tread their pedals. Hushovd had become a marauding, opportunistic, classy attacker. Behind him, in 2010, Alessandro Petacchi, another grisly veteran, slipstreamed his way into green. And Cavendish, wisely, offered only meagre opposition. The green jersey, we read into his apparent ambivalence, was some sort of weird, and somewhat arbitrary, consolation prize for sprinters, who were one pedal turn away from obsolescence. The fastest man had no need for such fool's gold.

But he could only convince us, or indeed himself, of his indifference for so long. In 2011 the points competition was reconfigured, reducing the number of intermediate sprints to just one, while loading more points onto them as an incentive. It had been carried out with Cavendish in mind. It was, I was given to understand, a mark of respect from the race itself. Christian Prudhomme confirmed as much when, to my great surprise, he told me, 'Mark Cavendish had been the starting point in our considerations. To imagine a rider of his exceptional talent going through his career without ever once winning the green jersey – that would have been unthinkable.' At least, I think that's what he said. He was speaking to me in French, as was his wont. So he might have been talking about lawn maintenance or home baking.

There was also the question of legacy. Cavendish knew very well his place in the developing history of the sport. After fifteen stage wins, and with another clutch on the way, there was a sense that new targets should be set, the green jersey being the next in line. And so it was that he found himself being asked the question again.

In retrospect, that pre-Tour press conference had been very revealing. We'd all made our way to the downstairs restaurant area of the Bar Italia in Soho, which Cavendish now chooses on an annual basis for his pre-Tour de France press day, in homage to his breakthrough successes on the Giro.

I arrived at exactly the appointed time, imagining that it would be easy to grab a seat at the last minute. I was wrong. The attendance was big. Bigger, by far, than in previous years. I had to push my way back through the seated ranks, nodding in surprise as I noted how many general (and very senior) sports journalists had shown up. It was packed. The PA system, such as it was, seemed woefully inadequate. When Cavendish began to speak we struggled to hear him, his quiet voice dying into the cluster of Dictaphones on the table in front of him.

With the press conference underway, he seemed to be conducting a guided tour of his disparate personality traits. One by one, he dished them out. And we ticked them off. There was the bullishness, the bratishness, the short shrift. There was the self-effacing charm, the humility, the respect, and the humour.

And then there was the surprising thoughtfulness. He took so long thinking about his answer to one particularly innocuous question from a Norwegian journalist that I genuinely thought he'd slipped into some kind of state of deep meditative trance. His gaze wasn't so much 'faraway' as utterly absent. He appeared to be mouthing his response, preparing it for broadcast, seeing how it felt on the tongue, before allowing it to pass into record. Fascinated, I craned forward to catch his extremely well-prepared words.

'No. Not really,' he said, finally.

We all scribbled down his answer, unable to remember what the question had been.

At one point, he stopped abruptly, mid-answer. He appeared to be looking over the tops of all our heads at something behind us.

'Look, it's me.'

We craned our necks around. On the back wall of the restaurant hung a plasma TV. The screen was filled with a two-dimensional, digital Mark Cavendish lounging across a television studio couch on some pre-recorded daytime show.

'He's good, he is.' Cavendish said of himself. He was goofing around now. And so we laughed along with him.

It had been a very Mark Cavendish affair.

On arrival at my final destination, Liam and Woody, my colleagues of numerous Tours, swung by to pick me up from the railway station. I greeted my old friends with the awkward palm-slapping shoulder-hug thing that we British blokes tend to use in lieu of any natural ability to express ourselves. I rounded on them for being late ('Don't you know who I am?'), flung my bag in the boot (the same red and black bag I had used for the last four Tours, so still a relative novelty on board our car) and climbed in to my usual seat in the rear, my hand reaching unconsciously but with infinite precision to the seat belt. It was telling how the hand knew exactly where to find the belt.

The job got underway in earnest with the filming of the Riders' Presentation. We stopped to drink a coffee en route to the absurd medieval theme park that had paid the Tour a vast sum of money to host the ceremonials. We took our seats at Routierscafé in the middle of a network of slip roads and dual carriageways, and settled down to our first act of menu perusal of the 2011 Tour. Moules-frites, and glaces artisanales. There, we were up and running.

Then, to my great delight, the top button on Liam's trousers pinged off. It was as funny as anything I have ever seen. For the rest of the day, he had to operate the camera with one hand and keep his trousers up with the other. One set of slacks down into a three-week Tour, he was in trouble. We took a great deal of pleasure in this.

Although Liam's primary concern was to replace his useless trousers, our first proper target before the start of the race was to sit down with Bradley Wiggins and get his thoughts on digital video tape. Big things were expected of him. He'd ridden all season as if freed from the arduous, if self-inflicted, pressures of the previous campaign. A few weeks previously Wiggins had won the 2011 Dauphiné, a prestigious race in its own right, and a significant form guide for the tour, as the Queens Club is to Wimbledon. He had beaten Cadel Evans into second place. His preparation had been exceptional, his ambitions were privately high, but his public utterances, muted. After the hyperbole of Team Sky's launch and his 2010 capitulation, he wisely chose the course of expectation management.

'You should never forget that I'm a track rider, really, who can time trial a bit. Or a time triallist who can climb a little. You won't seem me attacking in the mountains. That's not going to happen.' A shy grin, but earnest eyes. I twiddled my biro and listened. How well riders talk about their sport. Is it simply a result of the solitary hours in the saddle? Is philosophy at one remove from chamois cream?

We sat opposite one another, in a corridor next to the huge, busy Salle de Presse. Wiggins talking so fluently, that I could hardly get the question out before he jumped in with his answer, typically a fraction before the question was finished.

I was very aware that ITV's long-serving Producer/Director, Steve Docherty, was sitting behind me, rather disconcertingly, as I conducted the interview. It was a rare public appearance for a man who spends every July with his hands welded to the control panel inside a TV truck. This was probably because the vehicle, which was to be his home for the rest of the month, hadn't yet been fully booted up and plugged in, so he was effectively officeless and had nowhere else to sit. But equally, I suspect he just wanted to see for himself what shape Wiggins was in. Literally. Wiggins was thin, even more so than usual, if that was possible.

As soon as the interview was finished, Steve jumped up very suddenly from behind me and ambushed Wiggins.

'How much do you weigh then?' He growled, almost accusingly, without introducing himself. I thought about butting in to make the introductions (just the basics, really: 'Brad, this is Steve. Steve this is Brad') but already the conversation had moved on.

'Well, I'm six kilos lighter than I was at the start in 2009.' Wiggins looked understandably disarmed by Steve's tall frame standing inches from him, and demanding answers. It can be an intimidating sight, and one that I have had cause to be very familiar with over the years.

'Bloody hell. Six kilos?' I could see him calculating virtual odds in his bookmaker's brain. 'Right ho. Well, good luck.' And with that Steve turned away. So too did Bradley Wiggins. They went their separate ways, leaving me on my own scratching my metaphorical head at the strangeness of the encounter. It was the first time in nearly a decade covering the Tour that I'd ever seen Steve actually talking to an actual rider.

I ran after Wiggins, and gave him a copy of my book, *How I Won the Yellow Jumper*, which had just been published. He looked suitably nonplussed. He had approached France with his targets intact, but he would leave with an unread paperback and his collarbone in bits.

I had also given Mark Cavendish a copy, too, back at that faltering press conference in Soho. The book contained a reasonably (and perhaps riskily) frank unpicking of the occasional difficulty of working with Cavendish's unpredictable moods. I figured that, cycling being a fairly narrow gene pool, it was inevitable he would get wind of what I had written. So, in an attempt to head off his reaction at the pass, I decided to pre-empt any issues by confronting them directly.

'Mark, you know I've written a book? Can I give you a copy?' I slid the offending article across the table in his direction.

'Oh yeah! I've heard about this. I want to read this.' He picked it up and started to read the quotes on the back. I think I saw him smile at the point where he got to 'evidently he was clueless', the quote that David Millar had provided.

'Thanks a lot,' he said.

'Well, you might not be saying that once you've read it. Anyway, some of it might strike a chord.' I felt like I should be honest. He glanced up at me.

'Will you sign it for me, please?'

I fished out a pen, and scribbled something.

To Mark. You might want to skip the two chapters about some bloke called Cavendish. Cheers, Ned.

Then he kindly posed for a picture, holding the book. He looked like he'd just been subjected to a mild electric shock; just enough for his eyes to pop out, and to enliven his hair. And he hadn't even started reading it yet. I fretted a little. But then I reassured myself by considering how unlikely it was that he'd ever get around to reading it. He'd leave it in his hotel room probably and forget all about it.

Three days later, our paths crossed again. It was the eve of the National Road Race Championships. We were both watching a criterium race in Newcastle. He was standing at the finish line, patiently signing autographs and posing for pictures with an endless stream of fans.

When he saw that I was there, he nodded a coy hello at me. I went over and shook his hand.

'Hi, Ned.' He wore a curious smirk. Or at least I imagined that he did.

'Hello, Mark, you all right?'

'Yes, thanks.'

'Looking forward to tomorrow?'

He shrugged. But the smirk hadn't quite gone away. I could smell an elephant in the room.

'I read your book.'

'Ah. Right. OK. Did you read the stuff about you and me, then?'

'I've read it all.'

'Really?' I was amazed. 'And?'

'I thought it was good.'

There was a pause. He clearly wasn't going to elaborate. I thought I'd quit while I was ahead.

'Excellent. Thanks.' A change of tack. 'So what do you think about the course tomorrow?'

'I pissed myself when I read about Wagner.' He broke into a broad grin.

Wagner had been the imaginary name I had given to his erstwhile PR manager at T-Mobile, a man with whom I had experienced a few problems, and who had been on the receiving end of some fairly blunt treatment in the book.

'Yes, but what was his real name, Mark? I just guessed that it was Wagner. I couldn't remember what he was really called.'

'No, that was it. He was called Wagner. Stefan Wagner.'

'Really? And he did look like that, didn't he? He did have a face that was "loosely based on Michael Stich"?' I was being uniquely vain; quoting back a phrase from my own book. But it had been a description that I was particularly pleased with.

Cavendish shrugged. The smile suddenly went.

'I don't know who Stick is.'

'Oh, right.' I remembered that he was only twenty-six. Of course he wouldn't know Michael Stich.

'He's that German Wimbledon Champion, from the eighties. Or maybe the nineties. Anyway, he won it once . . .'

At that point someone approached him for an autograph, and it became apparent that he'd stopped listening. I was left feeling like Spike Milligan's overenthusiastic religious zealot in *The Life of Brian*, who only realises that he has been utterly deserted when he's halfway through proclaiming, 'Yea, he cometh! Like the seed to the grave . . .' But no one is listening any more. He shuffled off stage right. And so did I.

The Tour was underway. Instantly there was carnage. Contador crashed at the earliest possible opportunity, hurting his knee and obviating the need for us to worry about him winning it, with all the ramifications his dubious status brought with it.

Phillipe Gilbert, wearing the Marmite colours of the Belgian National Champion, threw himself all over the race, winning, attacking, misfiring and failing and all the while looking like an extra from *Mad Max*, with his craggy features and bottle-blond barnet.

Geraint Thomas snaffled himself the white jersey for a while by finishing in the top placings day after day after day. That gave us an interview banker in the mixed zone, and provided the viewers back home with a stream of boy-next-door quotes: no-nonsense Welsh wisdom in this fancy foreign whirligig of a race.

'How did you go out there today, Geraint?'

'It was pretty hard, really.'

Can't argue with that.

After a week or so of being brilliant, he was rewarded with a new five-year deal by Team Sky. A number of other teams had been sniffing around. Dave Brailsford had been forced to dig a bit deeper than he might have expected to retain Thomas's prodigious services. The morning they made the new contract public, I was there to get his reaction.

'You must be very pleased, Geraint.'

'Yeah, it's pretty good, really.'

Couldn't argue with that either.

Rider after rider crashed out. From Vinokourov to Van de Velde, through Horner and Van den Broeck, they were dropping like wind-tunnel tested, highly paid flies. We embarked on the usual round of vox-pops from riders about safety on the race. It's one of those complaints that surfaces annually. I cannot remember a Tour on which we have ever asked the question and got a different answer.

'What do you think about safety this year?'

A perennial favourite, and a good question to thrust at a rider whose thighs have been effectively rubbed up and down with a giant tarmac leg-grater.

'Perfect. Outstanding. Virtually risk-free. Next!'

But the weather was appalling. The sunny start melted away as we headed for the top left-hand corner. Brittany did as Brittany does, pouring misery on the race. Stage after stage finished in torrential rain, with riders spattered in mud. It lent the proceedings a retro feel. Old-fashioned valour.

Norway was having the time of its woolly-jumpered Scandinavian life. From the moment that David Millar's Garmin team had powered Thor Hushovd into the race lead after winning the Team Time Trial ('We just went out there to try and win the Yellow Jumper, Ned,' as David Millar had explained with a wink in his live post-race interview), the Norsemen were in raptures.

They only had two riders on the race. But what a pair. One tall and blond; the other blond and tall. Thor Hushovd and Edvald Boasson Hagen. Hushovd had the clothing dilemma from which cycling dreams are woven. For seven days he had to cast aside his iconic rainbow jersey (worn by the reigning Champion of the World) in favour of the yellow jersey. That's a bit like putting your half-eaten Crunchie to one side because someone's just offered you a Toblerone. Except even better.

Not content with hogging the knitwear, he won two brilliant stages. The first of those came about amidst the Catholic gaudiness of Lourdes, and very nearly conferred a spirituality that the town's nakedly commercial heart scarcely deserves. The second, into Gap, he rode out simply because he could. Not to be outdone, the considerably younger Edvald Boasson Hagen won a bunch sprint (of sorts) into Lisieux, and a Hushovdian breakaway across the border to Pinerolo on Stage 17. Two riders. Four wins. An amazing strike rate.

It didn't make Boasson Hagen any easier to interview. There is a disengaged serenity about the young Norwegian that makes you wonder if he has any inkling of just how good he is and what he can go on to achieve. He smiles politely and gives answers which pull up at least ten seconds short of the standard minimum reply duration, as set out in the rule book. If you want to get a minute out of EBH, you need to have six or seven questions ready, which can take you quickly into unusual territory.

'Edvald, congratulations. Tell me why you decided to attack when you did?'

'What are your ambitions now for the rest of the Tour?'

'Um. Ever been in a hot air balloon?'

Liam affectionately calls him Ice Cream Boy, in oblique homage to Hagen Dazs. It's a name that works.

Norwegian television's Dag Otto, whom you may recall drives a liveried car around France with his handsome leathery face plastered all over it, had upped the ante in response to his countrymen's achievements. His TV studio now featured a table-top map of France, on which sat a toy car replica of the actual car he drove. It too, had a tiny little replica photo of Dag Otto's handsome, leathery (but very small) face on it.

We suggested to Gary Imlach that he should get one, too. He didn't seem to be listening.

Of course, Norway's elation was short-lived. News filtered through overnight of the shootings in Oslo. A gunman, dressed as a police officer, had killed sixty-nine people at a Norwegian summer camp.

By the morning of Saturday, 23 July, the extent of the tragedy had become apparent. I made my way over to see the guys from TV2. They were standing around in the damp Grenoble air waiting for instructions from head office. I don't think that they broadcast anything from the Tour de France that day. Suddenly their golden summer had been taken away from them.

There are rare occasions when the Tour's self-important bubble is burst. This was one of them.

The finish line at Lisieux was another.

I had noticed an unusual proliferation of American cyclo-tourists. In general, clusters of loudly enthusiastic amateurs were the cue for considerable, and largely unwarranted, muttering from our crew. And this bunch was being particularly annoying. Partly this was because there were so many of them, partly because they were all wearing matching yellow jerseys (a BIG breach of etiquette), but mostly because they kept parading noisily through the back of the shot every time I tried recording a rather overwritten (and therefore complex) piece to camera at the finish line.

Looking more closely, though, I began to notice that they scarcely fitted the usual demographic. Many of them were black, which is shamefully uncommon on the Tour. They were all very young and, almost to a man, tattooed. And every other one had a limb missing.

I spoke to one of their number, a very polite, very hand-some Italian-American. He explained that they were all veterans from the Iraq and Afghanistan conflicts. Cycling together had become part of their rehabilitation. He told me how often these guys had been sent home to isolated communities with little or no support, and that only by meeting up on these cycle rides could they find kinship, and some chance to talk about their shared experiences. They were dropping in on the Tour de France, and riding the routes of the first few stages, often on specially adapted bikes for amputees. They avoided the Caravane Publicitaire, though, since its explosive noise had been far too close for comfort. The wars still rang in their ears.

When he left, one of his colleagues turned to me.

'You know who that was, right?'

'I have no idea. Sorry.'

'That's Sal Giunta. He's the first living man since the Vietnam War to receive the Medal of Honor.'

I watched Sal go on his way. Then I turned, and went back

to the truck to carry on writing a script about Andy Schleck. It was one of those chance encounters that are the speciality of the Tour de France.

Cavendish got round to winning, albeit a little late. Having missed out on one or two earlier opportunities, it was in Cap Fréhel, on an uphill drag to the line, where he notched his first win. A remarkable victory. But not what either Liam, Woody or I will remember Stage 5 for. It was about nine o'clock when we got the call. We had just arrived at a ghostly hotel with oak panels, a lame dog, lace curtains and a lingering smell of deep fat fryers. We were in Saint Malo, a torturous two-hour drive from the finish line in Cap Fréhel. We'd just performed the ritual unloading of the car, and had assembled in the grisly foyer, ready to hasten away towards the sea front in search of a restaurant that didn't serve human body parts.

'Ned, it's Mike.' Our technical supervisor sounded a bit frayed on the phone. 'Um, so now you have to get back to Cap Fréhel.'

'OK.' I looked at the others. A certain wide-eyed horror spread across my face and must have hinted at bad news. But just to reduce the room for ambiguity, I added, 'That's shit. Why?'

'The truck's broken down. It hasn't left the finish line yet. But we reckon we can still get an audio feed on air for tomorrow if you go back to the truck and get some kit off the trailer.'

Two hours later, we pulled up in the gathering darkness back at Cap Fréhel. It was a bizarre sight. Where there had been an entire broadcast village just hours before, now there was only a ploughed field. And our broken truck.

Woody spent the next hour scrabbling around in the pitch black (we had no torch) trying to retrieve the leads, cables, and nameless, numberless other bits of technical nuts and bolts that Mike had detailed.

Meanwhile I had to help Richard, our endlessly patient driver, talk French to a local firm of Breton emergency mechanics. The issue had something to do with tyres. I had a horror of this. After all, how do English speakers pronounce the word *'pneu'* without not only sounding stupid, but also being stupid?

'Bollocks!' shouted Woody from the back of the truck as he banged his head on yet another overhanging crate.

'All right, Woody. Don't get in a silly little tizzy,' Liam chipped in, encouragingly.

'Et il se trouve où, le camion?' The heavily accented Breton mechanic asked me on the phone. Where was the truck? A reasonable question, given that he had to find it.

'Ici.' I pointed rather inadequately at the field he was nowhere near, and I shrugged apologetically at Richard.

'Bugger'. There was a thud of kneecap on metal. Woody was no longer enjoying being in the back of the truck.

Eventually we had all the gear. There was not a cubic inch of space left in the Espace that didn't contain DIN leads and CODECS (whatever they were). I assured Richard that my telephone conversation with the Breton mechanic had been not only geographically precise, but also technically perfect, pinpointing the exact nature of the breakdown. Nothing could go wrong. We drove off, feeling furious, but nothing short of heroic. The show, *mesdames et messieurs*, would go on.

We didn't get back to the Saint Malo hotel till one in the morning. When we did, the lame dog snarled, and the foyer smelt even more strongly of fat. We set our alarms for 'stupidly early', and went to our various cells without a word.

But the next day, as we got to the finish line in Lisieux, our heroes' welcome never materialised.

'Have you got all that stuff, then?' Mike appeared, looking pretty serene.

We were greeted by the sight of the truck with all its wheels intact, the studio set already erected, and everything about to continue on its sweet seamless course. As if nothing at all had happened.

Apparently the problem with the truck had been instantly fixed, and Richard had set off shortly after us. What, we wondered, was the point in being saints if nobody acknowledged it? None – there was no point. So we sulked for the rest of the morning, and banged things around. Pointedly.

And that's one of the ways in which Mark Cavendish and I will take away different memories of the 2011 Tour de France.

And on Stage 7, Bradley Wiggins went home. The last I saw of him was in the car park outside Châteauroux's main hospital, teetering towards a Team Sky Jaguar with Rod Ellingworth, his coach, behind the wheel. He had broken his collarbone, gained a sling, and exited the Tour, all within a few hectic hours. Sky had chartered a plane to get him home, adding to their growing mystique as the best-funded, best-organised super-cycling team in the world.

We had arrived in the nick of time. It was a little applied wisdom, coupled with pure luck. A minute later and we'd have missed the Jag on its way to the local airport. As it was, we followed him on his wobbly journey from the hospital to the car, where he turned around and talked.

At first I was confused. If he was devastated to be missing out, he was hiding it well. He looked almost amused. Then, midway through his answer, I understood what was going on. The French medics had pumped him so full of morphine that he was struggling to see the serious side of anything. He did well not to burst into song. We commiserated, wished him all the best, and sent him on his way. He beamed back at us, narcotically.

The next time he appeared on our TV screens, it was August, and he was on a mad charge with his teammate Chris Froome for the podium of the Vuelta a España. It was a prodigious ride that belied to some extent the downplaying of his own abilities. And it begged the question of what he might have been capable of had he not crashed out in July. But that, disppointingly was another story, that will never be told.

If Wiggins couldn't ride in France, Chris Boardman and I would have to do it for him.

BAFTA were duly informed and sent scouts to France in order to validate our attempts to make some of the Best Television Ever Recorded. Staggeringly, the preparations for the shoot had begun months in advance. Back as early as March, there had been a flurry of emails exchanged between the show's directors, producers and cameramen, Chris Boardman and myself. There was even some worrying talk of aerohelmets.

This was the Big Idea: Chris, or 'Olympic Bloke', as he became universally known during this edition of the Tour, was going to teach me how to ride a bike. For the first time since my dad released his grip from my back wheel and allowed my five-year-old legs to teeter off onto the recreation ground outside our house, I felt myself quivering on the threshold of greatness. This wasn't Dad, though. This was Olympic Bloke, and so the pressure was notched up accordingly. After all, as Chris's increasingly irritating adverts on TV suggested, 'He didn't know what second place on the podium was for.' (Apart, that is, from the numerous times when he had to stand there looking up at Miguel Indurain, as we delighted in reminding him.)

I had been out running with Chris for years, admiring his relentless, sapping ability to be consistently 15 per cent better than me over all distances and across all terrains. I had become accustomed to the sight of his hairless Olympian legs pumping away in their fell-running shoes and dropping me on some alpine goat track, whilst he still happily chatted away about the problems syncing an iPad with a Windows-based desktop. Or something.

Running is not an uncommon transition phase for retired roadies. The urge to do something different when they finally stop riding is irresistible. And for many, like the recently retired Olympic rider Chris Newton who posted an alarmingly good time in his first ever marathon, this means running. They feel delightfully liberated by the simplicity of it: a pair of trainers, shorts, and off you go. None of this pump-in-the-back-pocket, chain-lube and Allen-key shenanigans. Not only that, but their entire riding career has been predicated on the principle of doing nothing that so much as even remotely resembles running. In fact, walking can present a problem for most of them. Even standing up a bit does them in. They are, it has to be said, wonderfully feeble individuals in lots of ways, with a propensity for catching colds. They boast weedy little upper bodies and hopeless one-dimensional physiologies. Pedal, pedal, pedal. They're very good indeed at doing that. But stand around for twenty minutes at a bus stop? Forget it.

Chris Boardman had also run the London Marathon. It galled me greatly that his time had beaten mine by fully twenty-six minutes. That crushing disappointment negotiated, I had been secretly relieved that the old ankle injury he had sustained when he crashed out of the 1995 Tour Prologue had flared up again. The doctor had told him to pack in the running and get back on his bike. I agreed with the doctor, by and large, and started to enjoy lonelier, slower runs during the month of July. By myself. Without him being better than me.

So Chris had rediscovered riding his bicycle. At first gingerly, then with increasing frequency and duration. The fact that he owned a mega-successful bike brand with a warehouse full of sleek black-liveried road bikes with his name all over them, must have acted as some mild incentive. Not that Chris Boardman ever lacks motivation.

So here he was, this born-again, lapsed, and then born-again cycling bloke, outside our hilltop hotel in the neatly panoramic Vendée village of Pouzauges. It was early in the morning as I left the breakfast room to find Chris out in the chilly morning air, down on his haunches and engaging in what he called 'fettling'. It was a word I was about to hear often over the course of the day.

Two bikes bearing his name in simple, minimalistic yellow and white letters had been loaded onto the TV truck back in England. Here in France they were being carefully unpacked in preparation for the day's filming. Handlebars, cranks, stems and brackets. I barely knew the names of any of the pieces. I certainly couldn't have assembled them.

Chris was appalled at my choice of footwear. I was wearing 'SPDs'. This was not good, it seemed. They are clipped shoes that come with their own special pedals, all right. But they are not designed for performance road cyclists riding 'performance' bikes in a 'performance' sort of way.

Instead of projecting out from the sole like a metallic bunion, making the footwear unwearable unless clipped onto a bike, SPDs are smaller cleats, embedded into a shoe that might even pass muster for normal, non-cycling use. Apparently, according to cycling purists, they are worn and ridden by idiots. So, naturally, I was wearing them.

I am used to being the only rider on organised rides not hobbling around like a penguin staggering back from the pub when off the bike. I had stopped off especially at a branch of Decathalon on my drive down from Brittany and picked

up a brand new set of SPD pedals (*Les Pédales des Idiots!*).
It was these that Chris was now taking a great lack of pleasure
in 'fettling' onto the 'cboardman' pushbike I was to be loaned.

Finally, after an hour or so of unbridled use of spanners
and ratchets (probably), and having sent me out in a car to
find yet another branch of Decathalon to buy an implausible
number of water bottles as props for the shoot, Chris declared
himself all fettled out, and we were good to go.

John Tinetti, my taciturn cameraman colleague of every
Tour I have covered, climbed onto the back of a motorbike
ridden by Jacky Koch, the long-standing moto-pilot of the
legendary Tour photographer Graham Watson. We rode down
the steep hill through the village and headed for the open
road. Instantly I encountered problems, which I was almost
too shy to mention to Chris. It seemed that every time I
touched my rear brake, I nearly died. It emerged that my bike
was equipped with a carbon rim thing, or something like that,
which meant that braking, far from being a safe course of
action designed to reduce speed and minimise the chance of
falling from your bicycle, had become an act of suicidal self-
loathing. We stopped, almost as soon as we had set off, while
Chris re-fettled some things.

A little while later, the filming got underway. Six little items
were to be shot. Six vignettes designed to bring to life the
basic underlying principles of certain aspects of road racing,
things like drafting, crosswinds, team time trials. The water
bottles were put to breathtaking slapstick use, when I had to
pretend to be his domestique. Chris had scripted them all
carefully. He would be the master. I would be the student.

Somewhere during the filming of the first little piece though,
things started heading in a certain and, from my point of view,
somewhat regrettable direction. I think it might have been
John's fault. He was filming a sequence in which I was riding
in front of Chris, giving him the paltry benefit of drafting on

my wheel. Filmed from the side, Chris delivered a line to camera, and then, with a slight acceleration of the motorbike, the shot panned forward to me, ostensibly working very hard at the front. The problem was that we had to fake it a bit. We couldn't ride at all fast, really, given that Chris was concentrating on delivering his lines, and I was concentrating on not dying. We were also on the open road, with the motorbike firmly on the wrong side of the carriageway. All in all, it would have failed even the most cursory health and safety audit. Which was a good job, because we hadn't done one.

The problem, as John informed me, stepping down from the bike, was that it didn't look even remotely hard. And because it looked too easy, it was failing to make the point. And because it was failing to make the point, it was pointless. And because it was pointless, we were all going to get into trouble etc.. etc. etc.

I should 'Ham it up a bit, mate.' That was John's suggestion. And that was where I ran into a bit of trouble.

For four years from 1991 to 1995, I had struggled under the illusion that I could make a living as an actor. I had cobbled together a CV consisting of sporadic low-key acting assignments. The highlight of my 'career' was playing one of the Montgolfier brothers to an audience of airline executives at the launch of the Airbus A330 in Hamburg. A glorified aeroplane salesman in a belle époque wig. I had scoured the German papers in vain the following day for a review of my performance. But it seemed that no critics had attended. Michael Heseltine, sitting alongside Helmut Kohl had appeared to enjoy it, as well as a posse of important South Korean airline types, who I had later spotted looking up at the Airbus and kicking its tyres as they pondered making an offer. But that was it, in terms of acting.

So here I was, the best part of twenty years later, being asked to rekindle a thespian talent, which had flickered with such a modest flame in the first place that it blew clean out at the first cold blast of rent arrears.

We re-shot the sequence, and this time I threw the theatrical kitchen sink at it. Cheeks-puffing, snot-wiping, legs-akimbo. I selected a ridiculously easy gear, so that I could best express the expended effort through the visual medium of spinning my legs ludicrously fast. I felt like I had captured the essence of suffering. This was a refined distillation of the very nature of the sport. I had brought the agony into people's living rooms. I felt artistically fulfilled.

Word had come back from the production headquarters in London, where these pieces had been edited together, that they were very pleased with them. I read in an email that 'my contributions had made them'. Irony never transfers well to the printed word.

Sadly, when I saw the pieces back, I realised that I simply looked an utter arse. There I was, all knees and elbows and silly gears, pretending to be out of breath, with Chris chatting away to camera and sailing along effortlessly in my wake. My one chance to measure myself alongside Chris Boardman, to gain in kudos and rub off a little reflected glory. And I'd blown out my cheeks for comic effect.

I thought of the impeccable Gary Imlach's vow never to be filmed riding a bike, and, not for the first time, bowed inwardly to his greater wisdom.

With all this shamefully camp messing around on bikes with Chris, I nearly forgot the main reason for my having been sent to France: to track Mark Cavendish in his attempt to win the green jersey. I was sure that he and I were about to enjoy an easier working relationship. He had, after all, read my account of life covering the Tour, and would perhaps appreciate the particular pressures we have, in our own little ways, to contend with. He would doubtless be full of sympathy for my midnight sojourn in a Breton field talking to a French mechanic about hydraulics.

Needless to say, it didn't quite work out that way. Talking to Mark Cavendish, both on and off camera, remained a curiously subtle enigma. Undefined, uncertain endings are a hallmark of our encounters. Beginnings aren't much easier either. He has an unusual way, for example, of giving the interviewer no clear signal as to when an interview should begin. Conventionally, with other riders, this will take the form of a nod, or a deliberate look up, a straightening of the shoulders or a quick, 'OK, then.' With Cavendish, you kind of drift into the procedure, unsure, even as you plough through your opening question, as to whether or not the interview has in fact begun. This is just the way it is; the way he is.

Mostly, we got on smoothly enough with our defined roles. We even negotiated our way through a most surprisingly delicate encounter. He'd just pulled on the famous green jersey for the first time that summer, and, with the cameras rolling, turned with a coy three-quarters smile, and simpered, 'Don't you think it suits me, Ned?'

I said I thought it did. Very much.

He was happy, by and large, to accept the media obligations of his trade. But not always. There was a tense little situation in a car park in Lorient, which ended well enough, but had started with Cavendish claiming we were treating him like an animal by filming him walking to the bus. There was some truth in that assertion, I suppose. The Tour de France can indeed be bit of a zoo.

But the 'walking shot', the 'car park photo opportunity' is the stock in trade of reporting the Tour. It might be slightly unimaginative, but it is quite normal, and quite essential. News channels call it the 'today shot'. It lends the story immediacy, giving the viewer a visual context for the unfolding narrative of the morning.

Riders expect it; sponsors and PR managers positively orchestrate it; the Tour demands it. Mark Cavendish has done it a thousand times. But that morning, it enraged him. I wondered what it must feel like to be subjected to that kind of scrutiny. He was there to win bike races, and certainly not to placate journalists. But the encounter told me everything I needed to know about our unchanged relationship, our unequal power play, the unique distance at which the athlete holds the outside world.

By now, of course, Cavendish was in race mode, and as such, he was a different man. I guess his dealings with me, their ease, or lack of it, are a finely calibrated barometer for the pressure he is under. When the bike bit of his life isn't quite right, the telly bit becomes a torture. I can understand that equation. But one-word losers are every bit as interesting as loquacious winners.

The return to winning ways changed everything, anyway. It always does. And after that sour little exchange, we cracked on with the usual routine. Time and time again, we played out the same pattern as previous years. The towel, the iced drink, the handshake of congratulations, the smile. The winning ride, again and again. It had begun in Cap Fréhel, it continued with Châteauroux, where I had to break the news to him that Bradley Wiggins had crashed out on the road behind him. It came as a genuine shock. 'Oh shit,' he said, daring Ofcom to get involved, and forcing Gary Imlach into a pre-emptive apology. He doubled up, then trebled up on these wins by taking the stages into Lavaur and Montpellier, and then dropped in another 'shit' during a post-race chat in Pinerolo, apropos of not much at all.

And on the Galibier, he put me in my place.

It wasn't a judo throw of an answer, swinging me over his back, and crashing me onto the floor with little birds tweeting around my unconscious head. But it was pretty smart, and it reminded me of how far I still have to travel before I understand the race without recourse to explanation.

He'd ridden up the mountain in the grupetto, the large clump of sprinters and assorted others who'd been detached from the head of the race, and whose sole ambition was to make the cut-off time. They failed. In fact, they failed by some margin. But the group was so large, that the Tour regulations allowed for them to continue in the race.

Shivering in the freezing winds of the Galibier, and without any means of contacting the rest of our production team stranded miles away in the TV compound halfway down the mountain, I was unaware that, although he had escaped elimination, he had been handed another penalty. So it came as news to me when he said, 'Obviously, I've been docked twenty points in the green jersey competition, which makes that a bit closer.' His nearest rival, José Rojas had comfortably made the cut.

How did he know this? Was he sure? 'So, just to confirm, you have been informed that you will lose those twenty points. Is that certain?' I wanted to make sure of what I had just heard.

'Anyone who knows bike racing knows that those are the rules.' He looked squarely at me, and allowed a little pause for the effect of the words to sink in. A hit, a very palpable hit.

When I got back to base, yomping miles back down the Galibier having missed the shuttle bus, I was relieved to find that Cavendish's answer had caught pretty much everyone on the hop, and had resulted in a frantic fluttering of the pages of the Race Regulations Manual. The gap in my understanding felt less yawning when I realised that Chris Boardman had had to double-check it too. But I was still chastened by the ease with which he had put me away. I wondered how many more years I would have to cover the event, before those gaps eventually silted up with knowledge. Decades more, I suspected.

* * *

The last time I sat down to write about Thomas Voeckler, a confession jumped spontaneously onto the page, rather catching me by surprise in the process. In July 2005 I had asked Thomas for his autograph. I just wanted it, because I was in awe of him. Because he was brilliant.

Asking for autographs, or rather, being asked by people to ask for autographs, is an occupational hazard for the sports hack. I still have bag full of football shirts from a chronically under-funded kids' team in south-east London, which I promised to get Frank Lampard to sign four years ago. I still haven't done it. I just can't bring myself to ask sportsmen to sign things as it instantly places you in the debit column: fan, and therefore not qualified as a journalist. Not a price worth paying.

So it was with another inner gasp of surprise, that I found myself shouting 'Thomas! Thomas!' across the cobbles of the Champs-Elysées. The 2011 Tour was done. My work was finished for the month. My family were alongside me. And yet I felt fit to descend spontaneously to the level of a whooping pre-teen *X-Factor* fan at the sight of the legendary French rider parading through Paris with his teammates.

'Thomas!' I trilled.

He caught my eye. I showed him the jersey I wanted signed and the pen I had pinched off someone standing to my side. Probably a child.

He smiled politely. But looked away and rode off.

'Yup', I muttered to myself. 'Let's just pretend that never happened.'

I handed the pen back, and created a diversion. 'Let's go and get a drink. I want a beer. Coke, kids?' My daughters trudged off with me in the general direction of fizz and sugar. Voeckler had done it again. For the second time, he'd turned me into a fan.

On Tuesday, 28 June 2011 Julie Voeckler gave birth to her daughter Lila. Her husband was at her side. He might have been forgiven for spending the previous few days gazing anxiously from the Europcar calendar on the Voeckler family wall, and back again to the sight of Julie's full-term shape as little Lila bided her time. For Voeckler will have been sweating slightly at the prospect of the mother of all fixture clashes. A new child and the Tour de France. Sometimes life does capricious things like that.

A lot was at stake. The previous autumn, Voeckler had rescued his team from extinction after their sponsor Bouygues Telecom had decided that the best way to market their prestigious B-Box (whatever one of those was) was no longer to stick its logo on the diminutive French Champion's Lycra. In short, they quit, taking their money with them. Voeckler had offers from a clutch of other teams, but remained loyal to the roster of riders who had been left high and dry.

Eventually, and solely because of Voeckler's very particular charisma, a sponsor came forward. Europcar, who charge people money to drive cars they don't own in an uncharacteristically reckless fashion, pinned their green flag to Tommy's bony backside. They did so, not out of any great sentiment, but purely in the hope that Voeckler would make enough of a splash on the

Tour for people like me to write sentences like this that contained the word 'Europcar' in future publications.

So the new father to a baby girl (he and Julie already had a son, Mahe) had added a considerable weight of responsibility on his slight frame. His teammates' jobs were saved, for now, but the Tour had to deliver. A bit like Julie had delivered on the Tuesday, only without the drugs.

Four days later, on the Saturday, the Tour rolled out of his home départment, the Vendée. Predictably, he was subjected to a welter of affectionate attention.

Eight days after that, and just twelve days into Lila's life, he crossed the finishing line in the main square of Saint-Flour, a town built on a rugged volcanic rock in the heart of the Massif Central. In that instant, and quite unexpectedly, he took over the lead of the Tour de France. Again.

The genesis of this story was, of course, the instant that Johnny Hoogerland and Juan Antonio Flecha were so famously wiped out by the French TV car. Overtaking the riders on a narrow, tree-lined country road, it suddenly swerved erratically to the right, and straight into the Tour de France. Flecha, who never stood a chance, slammed onto the tarmac with violent suddenness. Hoogerland catapulted over his handlebars, towards a barbed-wire fence and into cycling immortality. It was the defining image of the 2011 Tour. But there we will leave Johnny for now, unpicking the steely thorns from his backside. We will, of course, return to him, but up the road something else of huge significance was happening, almost incidentally.

Voeckler was the lead rider in the breakaway when the car struck. He looked over his shoulder, saw the crash, then stepped hard on his pedals and accelerated out of the shot.

Some of this might have been the pure adrenalin of the moment. Yet, like a darts player totting up the permutations of an unlikely checkout, Voeckler knew instinctively what to do. In that split second, he had calculated the consequences.

Hoogerland was just twenty-one seconds down on him in the General Classification, a gap that the Dutchman, a more naturally aggressive climber, could surely have attacked over the remaining inclines on the stage. That is, Hoogerland could have attacked, had he not ended up tangled in a barbed-wire fence. That kind of slowed him down.

In short, if the peloton let the break go, that crash meant the yellow jersey. Seven years after his improbable defence of the race lead, which had entranced the watching world, Voeckler was suddenly at it again. He didn't expect it. We didn't expect it. And little Lila will be told about it for many years to come.

The clockwork of memories rewound to 2004. Could it really have been 2004? A whole seven years ago? I was just thirty five! A mere, slightly podgy sapling, bending in the force-9 gale of events in just my second Tour de France. Armstrong was smashing the race apart. It was such a long time ago that people still thought Jan Ullrich might win. After a while, with this race ticking away in your heart, you start to measure out your life to its annual rhythm. Because it changes shape each year, more often than not with one defining feature, it tolls the bell of my irresistible ageing. 2007: London. 2008: Alpe d'Huez. 2009: Ventoux. 2010: Tourmalet. 2011: Galibier. The gaps in between are just so much padding. 2004: Voeckler.

Now he stood in open disbelief on the podium in Saint-Flour, his face scrunched into a smile devouring his every feature. He grabbed a fistful of the Europcar (there, I've done it again) logo on his yellow jersey, and kissed it with a passion not usually accorded to nylon-based weaves. The consummate professional.

Two Voecklers: this one, weather-beaten and scrawny. And that one: the 'baby-faced' little cheeky chappy Tommy V, who'd captivated the misty-eyed sporting sentimentalists some seven years ago. We drew breath, and wondered what the future would hold for Voeckler, Part II.

There is stuff both to admire and to fear about the sporting comeback, the repetition of former glories. It seldom passes well, if truth be told. To watch on, as an act of greatness is repeated at the fag end of a career, carries with it the uneasiness of a warm October day. It cannot be enjoyed with the same insouciance, since it doesn't contain promise in any measure, only fragility. So Voeckler's moment of triumph in Saint-Flour gave rise to just one thought. This moment seven years on was just a pale yellow pretender. I yearned to go back in time, and to witness the authentic, unfolding drama of 2004 once again.

A few days later, I looked aimlessly around the pastel-coloured, echoing lobby of the Mercure hotel in Albi. I was weary. It was the morning of Voeckler's third day in yellow. Behind me a French Eurosport crew were just putting the finishing touches to an edited feature on their laptop. In front of me, sitting patiently at a white plastic coffee table, Thomas Voeckler, already dressed from neckline to knees in acid lemon yellow, was being enthusiastically talked to by three besuited marketing reps. From what I could gather, they were pitching a new sponsorship deal for some kind of powdered glucose nonsense. Voeckler looked to be broadly delighted with their proposal. After a little while he shook their hands separately and, taking up a few free samples of the energy drink being discussed, he took his leave and headed back towards the breakfast room, where Julie was trying to get their son to eat yoghurt. This she was managing to do, whilst simultaneously rocking their new-born daughter back and forth in a pram. If she needed help, then it arrived in the form of the leader of the Tour de France.

After breakfast, he went outside. I stood next to Liam, who was filming Thomas Voeckler playing with little Mahe in the chilly drizzle outside the hotel in Albi. Wearing matching yellow jerseys, albeit in different sizes, the two male Voecklers were running from one side of the courtyard to another. Mahe squealed with delight each time his father set off, waddling like a sped-up Charlie Chaplin, bowlegged and feet akimbo for his son's amusement. He was running like he rode a bike: a bit strangely. In everything that Voeckler did on and off the bike, there was as much lateral movement as forward propulsion, defying all conventions of efficient technique. The 'awkward' gene was clearly very strong in his family. Back and forth and back and forth they went.

A little while later, after kissing his family farewell, he checked out of the hotel and, with a cursory nod of the head in my direction, consented to granting me a very quick interview. We rushed to his side and he continued walking. We talked from the front door of reception to the team bus turning its engine over some fifty metres away in the car park. It was one of those ferociously complex interviews conducted on the hoof, which drew on all the skill of the cameraman. Liam had to get in front of us, and walk backwards, keeping the framing, focus and shot steady, whilst having no idea what he was about to bump into. All this as we went across a courtyard, up two flights of stone steps, and then sharp left.

Voeckler was uncharacteristically grumpy that morning. I even felt, perhaps misguidedly, that there was a certain standoffishness between him and his unheralded teammates. They seemed to be keeping a little distance from the man who attracted all the attention. Perhaps they were simply horrified at the nauseating task of defending the jersey that awaited them. No longer could the team disappear in the pack. No longer would they, as single riders, be given licence to get in moves and look for individual honour. They would have to subjugate their efforts solely to protect their leader, a man who, let's face it, had done all this before and had no need to repeat it all over again. I glanced at Anthony Charteau as he climbed on board the bus. He had been on the Brioches la Boulangère roster in 2004, and had once memorably obliged us by giving a revealing interview in which he admitted to being the lowest-paid rider on the Tour de France. I forget the exact figure, but you could comfortably have earned as much stacking shelves in the local branch of Hyper-U. But this morning he looked a little downcast, and I found myself wondering what kind of money he was on now.

As the riders gazed through the rain-flecked glass at the few interested fans standing out in the rain to see off Team Europcar, they didn't look particularly optimistic. You could read their thoughts, 'Today a long flat stage. Then tomorrow to Luz-Ardiden. After that it really starts.' No, this would not be fun, and nor would it last long. In short, as the bus pulled away over the wet tarmac, it wasn't the same vibe. The glass-half-empty part of me mused gloomily that it was set to be a bitter little imitation of 2004, precarious, sapping and doomed to failure.

How wrong I was. On Stage 12 they tackled the Tourmalet, on whose slopes Voeckler contrived to lose control of his bike and dent a campervan. Then on the first summit finish of the Tour, he held on by his fingertips to the big-name climbers, trundling in just behind Alberto Contador, and only forty seconds behind Andy Schleck. He was in agony as he dismounted, his thigh muscles bruised from the earlier collision. It was a brave ride, which hinted that he meant business.

Two days later, though, we witnessed the extent of his reinvention. He finished in the group of favourites, without ever looking particularly troubled on the final climb to Plateau de Beille. This was no longer hanging on, this opened up the possibility that more was to come. My misgivings about his reign in yellow melted away. 2011 had returned to the scene of 2004's heroics, and trounced them. This was, arguably, better. We sat up and started to believe.

Voeckler, propelled by his splendid team, had already exceeded all expectations. His climbing, which had only ever been good enough for survival in a breakaway group of chancers at best, had changed beyond recognition. Not that he looked different, of course. He still threw his bike all over the road and gurned. But the speed, the ease with which he now rode. He comfortably matched the accelerations of the Schleck brothers and, far from losing time, actually looked as if he might have enough in reserve to launch his own counter-attacks. It was preposterous, thrilling, almost absurd. Voeckler was a man transformed. He hurdled the Pyrenees and then set his sights higher still.

Time after time over the coming days, before he eventually relinquished his status on the cacophonous slopes of Alpe d'Huez just two stages from Paris, I had the good fortune of interviewing Voeckler as his summer's story fattened into something mythical. He passed through the full range of sentiments: self-belief, humility, delight and foreboding. From aspiration to realism. But all with great patience and his trademark smile. He didn't need to win new friends, of course; he already had them in abundance. But he won them anyway.

'Thomas, you've been climbing with the very best, and you've not looked uncomfortable. In fact, today, you looked like you might be able to attack them.' I was speaking to him after he had climbed to Plateau de Beille. It was his fifth day in the leader's jersey and by an extraordinary coincidence, the same summit on which he had so improbably defended the maillot jaune in 2004. 'You're not just there by mistake, surely you must start to believe that you are a real GC contender.'

He looked at me with his head cocked to one side, and a smile spreading widely. 'Listen, I have a scoop for you. I am not going to win the Tour de France.'

'You sure about that?'

'The Alps will be very hard. The Galibier is a different climb. But I will try to defend it for as long as I can.'

And with that he was chaperoned from my sight, to face the next forest of microphones. His daily bread.

Five days, six, seven.

The Tour spanned the Camargue and then reached the Alps, dropping in on Gap for the millionth time. For Voeckler, who had survived the first two summit finishes with all of his unlikely lead intact, it was not without incident, of course. The race was too lively for that. Alberto Contador, who had fallen uncomfortably far out of the reckoning, kept trying to animate things. So too did Evans, who was attempting at every opportunity to put the Schleck brothers into difficulty (which mostly involved asking them to race their bicycles downhill in the rain). So the yellow jersey had taken some defending.

Weariness appeared to be taking hold of our plucky French hero. On the run in to Pinerolo, after two difficult and increasingly mountainous stages, Voeckler lost time with comic panache. It was one of those racing incidents that happen so unexpectedly that no camera captures them. All we get to see is the aftermath. And so it was when the helicopter suddenly cut to Voeckler riding around in circles on what appeared to be a disused petrol forecourt. He looked giddy. He looked knackered. Afterwards, he let us know that tomorrow he was finished. We nodded sagely. Tomorrow was the ascent of the Galibier. He was toast. Bernard Hinault, the last French winner of the Tour de France agreed when I spoke to him. '*Il est toast . . . un croque monsieur.*' Something along those lines.

This is what we believed. I walked three miles on my own up the Galibier to see his toasting with my own eyes. As if the mountain itself wasn't intimidating enough, the crest of the famous ridge where the finish line stood was wrapped in frozen cloud. Periodically, the gloom would lift, vertiginously. Either side of the Galibier pass, dizzying descents would burst rudely into sight, only to disappear a moment later. It was bloody cold. Clutches of tourists huddled together with Tour staff for comfort; unlikely allies against the chill.

The story of Stage 18 is well rehearsed. Andy Schleck's swashbuckling attack, which ended up with a little too much buckle for his swash. And there was Evans' quintessential, lonely ride. No one helped him pull Schleck back, so he did it on his own, head set to one side, hurting. And Voeckler, flanked by the fluid, young and increasingly prominent Pierre Rolland, grimacing his way to his finest hour.

As the mountain reared up ahead of them, Schleck began to fade. Evans remorselessly plugged away at the leader, keeping his losses within reasonable margins. And Voeckler held on. Although he lost touch just a little towards the end, he had done enough to defend his lead in the General Classification and, implausibly, to retain the yellow jersey through the sternest test of them all.

'Voeckler, ce héros!' L'Equipe declared the following day. They devoted the cover photo not to Andy Schleck, who'd made the big move of the Tour, nor did they dedicate their attention to Evans, who'd probably just done enough to win. They decided instead that Voeckler's image was the one that their readership needed to see dominate their front cover, squeezing aside all but a few adverts.

In the picture, he's just realised he's held on. His right arm is lifted in triumph at such an angle that his bike, unbalanced at the best of times on account of his extraordinary riding style, looks like it is about to topple over.

It's a photo that says, 'This far. And no further.'

And that, of course, is exactly what it proved to be, to the relief of certain people at ASO, I was astonished to learn. The following morning, I sat down for breakfast on Alpe D'Huez with a senior official from the Race Organisation.

'How about Voeckler, then? What'd that be like; a Frenchman in yellow in Paris?'

I expected his face to light up. But instead he slipped his shades further up his somewhat Gallic nose, and pulled a sour face, moving his tongue around his mouth as if cleaning his teeth of something unpleasant.

'Hmmm.'

'What do you mean, "hmmmmm"?', I asked, adding a couple of extra 'm's of my own.

He scratched his chin, in the style of Jean Paul Sartre.

'If he wins, we have a big problem, I think.' I stared at him, uncomprehendingly. 'It would be a little nicer for everyone if he loses the maillot today.'

It's the reality of the Tour de France, which we had been able happily to ignore in our euphoric appreciation of Voeckler. But every performance that rips up the form book raises eyebrows as it does so. For a great portion of the non-Anglophone world in 2009, it had been the same with Wiggins' unlikely fourth place overall. That is not to say that there was a shred of evidence to suggest wrongdoing with Wiggins or now, two years on, with Voeckler. Quite the contrary: a glance at their closest influences, their public utterances, and a sense of their privately expressed beliefs, stacked up overwhelming in their favour. British cycling and, more recently, the prevailing culture of the sport in France have been at the forefront of the fight against doping, with both Wiggins and Voeckler the public faces of those campaigns. But the ragged recent history of the Tour and the repeated unmasking of outstanding performances, have created an atmosphere of febrile suspicion. In a way, it was surprising that I had not noticed these darker mutterings earlier. It was a depressingly familiar moment.

My coffee companion clapped me on the back, got up and left me alone to mull over his words. Tommy? Really? Not a chance.

Besides, later on that day, he was exposed in all his familiar frailty, turning in the kind of collapse that spoke not so much of Superman, but of Mighty Mouse. On Stage 19, they tackled the Galibier again, from the other side, and from there they rode up Alpe d'Huez. The sight of him labouring up the first big climb all alone, after losing contact with the lead group and getting caught in no-man's land, was reassuring in its vulnerability. We knew this Voeckler more intimately than the sudden super-climber. We could relax now, and watch him lose the lead. His point had been made. Splendidly made.

He'll be back of course next year. Voeckler will lead his team across the month of July one more time, maybe once again in the colours of the French National champion, which he has worn with great élan (obviously, a French word works best in this sentence). And I am certain that he will be fêted (and there's another one) as he slips by stealth into a neatly composed breakaway on Stage 13 and is outsprinted by somebody from the Czech Republic with an unmemorable name. Perhaps we'll shout his name when he launches an absurdly overambitious attack on the peloton from twelve kilometres out. He can spend the remaining years of his career fostering the prodigious talent of Pierre Rolland, who may well win the Tour for the French before too long. And in doing so, we will witness his talent slowly fading until it disappears from the canvas of the Tour entirely, at which point he will take his rightful place as a stalwart of France Télévisions. I've got it all planned out for him, you see. He won't wear the yellow jersey again, though.

'This far. But no further' was a concept young Simon Carnochan singularly failed to understand.

'What is it you're planning to do?' I'd foolishly asked him back in June.

'Hitchhike round the route of the Tour de France.'

'What do you mean?'

'I want to hitchhike, um, round the route of the Tour de France.'

'Yes, I know. That's what you said.'

I paused to let this mad idea take shape in my imagination. It wouldn't. I needed more detail.

'How are you going to get to the start? It's a long way away, the Vendée.'

'I'm going to hitchhike.'

'Why?'

'Just to see if I can, really.'

This had been my first meeting with the unusual eighteen-year-old Simon Carnochan. I say meeting, but actually we were just speaking over Skype. I had been reluctant to make my number known by ringing him from my mobile or landline for fear he would prove to be a maniac. I was only semi-wrong. He did indeed prove to be a maniac. But not an axe-wielder. More an arch-blagger.

Simon had told me that he was taking time out after A levels before starting at college. Hitchhiking round France had come to him in a flash of inspiration watching telly one day. Such things, it seems, are indeed possible. I suspect that

Simon watches an unhealthy amount of televised sport. He seems to know all about it. He wasn't setting out with the aim of raising money for charity, but to test his powers of endurance. He simply wanted to see if it might not be fun.

At his age, I had completed a few epic hikes around Europe, and found that I was always being helped out by drivers who told me that, 'At your age, I completed a few epic hikes around Europe.' It's a generational thing, a self-feeding mutually assured system. It's how hitching works. One day, Simon Carnochan, sliding into whatever dysfunctionality middle age blesses him with and in an effort to reconnect with his reckless youth, will doubtless pull over without hesitation at the sight of some weedy chancer with a cardboard sign, or its Bluetooth equivalent, by a motorway slip road. And so it will continue.

I liked his story. I didn't believe it would be possible, but I liked it.

'OK. Keep in touch. Come and say hello at the finish line, if you get there. Good luck.' I hung up, with Skype's trademark swoosh, shook my head, and wondered briefly if I'd ever speak to him again.

By the time we had driven up to the top of the Mûr-de-Bretagne several weeks later, parked up in a ploughed field and trudged through the raincloud that shrouded the finish line towards our truck, I had long forgotten our conversation. It had been quite washed away by the more immediate demands of covering the race. I had consigned young Mr Carnochan to the notional and overflowing in-tray of vague medium-term obligations and projects that may or may not ever need to be accessed.

Entering our little compound, where the studio had been unpacked, I nodded ill-tempered hellos at the sad collection of colleagues sat around in waterproof tops and trousers, their chins buried in the warmth of their chests. When would this Tour warm up again? Nobody looked up at me. It was Stage

4, after all, so what did I expect. My God, unless things perked up, this was going to be a long month.

'There was some bloke here looking for you,' I was told. 'Some kid who said you'd invited him.'

I paused momentarily. No, I had no idea who that might have been, and could not recall any arrangement to meet anyone. I slipped into the darkened interior of the truck and went on with my task of writing a piece about Mark Cavendish's latest outburst.

When I next emerged, the mood had lifted. This normally only happens when someone from outside our immediate group makes an appearance to break up the monotony of our own company. A pale, very young-looking, blond-mopped boy (there's no other word for him) stood by our table. He was eating a madeleine cake, which I instantly recognised as emanating from the kitchen of Phillipe and Odette, our caterers, and regaling people with stories. He was wearing a pair of beige shorts, a Saur-Sojasun replica top, and was draped in a Union Jack. From head to toe, he was drenched. This was Simon Carnochan. He'd made it this far.

It was the beginning of our occasional fostering of his extraordinary campaign. After cake and coffee, Rob Lewellyn, our phlegmatic production manager, had seen fit to lend him a VIP day pass, which got him access to pretty much every area. He nearly wept with delight, and duly set off for the finish line.

Some time later, he was really weeping. It seems that his bizarre, and not entirely sanitary, presence alongside the great and good of the Tour in the hospitality areas close to the finish line had been cut short by an official. They had taken one look at the unwashed (and seemingly underage) hitchhiker wearing a wet flag and taking pictures of everything that moved, and had instantly removed his precious, borrowed accreditation, before kicking him out. Presumably with a cartoonish boot, and the words, 'And don't come back!'

By the time I saw him in tears, he'd blagged his way back into the compound. Simon was something of a master at Blagging his Way Into Things, and occasionally Out of Them. But he felt miserable here. Rob did his best to cheer him up, putting his mind at rest and insisting that ITV could easily get the pass returned. But for a while I could see the tiredness and the strain that getting as far as Brittany had induced in his slight frame. He would pitch his tent that night, somewhere. And prepare for another evening with as much food as his 1.50 daily budget allowed him to eat, and little or no idea how he would get to the next stage finish. We posed for pictures with him on the TV studio set, shook him by the hand, stuffed some more bits and pieces into his rucksack, and sent him on his way.

It kickstarted a sequence of sightings. He became known to us simply as 'Carno'. The next day we spotted him jogging along towards the finish line at Cap Fréhel, looking a bit dryer, a bit blonder and a bit more British than before, perhaps in anticipation of Mark Cavendish's maiden 2011 victory.

'Carno!' Woody had spotted him again. His hair was whitening in the increasing hours of sunshine, which had began to fall on the roads into Massif Central. Hanging over the rails at fifty metres to go. Sat on the grassy verges of a Category Two climb. There, here, everywhere was Carno, the Where's Wally of the 2011 Tour de France.

Every now and then, he'd drop in to see us. Chris Boardman took a particular avuncular interest in his journey, perhaps because his own eldest son was abroad as well during July, picking strawberries in Denmark, a wonderful activity designed to hedge against the inevitable onset of adulthood. His son had sent Chris the most amazing email detailing with finicky precision the best techniques for efficient berry harvesting.

I think Chris valued Carno's initiative. I think we all did, particularly because, as the weeks ground on, he would never arrive empty-handed. Opening his increasingly grimy and over-stuffed rucksack, he would hand out the goodies he had scavenged from the Caravane Publicitaire. Salty little biscuits. Tubs of cream cheese. Mini sausages. Cakes and washing powder. Hats. Hats and hats. And of course, Haribo. For us, these things were an amusing frippery – something of a quaint diversion. For him, they were subsistence. He had consumed his body weight in Haribo, and he had lived to tell the tale. The margins of his physiology had started to wobble gently. We respected him. He had become our gelatine friend.

One day we were filming in a start village.

'Carno!'

We looked over to where Liam had spotted him. He had plonked his giant rucksack down on the ground to the side, and was standing at a sponsor's stand chatting up an implausibly glamorous, well-manicured and tall French lady whose job it was to hawk her employer's wares (wine, in this case, I seem to remember) to visiting dignitaries. I don't imagine for a second that it was in her job description to fawn over a grubby English gap-year kid who had a precocious talent for stuffing fruit, bread, and yes, wine, into the pockets of his beige trousers. But the look on both their faces suggested that they were enjoying each other's company more than was decent, let alone explicable.

Blimey, he was a player. We watched on, highly amused. Our respect for Simon grew by the day.

Weeks later: 'Carno!'

'Where?'

'There! Holy shit!'

He wasn't hard to spot, actually, despite the fact that he was surrounded by a seething, beery, orange-clad, pissed mass of loosely cycling-related revellers pumping out the phattest sub-woofer mayhem into the Alpe d'Huez night air. Obviously,

Simon Carnochan had made it to Dutch Corner, the epicentre of the Tour's wildest excess, and he was *right* in the thick of the action. What else did we honestly expect?

As we forced our car through the crowd of intoxicated international zombies, Carno came leering out towards us. We were concerned on his behalf. It was obvious what had happened to our lad. He'd clearly been kidnapped by a highly boisterous posse of drunken oafs from the Low Countries, dragged backwards along a ditch, force-fed a giant frankfurter, and then made to gyrate wildly in the middle of the road in order to slow traffic down to walking pace. We vowed that we would make representations the very next day on his behalf to the British Consulate in Grenoble.

Actually, we just roared with laughter. He'd almost made it. Alpe d'Huez was the penultimate stage before Paris, and he had an epic journey behind him. He'd slept rough, spent a string of nights in the back of the van belonging to some Norwegian tourists who he had found particularly useful to his cause, and most memorably, he'd befriended a priest in the town of Saint-Paul-Trois-Châteaux who, in a spirit of biblical literalism, had invited the traveller in, and washed and fed him. Carno had blagged redemption, which, meta-physically, takes some doing.

At another point, he'd fallen in with the accredited organisation known as 'Les Jeunes Reporters du Tour', which trains journalistically minded French teenagers in the art of being Gary Imlach. Simon, presumably lying about his age by knocking off a good four years, was given free transport and lunches galore, and then sent out with a microphone to interview some of the English-speaking riders. He found it quite an eye-opener.

'Cav's a bit difficult,' he confessed to me one day, as he lolloped around in our production area.

'Hmm,' was my reply. 'Pass us a Haribo, Carno.'

But it was the Doublet and Movico guys to whom he owed his Tour. They are the army of boys and girls who set out the miles of barriers each day, and install the endlessly long PA systems at each finish line, and other such unsung activities. They invited him in daily to share their largely cheese-and-pasta-based affairs, which fuelled them for their tasks. Carno was all over them like a rash. They even ensured that, every now and then, he washed.

On the final transfer from Grenoble to Paris (some 600 kilometres), he played his trump card. Or rather, we presented him with his trump card, since it was not in his nature ever to ask favours of our team. We had discussed it among ourselves, and had reached the conclusion that it might be mildly diverting to allow him into our Espace for that final drive. We had long since run out of new ways of insulting each other, and the presence of an eighteen-year-old force of nature might make the kilometres pass more quickly.

So he threw his by now absurdly distorted rucksack, along with the obligatory half-inched 'Départ' sign, into the back of our car, and hopped in. The journey proved pleasant enough. Carno chattered away about the people he'd met en route, emitted a curiously goat-like smell, insulted our music choices by knowing the songs 'because it's all the same stuff that my dad plays', and then fell asleep.

When we reached the lovely little Hotel Alison in the Rue de Surène, it was the middle of the night. Carno had been awake as we'd hit the outskirts of Paris.

'Where you going to sleep, Carno?' Woody had asked him.

'I dunno. Probably won't. Think I'll just head for the Champs-Elysées, and wait till it gets light.'

'No, you won't.' It was nice to be able to trump his trump card. 'There's a spare room in our hotel. You have it. But don't come down for breakfast without washing,' I added. 'In fact, don't come down to breakfast at all.'

So it was that we checked him in under a pseudonym. 'You're Chris Boardman, if anyone asks, OK? You won the Prologue in 1994, and then again in '97 and '98. You run a multi-million-pound bike franchise.'

'Cheers, guys.'

'But don't come down for breakfast.'

He'd made it to Paris. The following morning, the Monday after it was all over, just as we were heading off in our separate directions, Carno came down to breakfast. Or rather, he swayed down to breakfast. In fact, he stepped in off the Paris street from a hugely extended night out, straight into breakfast.

'What the hell happened to you, Carno?'

He grinned, glassily. 'Went to the Team Sky party thing. Had to buy some trousers specially. Then went on after that. Somewhere. I think.' It transpired under interrogation that he'd ended up in some place of ill repute with a clutch of British cycling's finest talents.

We told Chris Boardman about Carno's final blag in Paris. He was deeply impressed, but also amused that he hadn't received an invite to the Team Sky party. I could tell what he was thinking: 'But I won the 1994 Prologue, and then again in '97 and '98. What's Carno ever done?'

But, Simon, if you're reading this, I take my hat off to you, my young friend! Just don't do it again.

The same could very well be said for Sammy Sanchez, who won the stage to Luz-Ardiden. And well done to him. Genuinely, we were all chuffed to bits for the bony little Asturian with the Olympic rings pinned to his earlobe. Having said all that, it would have been more convenient for us if he chose never to do it again. His victory led to a regrettable moment of broadcast confusion, in three different languages.

Cycling is the very hardest sport to televise. It does not take place within the cosy confines of a stadium. The logistics of covering an event which is played out along a very thin line stretched out over 200 kilometres of public road is one thing. But trying to guess when the game is going to end is quite another challenge. There is no final whistle after ninety minutes. And there can be plenty of extra time.

The Tour does its best to try and help, naturally. In the Race Manual, it prints a hugely detailed table of potential timings; the vertical columns are divided into three 'schedules': the fast, medium and slow timings. The horizontal lines relate to points on the map. In other words, the Race Manual helps you to predict that the head of the race will pass the level crossing between Saint-Pierre de Somewhere and St Jean de Somewhere Else at 14.58, provided they are going slow. The problem with this system is that it is well-intentioned nonsense. The race speeds up and slows down organically and often without rhyme or reason. A thirteen-kilometre climb with an average gradient of 9 per cent might take no time at all to get over. But it also might take an age if the heat is out of the race. And besides, there might be a lone leader going hell for leather, stretching out a lead over a wholly uninterested peloton. So who do the timings relate to? And when is the race 'over' for the day? When the leader crosses the line? When the yellow jersey group comes in? When the pre-race favourite struggles in five minutes down on him? Or when Tom Boonen finally hauls his sprinter's frame into view?

All this we have to predict and relay back to the transmission centre in London who fit in the commercial breaks, without which there is no is 'free-to-air' coverage. They are nightmarishly complex calculations. Ofcom regulates commercial breaks tightly. There are maximum and minimum numbers of breaks each hour. There are minimum part durations. There are under-runs and over-runs, with all the attendant chaos in the ensuing schedules. And as the race plays out during the afternoon, it is cycling clever-clogs Matt Rendell's onerous job to advise Steve Docherty, the director, on when to take breaks. Matt is a respected writer, a fine intellect, a phenomenally versatile linguist and a consummate Jazz Funk bass guitarist. Yet, this is the hardest of all his disciplines. He must advise on when it will be safe to come off the air, leaving Gary, Chris and myself enough time to wrap up the afternoon's events without spreading our content too thin.

But too thin was precisely what we were reduced to that day in Luz-Ardiden. Sammy Sanchez had stuffed Matt's best efforts at predicting the outcome, and we'd ended up with an interminable half hour of airtime at the end of the programme, which somehow we had to fill.

Gary and Chris had looked again at the key moves of the day, glanced at both the Stage Result and General Classification graphic, and talked over the daily parade of self-conscious riders on the podium clutching flowers and cuddly toys and looked forward to tomorrow's stage. Then it was down to me to get some interviews.

The first of them was easy enough. Straight away, the

increasingly shaggy-haired and elongated figure of Geraint
Thomas, with his new five-year contract stuffed in his back
pocket, made his benign, laid-back way over to the ITV microphone. He'd won the Combativity Prize after joining a mad
rampaging breakaway move that had ended in him flying into
a grassy ditch just after he'd sped past a bemused-looking lady
waving a Welsh flag in his face. Snaking a wildly unstable path
between a quad bike and a caravan, he'd executed a perfect
comedy fall over the handlebars. Minutes later, he was at it
again, this time a parked car was just averted. So, reflecting on
his great adventure, peppered with misadventures, Thomas did
his usual shtick. Big wide eyes, the flicker of a smile tugging at
the corners of his mouth and his usual humdrum phraseology.

'I lost it a bit in my head,' was his frank assessment of his
unusually inadequate bike-handling skills.

I thanked him, and he headed off to the podium to collect
his ashtray/enamel bucket/oil painting from the sponsor. The
rest of the press pack took little notice of him; such is the
fate on most given days of the winner of the Combativity
Prize. He's a footnote.

But the dead minutes of airtime still stretched in front of
us. It was clear that we would need another interview before
finally getting off the air, or Gary would be left to talk over
endless replays of Geraint's wonderful tumble.

From the TV truck several hundred metres away, Steve
noticed, by watching the output from Liam's camera, that
Sanchez was being paraded through the interview zone.

'Does he speak English, Ned?' Steve demanded in my ear.

'No idea,' I replied. Although I reckoned it was extremely
unlikely. 'I'll check.'

As Sanchez conducted a Spanish language interview with
the Belgian network Sporza, to my side, I caught the attention
of his ASO minder.

'Does Sammy speak English?'

'No. Why don't you British ever speak other languages.' It was a fair point.

'We do. I do.' I felt my linguistic hackles rising. 'Does he speak French?'

'*Oui*.'

'*Bon*. Bring it on.'

And then, before I could guess what live television horrors were about to descend on me, the Olympic champion and stage winner was brought before, looking undeniably very Spanish, and not even remotely French. Before I could say *Ola!*, I could hear Gary throwing to me. I turned to the camera, and effected an introduction.

'OK, Gary, we'll try this very quickly. I'm going to speak French, he's going to reply in French. He speaks Spanish, and I don't really. So this is going to be interesting.'

Beads of sweat were already building up. I turned to him. '*Une victoire superbe. Une étape extraordinaire pour vous*.' Not a question, more a poorly pronounced statement of the obvious, really. But it was French-sounding enough for me to feel like I'd got away with it. Sanchez understood perfectly, and launched into his reply. In Spanish.

Twenty seconds later, he'd stopped talking rapidly in a language I did not understand. So, I guessed, he didn't speak French after all. I turned and looked imploringly at his soigneur. Perhaps he could translate. All soigneurs can speak a bit of French after all.

I pushed the microphone his way. 'This had better be good,' I quipped, by now thoroughly alarmed at the prospect of having to listen to the soigneur's answer, and translate it back into English for those benefit of viewers at home who hadn't lost the will to live or kicked a hole in their HD-ready plasma screens. The soigneur, a short bespectacled chap clutching a bouquet and an umbrella, started to speak.

At first I thought I understood one or two words.

'*Pour l'equipe c'est incroyable. Il y a . . .*'

But that was the end of anything intelligible.

On he went, by now drifting into some ghastly Pyreneean hybrid of every major, and some virtually extinct, southern European tongue. '. . . *desinges arroyal lesciggarres ici paralos arablo importante corbaranarntohalinos haranquintonitntiones marrraqueltanimonositcallemntes . . .*'

Laughter exploded in my ear. Which didn't help. Facing away from the camera and towards my strange interlocutor talking utter nonsense at me, I narrowed my gaze, and wondered what my next move should be.

'. . . *jalamentariostoqui ameris cointabios bono bono lamareica . . .*'

Even Sanchez had stopped listening, too, and had by now started to drift his attention away to the next interview in the line.

'. . . *hamos barandos pinteria Luz-Ardiden.*'

He was done. I thanked him, using all the clipped English insincerity I could muster.

I turned to the camera. There was nothing for it but brute honesty. There was no wool to pull over eyes, and probably no eyes left watching anyway. I felt like I could say what I wanted. It was almost liberating. I didn't choose my words carefully. I just said the first thing that came to mind.

'That was the most confusing interview of my life.'

Which, in the polyphonic matrix of the Tour de France interview pen, is saying something.

The next day, and still reeling a little from my encounter with Sanchez, I was buying a coffee, which seemed like the right thing to do. An espresso, with a little sugar to combat an early morning, mid-Tour slump. Suddenly there was a giant clap on my shoulder.

'Hey. What about the Tour of Britain? Fucking great race.'

I turned round, and was face to face with the marvellous, nearly murdered, Johnny Hoogerland.

'Mr Hoogerland,' I said. And I put out my hand. I have no idea what turned me so formal.

'Call me Johnny.'

And so I did, feeling giddily blessed. After all, here was a hero. No doubting it. He sat next to me at the bar, and over coffee we spoke about Colchester and Swansea, Blackpool and London. He seemed fascinated by the plans for that year's Tour of Britain.

Hoogerland. Roll it around the tongue. It is a great sound. Marry it up with that classic Northern European rocker's throwback first name 'Johnny', and you're in business even before you've hurled yourself over your handlebars and into Tour Legend.

I have to say, that I'd seen the Hoogerland thing, or at least something like it, coming. Not literally of course. No one could have predicted that the France Télévisions' car would suddenly surge up the left-hand side of the road, and then swing violently right in an attempt to assassinate Sky's Juan Antonio Flecha. But I had come to the Tour knowing intuitively that one of that marauding mob who go under the collective umbrella of Team Vacansoleil would do something to leave us all both awed and aghast.

Some background is perhaps necessary. Vacansoleil, for those who don't know, are a Dutch campsite/mobile home-type holiday thing. I'm sure their advertising people have a snappier way of summing up their business than that, and indeed if you were to visit their gloriously blue and yellow website (no, I'm not on commission) you will get the gist straight way. Their main image is this: distant mountains, blue skies, birds a-flutter, kites a-flying, kids a-frolicking and young, beautiful couples lounging around in front of their sun-dappled wooden chalets.

But look beneath the surface. All is not what it seems. The

beating heart of Hoogerland Holidays is very different. There is, if you listen hard, Lou Reed blaring from a distorting beatbox across the road, where the parents have collapsed on half-deflated lilos in the pool with a bottle of Jack Daniels, a bong and a bargain bucket of fried chicken. This is what I fondly imagine to be the real Vacansoleil experience. Book now to avoid disappointment.

I have reached this balanced conclusion not because I have ever had the great good fortune to experience a Vacansoleil holiday (as I said, I am not yet on commission), but because I have observed at close quarters their raucous rise through cycling's ranks to the dizzy heights of the Tour de France.

I was certain that they'd try something at the Tour. Part of the reason for my certainty was their liberating lack of a leader. They had no 'A' List sprinter (unless you count Romain Feillu, or Borut Božič, which you mustn't feel obliged to). They had no 'captain on the road', and they certainly didn't dream of being so pompous as to protect a 'GC rider'. No, they just had a bunch of blokes with a propensity for unfettered aggression. They wound them up, they clad them in campervan-related logos, and they let them go.

Sadly, it didn't really work. The irrepressibly attack-minded Belgian Thomas De Gendt fell at the first possible opportunity, smashing himself up, and hauling his overdeveloped quads unconvincingly around the rest of France. Borut Božič and Romain Feillu weren't good enough to mix it with the rest of the sprinters. Wout Poels, who I erroneously tipped for every Gilbert-like uphill finish, had brought the wrong pair of legs to the party. He abandoned after hitting the tarmac once too often, and then getting sick.

So it fell to Hoogerland to fall. Sponsors, naturally, only have the best interest of the riders at heart. But I wonder if there's not a Hoogerland chart hanging on a wall in Vacansoleil's dark blue and yellow headquarters somewhere uninspiring in

Holland, with an arrow of interest in the brand rising strato-spherically from the instant that Hoogerland unclips his right foot, wobbles, and then shoots over his handlebars and into a barbed-wire fence, tearing his arse to shreds.

'Ouch' doesn't do it justice. Have you ever slipped while cutting a tomato, and nicked a little slice into your finger? That's 'ouch'. This was beyond description, but I should try, for the benefit of those who are too squeamish to look it up on Google Images, as I just have.

The impression it left, to return to the tomato slicing meta-phor, was this: Imagine Johnny Hoogerland lying face down on the kitchen counter. You rip open his shorts to reveal his left thigh and buttock (bear with me, I'm just illustrating a point). You sharpen the knife, and then you draw at least ten deep slices across his flesh. But your devilish work is not yet quite complete, and so you take a rolling pin and smack him on the head, the shoulder, the elbow, and probably just for good measure, the arse. Then he jumps down from your kitchen work surface, and hops onto a bike. After all, there's a race on.

I'm exaggerating. Actually, no I'm not. It was worse than that.

Hours later, Johnny, swabbed, bandaged, perhaps in a heightened state of pain relief (I hope for his sake he was), and clad in his blood-drop red polka-dot jersey, hobbled over to say his piece to my colleague from a rival network.

Normally I would have had an unseemly fight with them about this act of rank-pulling. Especially with this particular Italian colleague who sported hair oil, reflective shades and an unencumbered ability to kiss ladies on both cheeks without looking flustered, stopping inappropriately at just one kiss, going for an unwanted third, or bumping noses on the exit manoeuvre. Yes, he was that good. The Silvio Berlusconi of the Mixed Zone, turning the simplest post-race interview into a potential Bunga Bunga party. He wore a gold bracelet. He was the continental's continental TV reporter, and needed a smack, frankly (which Matt Rendell offered to provide a few days later, I forget why).

But on this occasion, I am reluctant to confess, he got it right. He had a bit of kit with him, attached to the front of his camera, which could play back footage to the interviewee. And so it was that Johnny Hoogerland, with the cameras rolling live on his reaction, watched back the moment that had nearly ended his career, and very possibly his life.

Hoogerland was visibly horrified. I have no doubt that it shocked him to see the violence of the incident. He looked genuinely scared for the rider he saw tumbling through the air like a rag doll. It must have been hard to believe that he was looking at himself. But when he spoke, he was calm, dignified, and resisted calls for punishment. He let us play the role of lynch mob on his behalf. We readily obliged.

That evening, at our hotel in Aurillac, a France Télévisions car, identical to the one that had done the damage, pulled up. They were staying in the same place!

We scowled at each of their team over breakfast the next day, working out which one we were going to dob in. Was it the pasty youth in the crumpled polo shirt or the brunette with the shades, who took too long spreading the butter? Was it the overly cheerful chubby bloke in the cheap supermarket jeans and the Greenpeace T-shirt who set everyone's teeth on edge by whistling Lady Gaga's 'Poker Face'? It was none of them. It was, in fact, the wrong car. The actual vehicle, complete with the actual culprit, had been successfully spirited away. They disappeared from the race, and were never heard of again.

I will never look at those France Télévisions Citroëns in the same light. They have always been driven recklessly. This year's Tour, despite the appalling incident with Flecha and Hoogerland, featured a definite, and marked return to the bad old (good old) days of driving at 100 kph down the wrong side of a road. Recent Tours had seen this desperately dangerous practice phased out by the police. But for some reason, this year, it returned, and the TV Citroëns led the charge, in particular from Bourg d'Oisans to Grenoble on the penultimate transfer. A thirty-mile stretch of occasional dual carriageway turned into a massive game of chicken with oncoming caravans and the sudden appearance of central reservations. My palms grow sweaty at the memory of that awful drive. Sitting in stationary traffic, you would suddenly become aware of blue flashing lights in your wing-mirror. Three or four police cars would come charging down the (almost empty) wrong side of the road. The trick was to pull out and slipstream them. It wasn't particularly legal. But it got you to your final destination fast, which, after three weeks on the road, was pretty much all that mattered to any of us.

The French TV cars, needless to say were the most fearless. They instinctively took their place at the front of the convoy, just behind the police vehicles, as a matter of national pride. I once had the temerity to position myself at the sharp end of the race in a spot that was rightfully theirs. I was nearly deliberately rammed. It was like being a Saunier Duval rider trying to mix it with Lance Armstrong's US Postal Big Blue Train. Not a good idea.

We waged war on them last summer, just as they seemed intent on waging war with the rest of the world. On the descent of the Plateau de Beille, stuck in an immobile snake of traffic, I opted to pull on my running shoes and see if I could get to the bottom of the mountain quicker than Woody and Liam in the Espace. Most of the time, I was running past stationary cars. But sometimes the line of traffic would move, and cars would overtake me slowly. On one such an occasion, I was passed by a France Télévisions Citroën, whose driver saw fit to spray me, quite deliberately, with windscreen wiper fluid. Already running on frayed nerves, I was instantly incensed. But the traffic came shuddering to a halt round the next corner, and at once I was granted the opportunity to make my feelings felt. I caught up with the offending vehicle.

There were four lads in the car, in their early twenties. They looked like production juniors. I tapped on the window. They wound it down. With exaggerated calmness, but with clunky French I asked them whether or not they would agree that France Télévisions had had an excellent Tour behind the wheel, when taken as a whole, and that their minor act of hooliganism just added a slight blemish to the impression of considerate driving which had so typified their corporate approach.

I'm pretty sure that's exactly what I asked them. They looked sheepish enough. I asked them if they wouldn't mind me noting down their registration. They looked worried. I told them that I would take the matter further the next day. They looked genuinely petrified. Or I imagined that they did. But on reflection, perhaps they were just upset at the sight of my puffy red face dripping detergent and runner's snot from the end of my imperious nose onto their upholstery.

I withdrew my righteous head, and felt as if I had planted a blue and yellow Vacansoleil flag on the moral high ground of the Plateau de Beille.

I'd done it for Johnny. We'd all done it for Johnny.

The day of his slicing, he stood on the podium and wept, as much in pain as in shock. I think the pride would have come later, if it came at all. That night he had thirty-three stitches to his wounds. But still he rode on. He carried the claret-spattered polka-dot jersey on his shoulders through the next two stages, then lost it, only to regain it again for a further three days. Sometimes he would become detached, suffering on his own at the back of the bunch. But mostly he held his own. Slowly he healed, and as Paris neared, he even featured in the occasional attack.

I wonder to this day if he realises the effect he had on people all across the world, watching the race. Within days an enterprising American website was knocking out T-shirts that declared 'Welcome to Hoogerland! Population: Heroes.'

I bought one.

Hoogerland's story summed it all up. His bravery told us what we all longed to hear about the courage of the riders. It rose above the noise of the race, and it drowned out the dopers, it crowded out the also-rans. The battle for the podium places, at times seemed second best. Yes, even the winner.

That isn't to say that Evans' victory won't be remembered. It was a victory rightfully greeted with joy by Mike Tomalaris and his Australian colleagues, who must occasionally have succumbed to the feeling that they were broadcasting only to drunks and insomniacs still awake at 3 a.m. in Canberra.

The winner was warmly applauded by most of the peloton. Despite his quirks and tics and occasional threats to decapitate journalists who threaten to touch his little toy dog, Evans is respected and liked; a man who has squeezed every drop of talent out of his bony frame. His valour on the climb to the Galibier won him the Tour. In some ways, it would have been wrong had he won the stage itself. That would have been uncharacteristic. Evans wins by limiting losses, by boundless grit and by quick thinking. A man at the limit of himself.

If only the same could have been said of Andy Schleck, whose frailties seemed to have turned in on him. They are attacking him from within. The ill-considered complaints about descending may have lost him PR points, which his hollow-sounding claim that the fifty-seven second advantage he held over Evans would be defendable in the time trial did little to recapture. In the end, I stood talking to him in Paris, worried that I might accidentally let slip his nickname, Andy Schleckond.

'I'm very proud to have finished second in the Tour de France.'

I looked quizzically at him. He should be furious to finish second, especially in a year when Contador's challenge went AWOL. He should have been enraged that he had squandered such obvious talent once again. He is a nice man, and has never been anything other than polite in his dealings with us. But that's not the point, is it? He is the most fluent, most obviously talented climber on the radar. Or at least, he should be.

Maybe he will win it one day. But maybe he simply won't. Either way it was Evans who took the 2011 win, his dimpled chin wobbling at the enormity of it all.

And Cavendish?

He roared up the Champs-Elysées. He made it three wins in three years in Paris. But this time, he did it in the green jersey that had so far eluded him.

I was waiting for him at the interview zone, already poised. I knew he'd win.

After the towelling and talking and smiling, he stepped away. I thanked him, shook his hand one last time. For the twentieth time after a Tour de France stage win.

A hurricane of noise was blowing in through the flaps of a white marquee designed to hide the riders from the crowds gathered out on the cobbles, waiting for the podium presentations to begin.

What memories will we all take away, when this imperious winning streak is over? What will remain with us of Mark Cavendish?

Standing in Paris to one side of the podium, watching the man (a little knock-kneed, and somewhat short, by the standards of immortals), I understood that not much had changed. Not since the first day I met him on the eve of the 2007 Tour, when he stated his aims, and articulated for the first time his quite unshakable faith. Nothing about him was different, except the colour of his jersey.

Only by being Mark Cavendish could you possibly imagine what drives him. And 'Being Mark Cavendish' necessitates being no one else, bending your will, tempering your heart, altering your course, for no one else. Not until every last target has been reached, grasped and locked away. And that, for the World Champion, is some way off.

I exited Paris, headed for the campsite in Brittany, reconnected my car's battery, and resumed my life.

It had been a riot.

And the answer to his question? Well, it's changed now.

Hushovd. Petacchi. Cavendish.

ACKNOWLEDGEMENTS

I should start by thanking Emily, who got me started on this journey. I owe a debt to Richard Moore, but I've already bought him a nice bottle of wine, so we're quits. Thanks to Stan at Jenny Brown, and to Matt Phillips at Yellow Jersey, for his alchemy.

Thanks also to Paul and Sue, who gave me lunch in 2003, and told me who Mario Cipollini is. To Josh for a word of encouragement in 1989. To Mike and Simon, for Monopoly in 2010.

Thanks to Brian Barwick, Mark Sharman, and Niall Sloane, all of whom have either signed or retained the TV rights to the Tour de France for ITV. Also, in a smaller, but no less significant way, I am indebted to Jim Clayton for the picture of me throwing a bike in a hedge.

To all those who have worked with me on Tours past and present, back in London and on the road in France, thanks for your dedication, and sense of adventure: Rob Llewelyn, David McQuaid, Steve 'Bilcoe' Blincoe, Freddie Morgues, Wrenne Hiscott, Chloe Deverell, Gary Franses, Pete Vasey, Andy Sessions, Revika Ramkissun, Sophie Veats, Tony Davies, Titus Hill, Peter Wiggins, Peter Hussey, Chris Littleford, Chrissie Jobson, Sarsfield Brolly, Patrice Diallo, Carolyn Viccari, James and Brian Venner, and all others in France and at Molinare who make the show happen. To other tourists: Matt Pennell, Stephen Farrand, Paul Kimmage, David Walsh, Phil Bryden, Bob Roll, Honie Farrington, Peter Kaadtmann, Mike Tomalaris, Simon Brotherton, Graham Jones, Phil Sheehan, Johnny Green, Simon Richardson, Frankie Andreu, Dave Harmon, Richard Williams, Brendan Gallacher, Daniel Friebe and Geoff Thomas.

To John, Steve, Gary, Chris, Glenn, Liam and Woody. Not

forgetting Philippe and Odette and Romain, as well as Phil and Paul.

And a huge debt, as ever to Matt.

Thanks to David Millar, Thomas Voeckler, Richard Virenque, Robbie McEwen, Lance Armstrong, Bradley Wiggins and Mark Cavendish: names I will never forget. Thanks also to Brian Nygaard, Fran Millar and Dave Brailsford.

And finally, to Kath, Edith and Suzi. They are my full stop.

LIST OF ILLUSTRATIONS

22.   Chris Boardman dons a bin bag on the Tourmalet in 2010.

24.   Chris Boardman pretending to lift a truck.

25.   Phil Liggett inexplicably snuggles up next to a statue.

26.   Phil Liggett, stripped to the waist, but still talking.

28.   Phil Liggett, Paul Sherwen and me in a fit of nationalistic fervour, in Paris 2009.

30.   Watching the closing stages on the set with Chris Boardman and Gary Imlach.
      On top of the Col d'Aubisque.

38.   Green, white and yellow. The Aussie national colours, worn by Robbie McEwen, Baden Cooke and Brad McGee in 2003.

39.   Lance Armstrong at the start line.

43.   Ben Woodgate sheepishly posing with 'Shirley' Crow.

45.   The front page of L'Equipe, 12 July 2003.

51.   Lance Armstrong, when I confronted him about his feud with Filippo Simeoni. Smiling.

52.   The same interview with Lance Armstrong. A few seconds later, the smile had gone.

54.   A traffic jam on the Hautacam.

57.   A typical suitcase, containing dirty clothes in the plastic bags. Note the bottle of wine.

58.   A typical Tour shirt, manifestly badly ironed.

60.   Producer James Venner joins Gary Imlach in bin bag chic on top of the Tourmalet in 2010.

61.   A typical ironing scene on a sideboard in a hotel.

62.   Liam MacLeod with a coy frown.

63.   Ben Woodgate enjoying a rapid-fire sneezing fit over breakfast.

64.   Checking the oil in the Renault Espace. Feigning expertise.

65.   Mike Tope admiring his handiwork after scratching his car in Paris.

268. Team Sky's fleet: the bus and one of the Jaguars.

269. Personalised number plates on one of Sky's Jaguars.

270. Geraint Thomas, wearing his British national champion's jersey, being interviewed on the 2010 Tour.

275. Mark Cavendish on the 2010 Tour.

281. Mark Cavendish, caught on a TV monitor.

282. Mark Cavendish, the centre of attention behind the podium.

288. The ITV truck parked up next to a toilet in Paris.

289. A beautifully worded, instructive notice in the Tour toilets.

290. A chemical toilet placed next to some sculpture in Paris.

291. A non French-speaking driver appeals for help.

294. A 'mushroom'.

302. Alberto Contador takes a long drink before answering questions on the 2010 Tour.

305. The note given to me by a police officer who had witnessed my accident.

307. A cheap photo opportunity.

LIST OF ILLUSTRATIONS TO
HOW CAV WON THE GREEN JERSEY

Slaying the Badger

Richard Moore

LeMond, Hinault and the Greatest Ever Tour de France

Heroes and villains, spectacle and controversy, mind-games and endurance – this is the 1986 Tour de France.

Greg LeMond, 'L'Américain': fresh-faced, prodigious, newcomer. This is supposed to be his year.

Bernard Hinault, 'The Badger': aggressive, headstrong, five-time winner of the Tour. He has pledged his unwavering support to his team mate, LeMond.

The team is everything in the Tour, so the world watches, stunned, as LeMond and Hinault's explosive rivalry plays out over three high-octane weeks. *Slaying the Badger* relives the adrenaline and agony as LeMond battles to become the first American to win the Tour, with the Badger relentlessly on the attack.

'So engrossing, you don't want it to end'
Scotland on Sunday

'Captivating'
Times Literary Supplement

'Entertaining'
Richard Williams, *Guardian*

'From the opening pages this is a book that grips. Combining great insight, interviews and anecdotes with wonderfully vivid writing, it is thoroughly researched and well written'
Scotland on Sunday

'The race and the book build towards a gripping page-turning climax which you don't want to end'
Daily Telegraph

My Time

Bradley Wiggins

On 22 July 2012 Bradley Wiggins made history as the first British cyclist to win the Tour de France. Ten days later at the London Olympic Games he won gold in the time trial to become his country's most decorated Olympian. In an instant 'Wiggo', the kid from Kilburn, was a national hero.

Outspoken, honest, intelligent and fearless, Wiggins has been hailed as the people's champion. From his lowest ebb following a catastrophic attempt to conquer the 2010 Tour and the loss of his granddad who had raised him as a boy, *My Time* tells the story of his remarkable journey to win the world's toughest race.

'Fascinating'
The Times

'Listening to Bradley Wiggins is a pleasure unmatched in British sport'
Sunday Telegraph

'Like the man himself, captivating'
Daily Express

'Revealing'
Observer

'Raw, thrilling Wiggins'
Sunday Times

Put Me Back On My Bike

William Fotheringham

In Search of Tom Simpson

Tom Simpson was an Olympic medallist, world champion and the first Briton to wear the fabled yellow jersey of the Tour de France. He died a tragic early death on the barren moonscape of the Mont Ventoux during the 1967 Tour. A man of contradictions, Simpson was one of the first cyclists to admit to using banned drugs, and was accused of fixing races, yet the dapper Major Tom inspired awe and affection for the obsessive will to win which was ultimately to cost him his life.

Put Me Back on My Bike revisits the places and people associated with Simpson to produce the definitive story of Britain's greatest ever cyclist.

'The best cycling biography ever written'
Velo

'An intelligent, perceptive portrait'
Guardian

'A beautiful explanation of why Simpson's legend still exerts such a powerful hold'
Sunday Times

'An enjoyable, clear-eyed biography'
TLS

French Revolutions

Tim Moore

Cycling the Tour de France

Self-confessed loafer Tim Moore, seduced by the speed and glamour of the biggest annual sporting event in the world, sets out to cycle the course of the Tour de France. All 3,630km of it. Racing old men on butchers' bikes and being chased by cows, Moore soon resorts to standard race tactics – cheating and drugs – in a hilarious and moving tale of true adventure.

'Bill Bryson on two wheels... A one-liner every other line... Not so much witty travelogue as self-examination in a joke-heavy trial by fire'
Independent

'Moore is a talented and funny writer, who, through a combination of slapstick, absurd simile and a healthy suspicion of French civilisation, gives us something to laugh at on almost every page'
Daily Telegraph

'Moore's floundering attempts to emulate the Herculean feats of his cycling heroes unfold with eyewetting hilarity'
The Times

'Moore unleashes a high-energy torrent of astute observation and hilarious self-deprecation. Hailed as the new Bill Bryson, he is in fact a writer of considerably more substance... The jokes come thick and fast'
Irish Times

'Hilarious and inspiring... It is embarrassingly laugh-out-loud'
Daily Express

'One of the funniest books about sport ever written'
Sunday Times

ABOUT THE YELLOW JERSEY PRESS

In cycling, the yellow jersey is worn by the leader of the Tour de France. It symbolises achievement, effort, bravery and quality. When Yellow Jersey Press was created in 1998, it was to publish sports writing with these same values. Since then it has established itself as the premier list of high-quality sports writing, publishing five winners of the prestigious William Hill Sports Book of the Year award.

Yellow Jersey Press's range of cycling books is second to none. It is the home to some of the peloton's greatest heroes like Bradley Wiggins, Tom Simpson, Stephen Roche and Laurent Fignon, as well as some of the sport's best writers like William Fotheringham, Paul Kimmage and Richard Moore.